BYOUNG CHO

BYOUN

Thames & Hudson

G CHO

SOON CHUN CHO

*with 610 illustrations, including 322 in colour and 270 drawings_*

CONTENTS_

BYOUNG CHO,
ARCHITECT OF A DIFFERENT SHADE_

BY SOON CHUN CHO

Architect Byoung Cho is a mild-mannered maverick. Unfailingly polite, welcoming and jovial, he is driven by his passions, deeply connected to nature, and stirred by the spirituality of life. In 1982, at a time when few in Korea were looking towards the West, Cho devoured the writings of Mark Twain while studying traditional Korean ceramic arts. His friends spent every waking minute cramming for the national entrance examinations for Korea's top schools, but Cho decided to attend college in the United States. Lured by photographs of the Gallatin Range, Cho studied architecture at Montana State University in Bozeman, Montana, where his professors made him feel at home and encouraged in him a love for the region's agricultural buildings. Years later, after he had completed graduate work at the Harvard Graduate School of Design, taught in Germany, and practised architecture in Korea as well as in Boston, he was invited back to Montana. For twelve years he shuttled back and forth between Bozeman, teaching at the architecture school, and Seoul, where he runs a thriving practice.

Born in a cramped and bustling metropolis and steeped in the Asian philosophies, Cho has built dozens of projects, from concert halls and museums to kindergartens and intimate group residences for the mentally ill, that show a profound empathy for the way their users and inhabitants interact with each other and use their surroundings. One important example is his Twin Trees project, an office complex situated next to Gyeongbok Palace in Seoul, once the primary residence of Korea's kings. Due to their location within the old footprint of the palace compound, the Twin Trees towers were fraught with controversy even before Cho began designing them in earnest. The first palace was built on the site in 1395. During the Japanese occupation of Korea (1910–45) almost the entire complex was destroyed and less than half of the original structures have been restored. A succession of Korean presidents have made it a priority to rebuild the lost buildings, and the people view the palace at once as a source of pride and defeat, glory and loss, past and future. It may have been unfair to have any architect build on a site imbued with such history and emotion, but Cho's ultramodern design, with brilliant glass panes that literally reflect the beauty of Korea's past while signalling the optimism of a country looking towards its future, is widely considered to be a resounding success. The towers are especially popular among the young, who have taken pictures of themselves in front of the buildings and uploaded them onto Korean social-networking sites by the thousands.

Cho grew up in Seoul in a *hanok*, a house built in the traditional Korean architectural style. Often referred to as "houses that breathe", hanok are not only beautiful and comfortable, but also environmentally friendly. Based on the feng shui ideal of having a mountain behind the house and a river in front, they are laid out in square, L-shaped, or I-shaped formations, depending on the climate. Hanok are made with raw materials such as clay, wood and stone, which are recyclable and sustainable. They feature an ingenious 3,000-year-old heating system called *ondol*, which uses direct heat transfer from wood smoke through a masonry floor, and the doors and windows covered with *hanji*, traditional paper made from mulberry bark. Hanok are remarkably cool in summer and warm in winter.

Cho's childhood was filled with memorable experiences living in the hanok, which for him felt like living within nature. The sky, water, wind and earth were accessible to him. Sitting in the *maru* – an open-style living room that connects rooms and serves as a space for entertaining – or hanging out in the open-air courtyard, called a *madang*, he would gaze at the stars at night and cherish the feeling of connectedness with his surroundings. It is not surprising that the signature elements of Cho's architectural projects are inspired by the classical, natural forms found in the hanok – the grids of wooden framed paper doors and windows, the clean lines of the tiled roofs and beams, the purity of materials.

OPPOSITE_ *Concrete Box House sketched by Cho.*

"I believe that houses are better if they are simpler
and their relationship with their surroundings is richer.
A house can be comfortable if it satisfies
those two conditions."

– Byoung Cho

With all of Cho's projects, their placement in their surroundings is of primary concern. Even for an office tower in the middle of Seoul, he seeks to create an environment that promotes some sort of relationship between its inhabitants and nature – views of the sky, perhaps, or a place to catch a light breeze. Robert Ivy of the *Architectural Record* observes, "Cho examines space that defines, surrounds, and occupies in its own right, creating void, or absence, place, or presence. Simultaneously, he creates space through the manipulation of materials. . . . His work is grounded in the power of space to create relationships, a human quality."[1] Cho built his Earth House as a "house of the sky" in tribute to the Korean poet Yun Dong-Ju (1917–45), best known for his resistance poetry during the Japanese occupation. Arrested for being an "ideological offender" and "thought criminal", Yun died in prison in Japan. His poem *Sky, Wind, Star, and Poem* is still one of the most revered pieces of Korean literature today.

When designing the Earth House, Cho intended to observe nature as Yun's poem did: sky, wind and stars. The small, 14 x 7 metre (46 x 23 ft) house is essentially a box placed in the ground, with a courtyard open to the sky. Some of the walls are made from the earth dug for the house's foundations. There are six tiny rooms, including a study, kitchen and bathroom, each about 3.3 square metres (35.5 sq ft). It is a transitional space between inside and outside. It is a place designed to facilitate man's encounter with nature, a contemplative space in which one can smell the fragrance of the earth and observe the moon as it glides through the heavens. In a site so attuned to its surroundings, one's mind wades through pools of memories turned into emotions, whose traces echo the lines of the house. Cho's love of ceramics influences his use of material. The Earth House features a rammed earth wall, which, for Cho, was akin to a piece of ceramic art. An architect concerned with sustainability from the very beginning of his career, he built the wall from the earth dug at the house site, leaving out additives and other foreign materials. That way, the earth wall will one day return naturally to the soil.

Cho is an architect who adeptly captures the moment a ray of sunshine falls on a courtyard. Many of his counterparts, especially in the West, design buildings that are meant to be seen; Cho generates spaces in buildings from which to see. He learned from Le Corbusier and Ludwig Mies van der Rohe that the interior of a building is intimately linked to the exterior site, and vice

TOP LEFT_ *A watercolour on newspaper, entitled* Landscape, *by Cho, 1995.*

ABOVE RIGHT_ Skull, *1991, by Cho. Black ink on newspaper.*

ABOVE LEFT_ Hanok, *a traditional Korean house.*

OPPOSITE_ *The view from the roof of Concrete Box House, Yangpyeong, Korea.*

versa. In Montana, he learned that "agricultural buildings aren't really designed, someone just made them. I try to design like that – so it looks like it's not designed at all, it's just there".[2] Joining these views to those of the Asian philosophers, he is inspired to commune with nature, and his buildings become part and parcel of the landscape. His fundamental materials are sound, water, light, earth and wind. Before he starts to work, he considers the energy and flow of a site, from the ground underneath to the harmony or cacophony of its surroundings. Cho believes that his experience and perception of space through the accumulation of memories have transformed into emotions, which leave traces in his architecture.

According to Cho, the buildings he designs are "the architectural equivalent of Korean *buncheong* ceramics". The architect is well versed in the spirit and philosophy behind this traditional form of Korean stoneware. More informal in style than the celadon coveted by Chinese and Japanese royalty, buncheong enjoyed two hundred years of popularity during the Choson Dynasty, which began in 1392 and lasted until 1897. Buncheong ceramicists brought inventive changes to traditional forms, while bold decorative techniques and motifs responded to consumer preferences and facilitated mass production. At the same time, buncheong flaunted its materiality – the tactile, often uneven appearance that set it apart from the more refined ceramics of the court.

In the wake of the unsuccessful Japanese invasions of Korea at the end of the sixteenth century, buncheong, adopted by Japanese tea connoisseurs, would inspire generations of Japanese potters. Sen no Rikyu (1522–91), founder of *wabi-sabi*, a Japanese philosophy that promotes the beauty of the imperfect, the incomplete, and the impermanent,[3] was an avid admirer of buncheong and used it in his tea ceremonies. In Korea, however, buncheong fell out of favour in the eighteenth century. Nearly two hundred years later, twentieth-century Korean artists rediscovered their buncheong heritage, intrigued by the medium's visibly handmade aesthetic. Ceramics lovers who encounter it today are struck by the familiar yet refreshing quality of these vessels, which evoke the force of modernist gestural pieces and abstract expressions.

Buncheong bowls are now considered national treasures in Korea, but they were invented by common potters and used by commoners, who were not allowed to use the white porcelain made with kaolin favoured by the royal families and the ruling class. Cho prefers buncheong to white porcelain and even the graceful and delicate ninth-century Koryo Dynasty celadon. He states, "I enjoy the earth-toned bowls of buncheong, made quickly by a potter's rough hands. . . . Through that technique I can feel the heartbeat of the artist."[4] Like buncheong, Cho's architecture quietly revels in the natural, the unpretentious, and the material.

Minimalism in architecture can be described as the use of basic geometric shapes, with little or no ornament, stripping everything down to achieve simplicity. Many would place Cho in the minimalist camp, but the architect smiles and shrugs at the idea of belonging to any category or putting a label on his work: "I seek to build economically and sustainably, and to have the finished work achieve harmony with its surroundings. What that is called is beside the point." In doing so, his architecture conveys the simplicity and unpretentiousness of nature, and this makes him a successor to the anonymous potters of buncheong.

Cho's architecture shares the aesthetic philosophy of another contemporary artistic movement in Korea, monochrome painting. In *The Color of Nature: Monochrome Art in Korea*, art historian Barbara Bloemink remarked, "The Korean monochrome artists consciously focus on reducing their art works to the essentials, eliminating external references. . . . Their works are based in the traditional Korean aesthetic term *gozol*, roughly translated as plain, simple, and modest; but also elegant and graceful."[5] Monochrome art's greatest practitioners, including Seo-Bo Park, Chong-Hyun Ha, Chang-Sup Chung and Tae-Ho Kim, merge Western monochrome art with gozol and other traditional Asian methods and materials, such as *hanji*. A traditional paper handmade from mulberry bark, hanji was invented more than 1,600 years ago. Pliable, sturdy, and extremely versatile, it is the material that covers doors and windows in a hanok. Chang-Sup Chung and Seo-Bo Park use hanji as their main medium; Suh Seung-Won claims he has always been drawn to the square motif.[6] Like the monochrome artists, Cho is intimately familiar with the principles and concepts behind Western monochrome art. They have actively participated in the artistic exchange between East and West. But while much of Western monochrome art is grounded in the scientific, social and the political, Cho and his Korean monochrome elders' art is grounded in communion with nature. Descendants of a 2,000-year-old tradition, they are poets of eternity, for whom the white space is as important as the black line.

Korean artists emphasize the virtue of the materials they manipulate, and achieve beauty and a profound spirituality through simplicity, repetition and gesture. A brushstroke, a scrape is a vigorous manifestation of the vitality of nature. Cho aims to create transcendent, rather than merely intellectual, experiences. Close inspection with an open mind is the key to understanding Cho's architecture and the energy that flows through it and its surroundings.

"Letting nature be" is the main philosophy of the *Tao Te Ching*, and it represents Cho's work well. In particular, a line from chapter one, "The name that can be named is not the eternal name", is consistent with his architectural view of the world. Cho asserts, "How to stay and live inside it, rather than how to decorate it and what to display in it – that is what I plan for as an architect." His Concrete Box House, a vacation house he built for his family, is in essence a square concrete box. Similar in design and style to his Earth House, the Concrete Box House has a courtyard open to the sky. Located on the side of a mountain, it is an austere, simple space embedded at an angle in the hillside. The courtyard has a small pond and is surrounded by frameless glass walls, so that one may look into the courtyard from anywhere in the house. Cho can watch the reflection of the clouds by day and the moon and stars at night – a real-time screen of natural beauty.

Ten columns of recycled wood support the flat slab roof. The courtyard and wooden beams are reminiscent of a traditional hanok. In his book *In Praise of Architecture*, architect Gio Ponti wrote, "They must not follow the styles of the past (that is easy), but they must perpetuate the nobility of those styles as exhibited in the enchantment of their purest works (that is difficult)."[7] For Cho, each building project encompasses the hanok's essence, to be the place where humans live with nature. Like James Turrell, an artist whom he admires, Cho is fully aware of the importance of how people perceive their environment. It is his vocation to frame the reality they see.

OPPOSITE_ *Sketch by Cho showing the relationship between Twin Trees and the lookout point of Gyeongbok Palace, Seoul, 2006.*

Notes

1 Robert Ivy, "Cho Byoung-Soo: The Spaces In-between", in *Architect 03: Cho Byoung Soo* (Seoul: *Space*, 2009): 205.
2 *Dwell* magazine profile, http://www.dwell.com/profiles/article/byoung-cho.
3 See also Leonard Koren, *Wabi-Sabi: For Artists, Designers, Poets and Philosophers* (Stone Bridge Press, 1994).
4 *Architect 03: Cho Byoung Soo* (Seoul: *Space*, 2009).
5 Soon Chun Cho and Barbara Bloemink, *The Color of Nature: Monochrome Art in Korea* (Assouline, 2008): 16.
6 Interview between Suh Seung-Won and Kim In-Kyung, *Art Monthly* magazine, 2007.
7 Gio Ponti, *In Praise of Architecture* (F. W. Dodge, 1960): 4.

BYOUNG CHO'S BETWEEN_

MARK RAKATANSKY

It seems telling that the times I have sat in Camerata Music Hall with Byoungsoo Cho, we sit not in the triple-height space of the café, but back inside the single-storey area that is set outside of the defining edge of the main hall. This intimate setting is indeed experienced as being outside, as its ceiling consists entirely of glazing. So paradoxically this compressed space feels expansive in its bright light, even as we sit viewing the collective tables of the grander hall through a light first muted by the compressive effect of the hall's suspended mezzanine platform, then sharply defined on the opposite three-storey concrete wall by the raking uplift of illumination from the high skylight. Sitting outside to look back inside: this syncopated sequence of the compression and expansion of vision and space is first a disorienting experience but then a reorienting one, as in so much of Cho's work. As he said in our published conversation in the journal *Space*, it was his desire to keep the central space pure by pushing this seating area and the DJ room out from the main volume. This is ironic in that in order to maintain and perceive this desired purity one has to be positioned outside of it. But desire, by definition, is always elsewhere, in some other place from where we are; otherwise we would not be in the shifting position that is desire, this oscillation between us and the object of our desire, between the here and the there, separated from in order to seek to be reconnected.

There is a similar telling moment in the midst of his short text "Thoughts on the Apple Box", where there suddenly appears a series of terms that shift from its more pervasive essentialist terms and tone. This text, published in 2007 in that same issue of *Space*, is an acclamation to "the purity that comes from utility and honest material" exemplified by a "rudimentary" wooden apple box, professing notions of purity and utility and material and place and nature and silence and abstinence. The belief in those notions has certainly played a significant role in the shape and shaping of Cho's architecture, but their meanings shift through time and circumstance. Say, when Cho was growing up in the socially and politically restrictive regime of post-war Korea, in the pressure of a nation divided with a Demilitarized Zone (DMZ) created four years prior to Cho's birth in 1957, a time indeed when matters of purity and silence and abstinence had poignant political as well as aesthetic connotations. Or when he left the country in 1982 to learn the art and craft of pottery at Western Illinois University, seeking as he has said to be near the Mississippi River birthplace of one of his favourite authors Mark Twain. Or when he transferred to Montana State University later that year to study architecture (immersing himself in rural vernacular architecture), graduating in 1986 (and yet again when he returned to teach there from 1999 to 2006). Or during the two subsequent years when he worked for a corporate firm in Boston before continuing as a graduate student at the Harvard Graduate School of Design and an exchange student at the ETH in Zurich, completing his formal education in 1991.

Certainly within these four decades the various meanings of those "essential" terms for Cho had developed and transformed, particularly, as he has noted, in his encounter with Swiss Neo-Rationalism in his Lugano experience with Mario Campi (a member of the Tendenza group, along with Mario Botta and Luigi Snozzi) during his ETH semester in Spring 1990, where these terms would be aesthetically codified as best conveyed through single (or arrayed) volumes of "pure" geometry (usually rectilinear) and "pure" material (usually concrete). This mode was further reinforced during the year he spent in the mid-1990s teaching at the Kaiserslautern University of Technology with Wolfgang Böhm (a former colleague of Campi at the ETH), in a place 320 miles southwest of Berlin where five years before the Wall had fallen, and thus in the time of the complex early years of German unification.

Yet Cho's Ticino school experience stands in contrast to his two principal influences at the Harvard Graduate School of Design: the historian and critic Robin Evans and the architect Mack Scogin (then Chair of the Department of Architecture and Cho's thesis advisor). They both shunned any conceptual or design notions of essences and purity in favour of the relational

OPPOSITE_ *The interior of the Camerata Music Hall, Heyri Art Valley, Paju, Korea.*

exchanges they discovered in the complexities of high history and vernacular life, and their work remains among the most exhilarating examples of criticism and of architecture produced in the last thirty years. What is particularly interesting is the way Cho's work continues to negotiate between these two poles, poles already established through his considerations of historical and contemporary Korean social and cultural sensibilities. By project, and by turns in each project, Cho develops a mix of pure formal refinement and impure informal roughness, pure centralized forms pushing a seemingly auxiliary program outward only to instigate informal articulations as they encounter their sites. Informal, it needs to be said, is not not-formal. The white celadon and earth-toned Yi Dynasty pottery Cho favours, in his perception of their range between pure and rough, both have particular formal sensibilities as exacting and identifiable as the degrees of rigour and flexibility he maintains in the range of textures he develops in his concrete surfaces.

Indeed, I would say the only essential thing that can be said about the very essence of terms such as purity and utility and material and place and nature and silence and abstinence is that they remain instable in their essential meanings. The proof of which is the empty Korean water bottle I keep right next to me here on my writing desk to remind me of the poignant – humorous and heartbreaking – ironic mutability of Big Symbols. In this particular case, it is a symbol that began as a representation of destruction, division, and divisiveness, a tragedy of national and social and civil proportions, which some fifty years later in 2009 would be marketed, in the form of a "natural" mineral water, as signifying the very essence of purity, under the brand name *DMZ*. Bottled by the largest beverage corporation in Korea, this example of a seemingly antithetical plasticity of essential meaning strikes every Westerner I show this plastic bottle to as akin to as if a German corporation in the 1970s had attempted to market a product called *Berlin WallWater*. That the abstinence of culture in and throughout the 2.5-mile wide and 160-mile long division of country and society and family that is the DMZ would indeed result in an ecologically less contaminated zone that could be marketed as *pure* is just one of the many tragicomic narratives of history, one that Mark Twain would have appreciated. This is something you may sometimes think about even and especially in the powerful uplift and outsweep of Camerata Music Hall while the owner's collection of classical music or jazz is playing, located as it is just 3.5 miles away from the DMZ at the 38th Parallel, in the Heyri Art Valley, one of the most intensive collections of contemporary architecture in the world (currently nine times the number of buildings created for the Weissenhof Siedlung, the 1927 demonstration modernist settlement). Certainly a disorienting and reorienting experience for the viewer and the listener. In that impure distance between the North and the South of this divided country, that span of cultural space and time from the Korean War until now, what is shared and what is secret, what separates and what connects two such entities?

It is this last set of terms that suddenly appear midway through "Thoughts on the Apple Box", in a section whose subtitle is "The story of the society and culture the two apples boxes create". What is important, as Cho states, is not the two entities, but the experience *between* the two:

Experience of relationship between A and B: What you are to me, what I am to you
Experience of span between A and B: The distance from me to you
Experience of sharing between A and B: Us together
Experience of secrecy between A and B: Between you and me
Experience of separation between A and B: I am me, you are you
Experience of connection between A and B: You and me

Cho proposes here a list of six experiences, although the first establishes a more overarching category ("Experience of relationship between A and B: What you are to me, what I am to you") and the remaining five suggest terms that specify more particular articulations of these relations (spanning, sharing, secrecy, separation, connection). While it should be noted that the Korean word 사회성 (sahoeseong) in the subtitle translated as "society" may be more literally, if awkwardly, translated as "sociality", or perhaps better as "social relations", it does seem that Cho is attempting in his metaphors of the boxes to tell a tale of a society and a country, a "woori nara (우리 나라)", a nationhood of linked "surrounding neighbours", as he discusses later in the text. The common English preposition in these six sentences is "between", and the Korean particle that performs the role of this preposition (사이 sai) conveys the same seemingly antithetical range in the sense of meaning in relation to neighbouring entities as does the English word. For example, the meaningful space from this book to you as you are reading it now, as compared to the meaningless gap from you to whatever other object that just happens to be nearby you that you are not engaging with in this moment of reading.

OPPOSITE_ *The façade of the Be-twixt school.*

Prepositions act to convey relational positioning in time or space, regardless as to whether they are pre-positioned before the related entity or, as is sometimes the case in Korean grammar, post-positioned after the entity. In either case for the concept of "between", it is not as an abstract gap but only as relational distance that social and cultural positions are conveyed, likewise for an aesthetic sensibility that might arise out of this social and cultural sense.

This relational sense is conveyed in "Experience of span between A and B: The distance from me to you" even as the first half of the sentence in Korean uses a word whose definition is closer to "distance" than "span", while the second half says just "from me to you". But the translation as given is once again useful because it indicates not just some measurable but meaningless distance – 2.5 miles does not indicate the meaning of the distance from North Korea to South Korea that the DMZ represents – but the possibility of imagining the desire of one entity to span towards or away from another. Measuring a distance is not important, what is important is measuring the meaning in and of the distance. In his Village of Dancing Fish, the living distance between the dormitory boxes becomes not a gap but a living room on the ground level, and the open space above the living room provides an enframing to measure the relational distance and closeness of the Paju landscape and the community compound.

Measuring the distance between entities that are in relation with each other leads to the "Experience of sharing between A and B: Us together". And so in Cho's larger collective complexes he develops means to enact that sharing, as again in this case of the Village of Dancing Fish where the individual dormitory boxes and their living rooms are gathered under a series of elevated thin roof planes, or the Pai Chai University College of Arts building in which the three departments (Architecture, Music, Painting) are drawn together through a series of collective class rooms and public spaces.

This sharing then may give rise to an intimacy that is the "Experience of secrecy between A and B: Between you and me". While the seemingly reserved and principally opaque exterior of many of Cho's projects has been noted as creating interior intimacy, it may be said that often their secrets are revealed in plain sight. Revealed indeed in some of his most ingenious tectonic inventions, such as his skylights made up of stacked layers of glass, presenting not their face for us to look through but their edges illuminated from the life within. But even the cantilever boxed windows of many of the early projects (as well as in the Two-box House and Camerata), which one would not imagine would need to be projected outward in order to keep the house volume pure, intriguingly draw the view out rather than in. And in the Be-twixt school building it is not only the oblique resin windows that offset vision, but also the large glass boxes embedded into the building surface which seemingly invite the view in but through offset sanding on either side of the glass in fact screens it, suspending our vision in between in a volume of light revealed at the building's corner.

In a number of Cho's projects this intimacy generates the counter need for the "Experience of separation between A and B: I am me, you are you". Projects that could easily be developed as single volumes are separated into multiple formations to manifest individual programmatic identities: Two-box, Three-box, Four-box, Stone Wall, Oisoo Lee, E-shaped, U-shaped houses, as well as in institutional buildings like Be-twixt and the Sagan Gallery. Even internally in projects such as the Three-box House and Be-twixt vision across the divide is offset to maintain separation.

In the final turn this very separation instigates a desire to reconnect and so Cho draws these entities back together in an "Experience of connection between A and B: You and me", not only through the screens he wraps around the separated volumes, but through visual, spatial, material exchanges. In this regard the Stone Wall House and the Hanil Visitor complex enact intensive dynamic interplays between separation and connection, while the most recent project, the Louis Vuitton flagship store in Seoul, suggests even more synthetic evolutions by inverting the earlier mode of pushing auxiliary programs outward through involutions now inward eroding the prior pure form of the box, as new relational spatial complexity is developed internally. The Korean second half of this last phrase actually says "You are me, I am you", but again the printed translation perhaps serves circumstances better. The total collapse of two entities into each other is not possible – although it has been almost 150 years since the end of Civil War divisions into North and South of the nominally United States, the traces of those differences remain deep, certainly evident in any national election, remain an ongoing and evolving drama of distance, sharing, secrecy, separation, and connection. What is exciting in Cho's work is the ongoing and evolving drama of the between of these terms in the complex and relational states inherent in every type of building.

OPPOSITE ABOVE AND BELOW_ The fabric cast concrete façade, and the interior, of the Hanil Visitors' Centre and Guest House, Danyang, Korea.

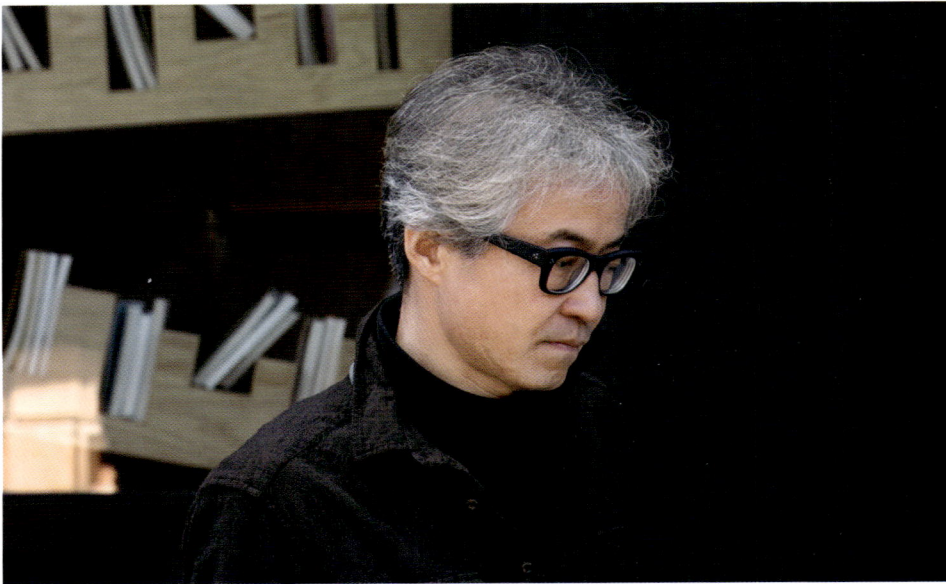

INTERVIEW WITH BYOUNG CHO_

BY CHUL R. KIM

CK: What was the Korean architecture scene like when you began your career, and what is it like now?

BC: These last two decades since I opened my office have been probably the most dramatic years for contemporary Korean architecture. I have noticed a lot of creative energy leading to new, meaningful work. I started my own practice in Seoul twenty years ago, in 1993. I had returned to Korea after ten years of studying and working in the US. In the early 1990s, many of us went abroad and filled our minds with beautiful buildings, lasting friendships, and valuable lessons in the US and Europe, and then came back to Korea with fresh ideas and passion. We were relatively young, in our thirties, and eager to test our theories and visions.

One interesting group that gathered at the time to share ideas was the 4.3 Group led by architects such as Hyo-Sang Seung and Min Hyun-Sik. I remember a fresh and exciting exhibition the group mounted twenty years ago in Seoul, with a gorgeous catalogue that had a blue corrugated cardboard cover. It was my first significant encounter with contemporary Korean architecture and architects, the so-called "second generation", following in the footsteps of Kim Swoo-Geun.

CK: Kim is generally considered to be the grandfather of modern Korean architecture. He designed the main stadium for the Seoul Olympics in 1988 and he started a magazine, *Space*, Korea's first art journal.

BC: He certainly left big shoes to fill. The 4.3 Group struggled with the question of how to express their Korean identity through contemporary architecture, as defined and understood by the West. The group seemed unified in philosophy and attitude, although the members' individual projects varied greatly in detail and characteristics. One principal belief was the importance of "architectural emptiness", the voids and spaces in and around the buildings themselves, as places that hold a power all their own. It is something I am keenly interested in: how do areas created inside and outside a building – the interstitial spaces, courtyards, hallways – occupy the space? How do they add to or detract from the overall feel of a structure? I appreciated the fact that these smart, accomplished architects were tackling many of the same questions I was, and setting the foundation for the work to come. Not much was expected of

OPPOSITE_ *Montana's mountainous terrain can be seen in the background. Cho has studied the agricultural and industrial buildings in Bozeman.*

us, in Korea and elsewhere, and experiments in contemporary architecture were still few and far between. Today, the scene in Korea has grown tremendously and, especially among the general public, there is a greater awareness of contemporary architecture. There is a greater diversity of practitioners, in both the residential and commercial realms, and there are lots of incredible buildings to see throughout Seoul and in other cities. The change has been truly multi-faceted and profound. Also, Korean architects are well connected internationally, having kept and nurtured those bonds made overseas years earlier.

CK: Who are your greatest influences?

BC: When I was an undergraduate, I revered Ludwig Mies van der Rohe, Alvar Aalto, Peter Zumthor, and Jacques Herzog and Pierre de Meuron. However, since I wrote my thesis while at the Harvard Graduate School of Design, the Taoist philosopher Lao Tzu has probably most influenced my architecture as well as my everyday life. From a very early age, I have always been interested in philosophy and nature. I don't think I have ever fully believed in God, but I've thought a lot about birth, life and death. I came to believe in the reasons behind actions. I was curious about intuition. I used to read over and over a book entitled *What Is Man* by Mark Twain, a writer who has affected me deeply. Intuition and emotion, matter and logic – these philosophical questions have helped frame my work in architecture. A class I took at Harvard, Robin Evans's "Intuition and the Rational" seminar, helped me realize that these two disparate concepts are connected. Neither one can exist or be recognized without the other. That is basically the underlying concept of the yin and the yang, which oppose each other but exist as one common body. In the *Tao Te Ching*, everything is relative, and understood through relationships, rather than through its own absolute values.

CK: For example, light is understood in relationship to darkness, and vice versa.

BC: That is my intent in practising architecture. The building is never a thing or a form in and of itself; it is a being that occupies a space, interacts with its environs. It transforms and is transformed by what is around it, constantly and simultaneously.

ABOVE AND OPPOSITE_ *Agricultural buildings in Bozeman, Montana.*

CK: What other forms of art do you practise, and how do they relate to your architectural work?

BC: To me, art and architecture share many aspects, and they stand on common ground. I paint, I sculpt, and I create installations. These activities inspire my architecture. For me, artmaking offers more interesting experiences, making me feel more alive. I love using my body to create paintings, sculptures and prints. For example, when I paint skulls, I use my fingers, hands, and other parts of my body, but no brushes or tools. To me, the only difference between art and architecture is the use of the body. I do not plan ahead in art; I make it by following the flow of my body and intuition. Art has certainly been an exploratory process that has helped me find myself.

One work that exemplifies the thoughts and feelings I address in my art is the Apple Box. Anyone who knows me and my architecture knows that the box is a fundamental shape in my repertoire. The box can symbolize a separation – between what is inside and what is outside. But for me, the box represents what I call "us" (*woori*). The boxes I have made are linked, tied, and, at times, modified in relation to each other. I am in awe of the emptiness inside the box, its purity and abstinence. I am attentive to its effectiveness and its possibilities. I like how it absorbs the sun and the wind. I hope to express through the box the resonant universe that exists in me, in all of us.

CK: After studying at Montana State University in the 1980s, you returned to the university in 1999 to teach. How has Montana affected your view of life and of your work?

BC: Montana is my second home. I love the place, the people, and the architecture, especially the industrial and agricultural buildings found throughout the state. I spent my twenties there as a student and my forties as a professor in the architecture program. As a student, I enjoyed the slow pace of life away from big cities, and I met friends whose families were involved with the region's agricultural economy. I loved the region's industrial and agricultural buildings, but I guess I was too busy with schoolwork to study them very closely.

CK: That changed during your second sojourn in Bozeman.

BC: Yes, very much so. As a teacher, I focused more on my own interests, and I had more of an opportunity to explore the agricultural and industrial buildings: farmhouses, silos, grain-storage facilities made of corrugated steel and gabled roofs. I always thought the honesty and straightforwardness I perceived in people were faithfully reflected in the region's architecture. In fact, their characteristics are in many ways similar to those of the people of Korea. I find that I am comfortable, that I am myself in Montana. Certainly, my experiences in Montana helped develop my admiration for nature, and they also helped form my love of simplicity.

CK: Can you describe the process by which you conceive of and arrive at a design for a building? Does this process change from project to project, or are you a creature of habit?

BC: As I hinted at earlier, I am both rational and intuitive. In his short essay, "Mountain Streams and Trout", Alvar Aalto writes that his moment of creation, or "crystallization", comes from intuition, but it comes only after the rational understanding of a site and its qualities. I start designing for a building in a similar way. I start with the peculiarities of a site, and then apply the program. To me, observing what the given site has and doesn't have is the most important foundation of a design. Once I accomplish that, I turn to questioning and reorganizing the given program. Often I propose to my clients that they adjust their requirements to fit into the site more comfortably. First I form a relationship to the site. The shape of the building usually comes later.

When I start to form ideas about a building, I use sketches to visualize and to imagine what it may look like. Almost at the same time, I select and test materials and construction details. I feel strongly that the creative use of materials and methods is as important as the form on which they are being used. Sometimes, I have to change my entire notion of a building when a construction detail or material does not work as expected. In my structures it is especially in the details that one can see and understand me as an architect and as a human being.

CK: How do you want people to interact with your buildings?

BC: With any building I have built, I want people to experience it in a way that goes beyond merely the visual. I would like them to "feel" it – that is, feel the shape of the building, feel how it fits into nature, how it becomes a part of its environment. I want them to envision living and working in it. I want them to feel what it's like to be inside the structure, outside the structure, and everywhere in between. I believe that my architecture endeavours to describe in a thoughtful manner the relationships between humans and buildings, humans and nature, and humans with other humans.

CK: Sustainability and the impact of your buildings on their surroundings, both during and after their construction, are of the utmost importance to you. When did you first come to feel that way? How does sustainability insert itself into your work?

BC: I guess I've had that attitude from the earliest stage of my career. My early projects, such as the I-shaped House and L-shaped House, explored those qualities. In both, the built structures stay rather simple, allowing surrounding voids to dominate, flow and play. I'm sure that my attitude has been influenced by the cultural heritage of Korea. The big idea behind Korean architecture of the last five hundred years is the notion of site design. How does one deal with the surrounding environment? Koreans have long sought harmony in the way a building is situated and laid out. This is called *poong-soo* in Korean; it is known in China and the West as feng shui. Even though I did not study architecture in Korea, I must have absorbed its elements by growing up in a traditional house and village. "Wind-and-water" is a theory of site selection – planning a site or laying out a room in relation to its surroundings.

Sustainability has been of the utmost importance to me for a very long time. I have seen first hand how much is wasted and lost in every architectural project, in every construction site. I insist on using materials and construction methods that are available locally. The best part is, they often cost less. I frequently use recycled materials, such as woods and concrete. My team and I are interested not only in the use of so-called "sustainable materials", but in the

OPPOSITE_ *Sketch showing the relationship in the E-shaped House, Seoul, Korea, between the water garden, the concrete and the low window opening.*

sustainable applications of conventional materials. For example, in the Hanil Visitors' Centre and Guest House, we used abandoned concrete in a unique and truly sustainable way. In Korea, as in Japan, pour-in-place concrete has been the most commonly used material since the Second World War. I believe that finding ways to recycle concrete is crucial, particularly in our region, for at least the next fifty years. We tested and developed several different applications of concrete from demolished buildings and we noticed that crushed concrete absorbs moisture very well. We placed it in gabion baskets to absorb moisture, and sprinkled seeds taken from the surrounding plants, and soon the entire wall turned green. Thus concrete saved from environmental waste provides shade to the west end of the building. The green wall helps cool the building in Korea's hot summers. Our thought is that recycled concrete can be rehabilitated and used to at once control and be in visual harmony with the environment. In my definition, for something to be truly sustainable it has to be culturally, socially, and environmentally so. Any construction material or method should be carefully analysed and studied from multiple angles – physical and environmental as well as social and cultural.

CK: As you find yourself in the middle of your career – with lots of buildings behind you and, one hopes, lots of buildings still before you – what more do you want or expect to accomplish?

BC: My goal is to achieve more consistency in the direction of my works. I would like to believe that the projects my firm and I have built over the past twenty years were along the same path. They were simple structures that framed and connected people and nature. The underlying philosophy for them came from the traditional values found in traditional Korean poetry, paintings and architecture: purity, modesty, elegance, and spontaneity. But the idea of the simple structure has also been a fundamental part of Western culture, especially in the agricultural and industrial environment. I would like to continue these traditions and examine further the ways in which "simple architecture" can connect us to the earth. And I hope my buildings reflect that more clearly and uniquely. That is all that I would like to accomplish, to contribute to better living and a more sustainable planet.

OPPOSITE_ *The western wall at the Hanil Visitors' Centre, Danyang, Korea.*
The project promotes the environmental benefits of recycling concrete.

AN ORIGINAL WITH NATURAL SENSIBILITIES_

BY BONG-RYUL KIM

An architect who has worked in architecture all his life arrives at some point at a crossroads, where he must choose a direction in which to continue. One path may lead him to new projects based on new concepts. To build with materials that have not been used or seen before is to take a risk, but also to invite a creative adventure. The architect can then make a newly created space. The architect does not know exactly what the outcome might be. He might know what he wants, but cannot express clearly what it is. But during the work process he may sense, "This isn't it." Ideas flow out endlessly for every new project. Even if the bank of ideas eventually runs out that will not stop him. If he has support from his partners and employees that can fill in his shortcomings, then he might be able to continue on his path as an inventor-architect.

Another path the architect can take is to choose one model and pursue it doggedly until all possibilities have been exhausted. This is the attitude of an architect-in-training. He knows precisely what he has accomplished, what he has lost, and what he needs to accomplish. In each new project, he will use similar concepts and space, and even materials and details, repeatedly. His work may be criticized for being repetitive, but he continues to work towards his ideal. To him, "new" does not mean creating something new for the first time; newness is about evolving towards his goal. Thus, the results that accumulate from his progression take him closer, with each work completed, towards a state of perfection. Such an architect needs partners who agree with and support his ideas and direction. But fundamentally, no one can do the work for him. Byoung Cho is an architect who pursues the latter of the two paths.

REPETITION AND DIFFERENCE

Cho's first project upon returning to Korea, after more than a decade abroad, was for a residential complex in Shindang-dong, a neighbourhood in Seoul. After taking an interest in the spontaneously built structures in the hillsides of Shindang-dong, he published a small book, *Contemporary Vernacular*. In the book, Cho made the point that the area was rich in architectural details – rugged stairways, recycled doors, the juxtaposition of unrelated materials – that went largely unnoticed. Given his study overseas and the unfamiliar passion in his work, people wondered whether Cho was a bit obsessive.

When Cho built the L-shaped House in Seoul and another similar residence in Ilsan, the originality of these designs was evident. They looked like they were a new attempt to explore one's existence. But looking back fifteen years later, I feel that they were the unleashing of a rather more powerful and sustaining interest and passion. Many of Cho's houses – the I-shaped House, the L-shaped House, the U-shaped House and the Box House, among them – are names originally coined from *hangul*, the Korean alphabet. (For this book, English letters with similar shapes have replaced the Korean letters.) The architect uses their angular configurations to maximum benefit, especially in his projects located in urban areas, and in this way they are descended from traditional Korean houses. The U-shaped and the square-shaped traditional houses in the northern part of Seoul protect their inhabitants from the noise of the streets and neighbours. Such an arrangement also follows the principle of having all of the flow lines originate in the inner court. From his perspective, Cho's box styles could be interpreted as having derived from city construction or residential circumstances.

OPPOSITE ABOVE_ *The skylight and concrete detail of the Two-box House, Heyri Art Valley, Paju, Korea.*

OPPOSITE BELOW_ *Concrete Box House in its surroundings, Yangpyeong, Korea.*

For projects in less dense areas, the shape of a building is not determined so much by external factors. Rather, it comes from the vision of the architect; the inspiration comes from deep within him. The square-shaped Earth House, built on a secluded hill in the Seoul countryside, is a summer house, a kind of studio. It is situated in nature, but Cho has sheltered it from the elements by minimizing its external opening. The architect placed the inner court in the middle of the box and surrounded the four sides of the court with transparent glass. The structure is completely closed off externally, but it is opened internally, like a box with double-sided construction. The inner court is buried in the ground. The structure has no external walls: the inner court is dug out of the ground. The only aspect that opens out to nature is the sky above the inner court. Cho's houses do not come in direct contact with the landscape or the environment. Instead, they construct rim boundaries and provide a valuable perspective to "a rite of passage" that crosses such boundaries.

Cho's Pai Chai University College of Arts building repeats this box shape. However, unlike in his residential structures, the inner court of the museum becomes an enhanced public space. Cho has placed the box in the air, focusing not only the flow line, but also the sight line on the inner court. Incorporating the slope of the site into the courtyard, he has created an interesting experiment in the flow of people through the space. It may seem as if he were repeating his own prototype, but Cho's works contain many delicate differences. The vertical movement of the inner court, for instance, changes the relationship between the individual spaces. In the Earth House, the rooms that branch out in all directions from the centre of the court are facing each other. In contrast, the space at the Pai Chai University College of Arts building is more independent. In order to bring a sense of individuality to the building's more private areas, Cho felt it was important to centre the public's attention on the inner court and make it a place where people naturally want to gather.

Working on both private residential houses and public buildings has given Cho the opportunity to see the advantages gained through repetition. By using the same elements in multiple buildings, yet altering each one to suit its individual needs, the architect is approaching a state of perfection. Such differences are valuable, since they result from the architect's innermost desires. The house he built for the novelist Oisoo Lee, in Hwacheon, Korea, is a powerful example, and may even be misunderstood as not being part of the same series. With a hard skin like a crust and divided segments, the structure looks different from Cho's prototypical boxes, but the house maintains the concept of being closed off to the exterior and open to the interior, echoing the prototype of the double-sided construction. It repeats a theme, yet is strongly individual in character.

PROTOTYPE AND EXPERIENCE

As we see the box reiterated and subtly transformed, we wonder where the prototype came from. The architect often recalls the times he played in his mother's traditional hanok house, located in Seoul. He remembers not only the spatial schemes, but also the feel of the materials, such as wooden posts and doors. In the repeated concrete box arrangements in his work, the prototype of the traditional hanok can be found. His use of wooden posts, abruptly placed, provokes comparisons to the hanok's signature features. Also, Cho has been influenced by the shape of the wooden apple boxes found in Korea. However simple they may be, Cho has cited them as a representation of his architectural ideal. His sophisticated boxes echo the coarse and rough marks left by the power saw, the joining of pieces by nails that resist any signs of craftsmanship.

The Two-box House and the Three-box House conjure the image of apple boxes stacked on top of one another. Their textured surfaces evoke sawing marks. Cho has remarked that the rough concrete "provokes primitive senses that lie deep within humans". Perhaps Cho's interest in the contemporary vernacular is not sociological, but rather has to do with archaic materials and a dormant architectural nature. Primitive nature like this is found in such places as the barns and factories of Montana, the back country of the American Rockies, with which Cho is intimately familiar.

OPPOSITE_ *Pai Chai University College of Arts building, 2002.*

Like the apple boxes made solely from joined wooden materials, Cho's architectural materials join together naturally, without adhesives. For instance, he builds ceilings by stacking glass and placing it in the concrete holes. In other instances, concrete and steel plates are joined together, and from them wooden materials protrude. At times, he refuses to cover the concrete roof with waterproof agents or a parapet.

While at the Harvard Graduate School of Design, Cho exhibited seven geometric pieces based on his architectural prototype, entitled *Experience and Recognition*. One work was a wooden mass into which a stairway had been carved; another featured a rectangular shape half-buried in the ground. The objects not only showed variances within the framework of a double-sided box, but they were also much closer to a prototype of experience. If his double-sided construction is a form that penetrates through the external and the internal, the stairway buried in the ground is a form that recognizes the experience of penetrating the boundary of the ground level and entering the underground.

The starting point for Cho's architecture is neither abstract theory nor geometrical manipulation. It springs forth from his personal experience and memory. Therefore, they are not fragmented elements, but ones that exist in certain circumstances and relationships. For instance, the thin layer of water that often appears in Cho's design for the Sagan Gallery in Seoul is devised so that natural light reflects onto the surface of the water, rather than the form itself. The square-shaped box that closes off to the exterior may be seen, in this context, as an attempt to capture a piece of the sky. The low-lying windows serve as a type of frame, which controls what is seen on the outside. In the end, these factors derive from what humans have experienced and recognized. Why Cho is so overtly fixated as an architect on the properties and potential of matter is understandable in this context. His latest obsession is creating a new expression using wires, but his usual tools are concrete, plywood, glass and steel. By using unique construction methods on these common materials, he invites new experiences.

Through special details the architect reveals his method. When Cho juxtaposes disparate materials, he acknowledges there is a need for hidden sophisticated details. His architecture might seem devoid of details, making it look rough and slightly rustic, but that is his intention: it hides sophistication. Lao Tzu once said, "Grand craftsmanship looks awkward from a certain angle." Cho's architectural ingenuity is on the verge of achieving perfection through repetition and difference. His Earth House has no structure exposed at ground level. There is only the inner court buried in the ground and the stairway. The low entrance requires one to be careful when entering and the walls and the floor have no covering – to build this rustic, seemingly clumsy structure, a wooden frame was planted deep within the ground, and thick, complicated moulds had to be changed on several occasions.

For Cho, architecture pursued repeatedly, with the determination of an architect-in-training, has yielded noble attributes. Such efforts have allowed him to leap over the mediocre in all of his work. Regardless of who makes what structures in Switzerland, or what epoch-making architecture is debuted in England, Cho has kept on the same path of pursuing his own architectural ideal. But completing his works is not the only present he offers us. His repetitions always accompany new differences; they lead others to forget repetition itself. He proposes a new way of architecture, something that is traditional, but difficult to find in Korea's architectural landscape. Repetition leads to difference; when the differences accumulate, newness transpires. Is it not time for such new changes? This is why we expect the era of change when we contemplate Byoung Cho's architectural creations.

OPPOSITE_ *Community House, Yangpyeong, Korea, 2008.*

THE PROJECTS_

01. I-SHAPED HOUSE_

SEOUL, KOREA, 1997

Seoul is a city that has experienced a series of dramatic changes in the last hundred years or so. It has witnessed the end of the six-century-long Choson Dynasty; thirty-five years of Japanese occupation; the hellish Korean Conflict in the 1950s; three decades of painful reconstruction; and the miraculous economic boom of the past three decades. Traditional Confucian culture has yielded to a post-industrial, information-oriented society, and Korea is one of the most tech-savvy countries in the world. The changing times have meant more and more construction, but that comes at a price. Over five thousand years of history the city has built on top of itself, again and again, leaving layers of buildings and other elements, not to mention values and beliefs, buried underneath.

Cho observes, "Every day, we produce what we are required to produce, and we try to do it more efficiently. But we don't ask what it means for our inner selves. Through architecture, I want to restore our lost qualities by providing a place where one can escape from our increasingly mechanized environment. I would say that my architecture is successful if it provides the room for us to think about ourselves, to ask what and who we are, to what we belong, and toward what we are running."

The clients had two conditions for this two-family residence and art studio. The first was that one should feel calm and relaxed when one entered the house. Secondly, they wanted a simple plan incorporating a *madang*, or open courtyard. Cho's solution was to invoke the "I" shape in his design. When horizontal, the character signifies the number one in Chinese. An auspicious number that symbolizes the beginning, initiation, growth and potential. A horizontal I-shaped plan with a courtyard is the most common plan in traditional Korean residences. Cho selected it because he found it direct, calm and simple. He designed a box shaped like the character and placed it within the natural contours of the site.

Cho laid out the interior so that all of the major spaces would have a direct relationship with the courtyard. "When one rests looking out the window, the sky comes in over the concrete wall and the courtyard," he says. "One comes back to a place where one belongs, between nature and architecture – an organic and minimal straight line."

OPPOSITE, CLOCKWISE FROM TOP LEFT_ *The open courtyard of the I-shaped House. The house seen from the east and from the street.*

OPPOSITE, CLOCKWISE FROM TOP LEFT_
The bedroom of the I-shaped House seen from outside, the view
of the bedroom from the living room and the bedroom itself.

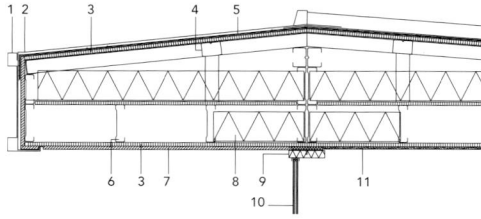

PROJECT TEAM: Jin-wook Lee
LOCATION: 475-35,4, Pyeongchang-dong, Jongno-gu, Seoul, Korea
USE: Residence and art studio
GROSS FLOOR AREA: 194 m² (2,088 ft²)
STRUCTURE: Reinforced concrete, light steel

SECTIONAL DETAIL: EXTERIOR WALL

1. THK 1.2 mm zinc-plated steel plate
2. THK 0.6 mm stainless steel plate
3. THK 12 mm OSB plywood
4. 64 x 45 x 1.4 m steel stud
5. THK 3 mm sheet waterproof
6. 127 x 30 x 1.4 m steel stud
7. THK 12 mm Douglas pine plywood
8. THK 100 mm glass fibre heat insulating material
9. THK 1.2 mm zinc-plated steel frame
10. THK 16 mm double glazing
11. THK 9 mm gypsum board
12. THK 20 mm red pine rectangular lumber
13. THK 3 mm steel plate
14. THK 200 mm RC concrete slab
15. THK 10 mm ondol floor
16. THK 40 mm pine ondol
17. THK 70 mm insulative foam concrete
18. THK 10 mm plaster mortar
19. THK 120 mm RC concrete wall
20. THK 15 mm plaster mortar
21. 60 x 40 x 2.4 m steel rectangular pipe

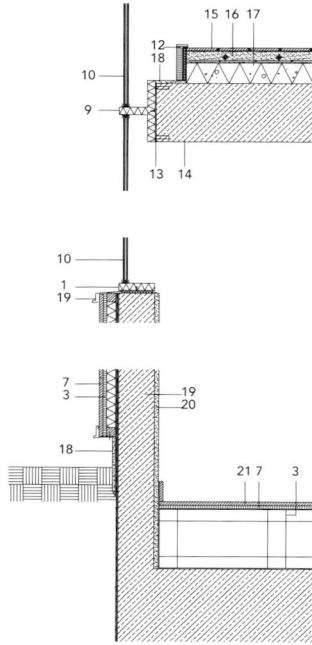

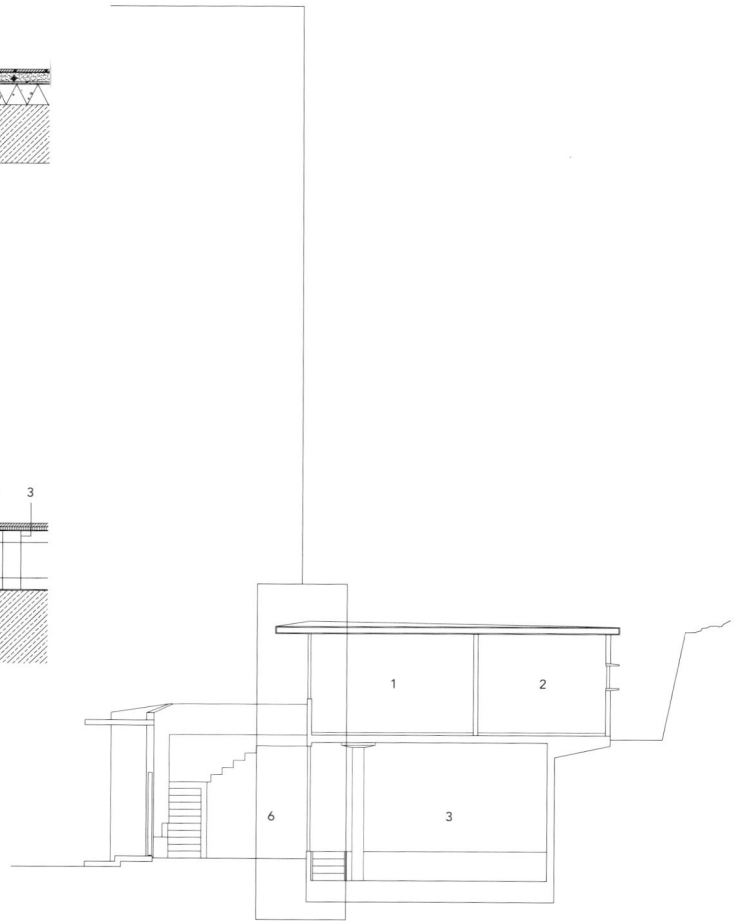

1. Living room
2. Kitchen and dining room
3. Room
4. Master bedroom
5. Children's room
6. Studio
7. Parking
8. Boiler
9. Courtyard

SECTION A

0   5 m

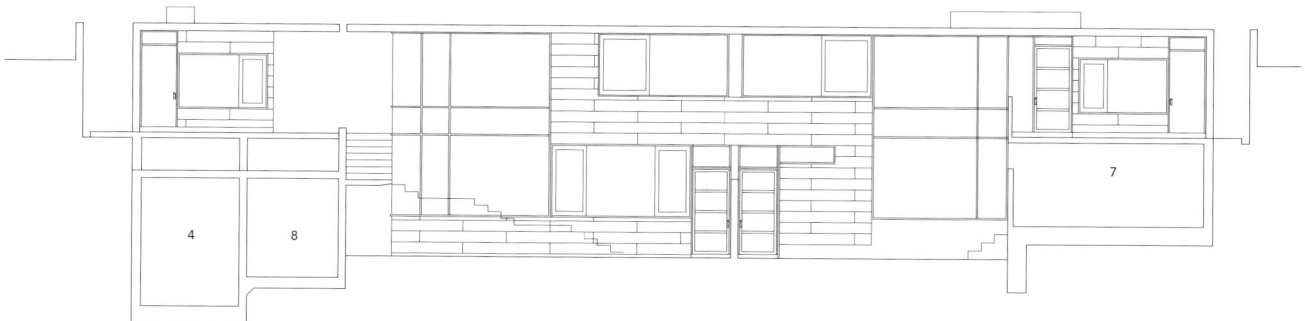

SECTION B

0   5 m

A'

A

8 m main road

FIRST FLOOR PLAN   0   5 m

4 3
4 3
5
1 2 2 1 5

6   6
7
8 9 9
B'
B
8

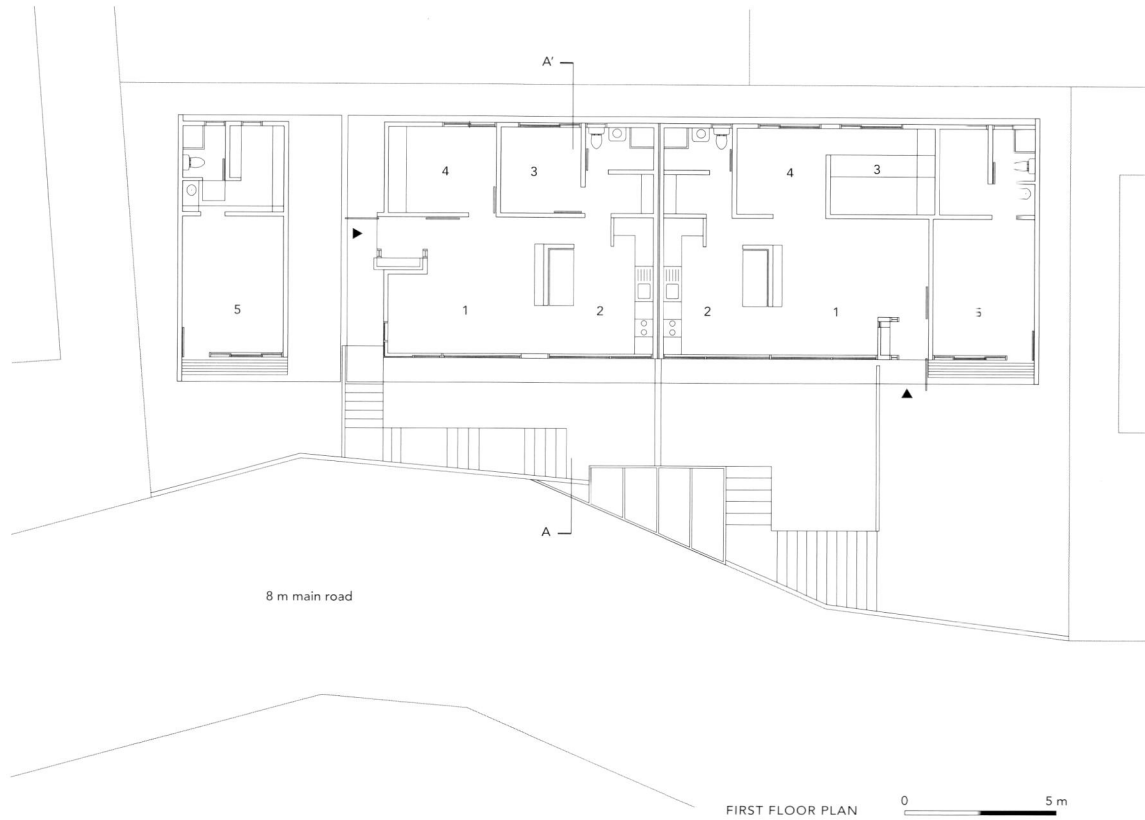

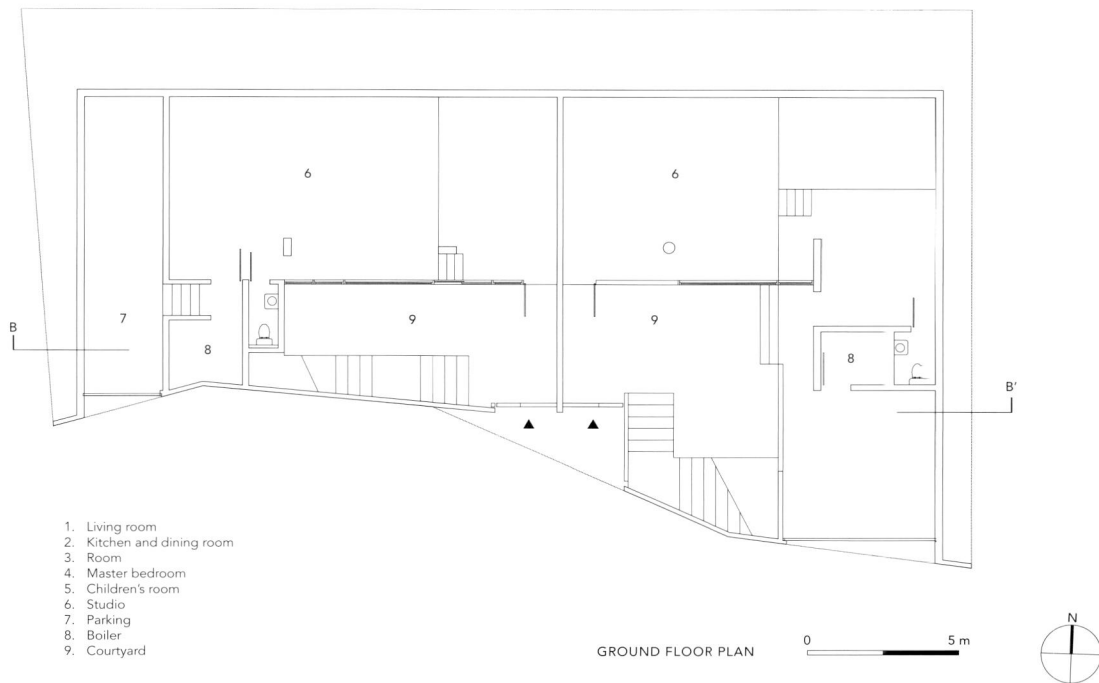

1. Living room
2. Kitchen and dining room
3. Room
4. Master bedroom
5. Children's room
6. Studio
7. Parking
8. Boiler
9. Courtyard

GROUND FLOOR PLAN   0   5 m

N

02. THE VILLAGE OF DANCING FISH_

PAJU, KOREA, 1999

The Village of Dancing Fish is a private facility in a semi-agricultural area in Paju, northwest of Seoul. The village offers housing and care for mentally disabled adults, with an experimental program that teaches residents agricultural work. It is situated on a serene hill whose name translates to the "hill where fish play". Woods gently embrace the campus and open into rural fields.

The dormitory was designed to retain and echo the gentle gradient of the hill and the woods surrounding it, as well as to provide a village-like atmosphere for the inhabitants.

This was achieved by the use of simple, light "boxes" perched delicately on the site, which allow views of the landscape to flow through like a breeze. The visual continuity of the hill and the units creates a dialogue between the surroundings and the manmade construction. A lightweight roof and a walkway unify and organize the boxes.

The villagers help run a farm during the day, and the produce grown on site is sold in a portable pavilion, providing an organic food source for the area's communities. Ample gathering spaces encourage social interaction among the village's residents, which greatly aids many patients' efforts towards reintegrating into society.

Cho placed visually distinctive particular areas in spaces throughout the complex where people with a reduced sense of direction, height, and time can orient themselves.

In keeping with his commitment to minimizing his imprint on the landscape, Cho built the facility using unprocessed materials wherever possible. Douglas fir plywood is the main exterior material for the living quarters. It required special attention at the joints and corners, where Cho decided to employ aluminium strips to make the composition tidy. Cho also used galvanized steel – its rustic quality was his nod to the Gyeonggi regions farming facilities. Timber was used for the horizontal lines in doors and windows, making it easier to distinguish between the different materials.

"Between the natural and humanistic elements of life, there exists a void, an 'in-between' that I believe can be filled and connected by architecture," states Cho. 'Furthermore, there exists a relationship between nature and being, which forms the basis of an integrative environment meant to successfully treat the patients."

OPPOSITE_ *The boxes of the dormitory set in farmland.*

PROJECT TEAM: Jea-ha Lee, Jin-wook Lee
LOCATION: 241, Eoyujiri, Jeokseon-myeon, Paju, Gyeonggi-do, Korea
USE: Educational and welfare facility
GROSS FLOOR AREA: 1,259 m² (13,551 ft²)
STRUCTURE: Reinforced concrete, wood, steel frame

NORTH ELEVATION

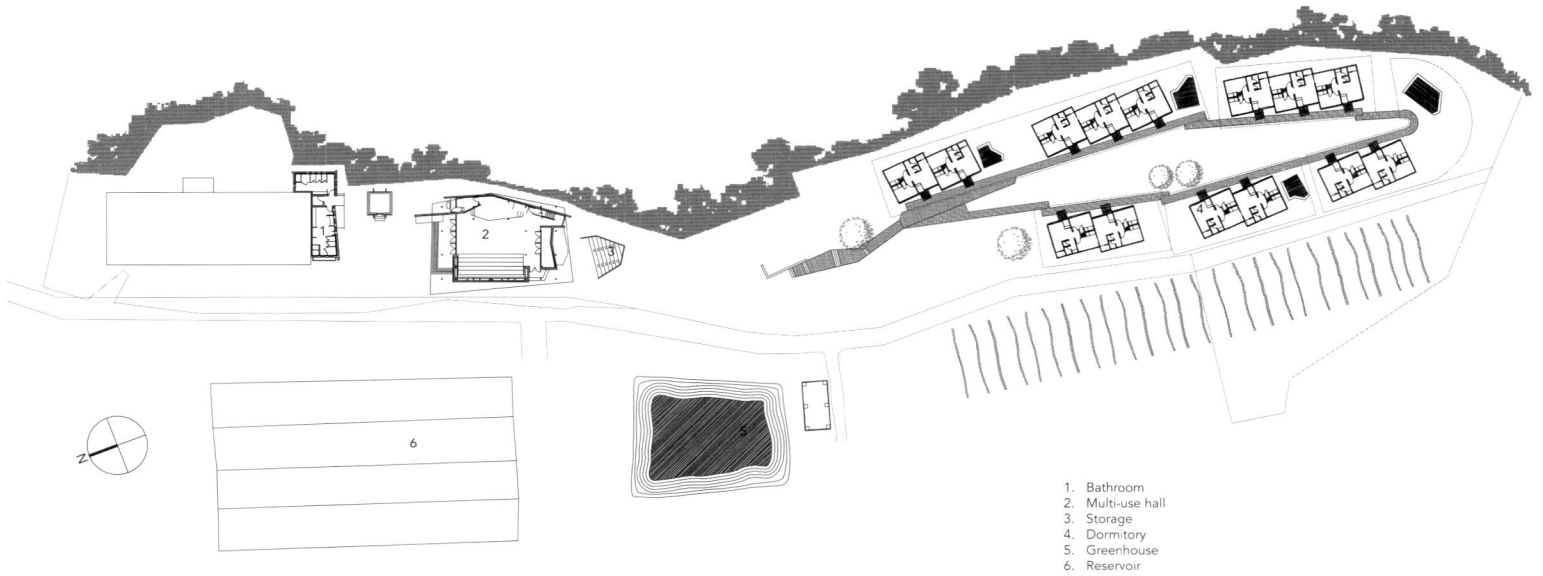

1. Bathroom
2. Multi-use hall
3. Storage
4. Dormitory
5. Greenhouse
6. Reservoir

GROUND FLOOR PLAN   0   10 m

CLOCKWISE FROM TOP LEFT_ *A detail of the roof, the living units and the interior of the multi-purpose building.*

CLOCKWISE FROM TOP LEFT_ *The dormitory roof corresponds to the semi-agricultural background of Paju, the walking deck in the courtyard and the multi-purpose building.*

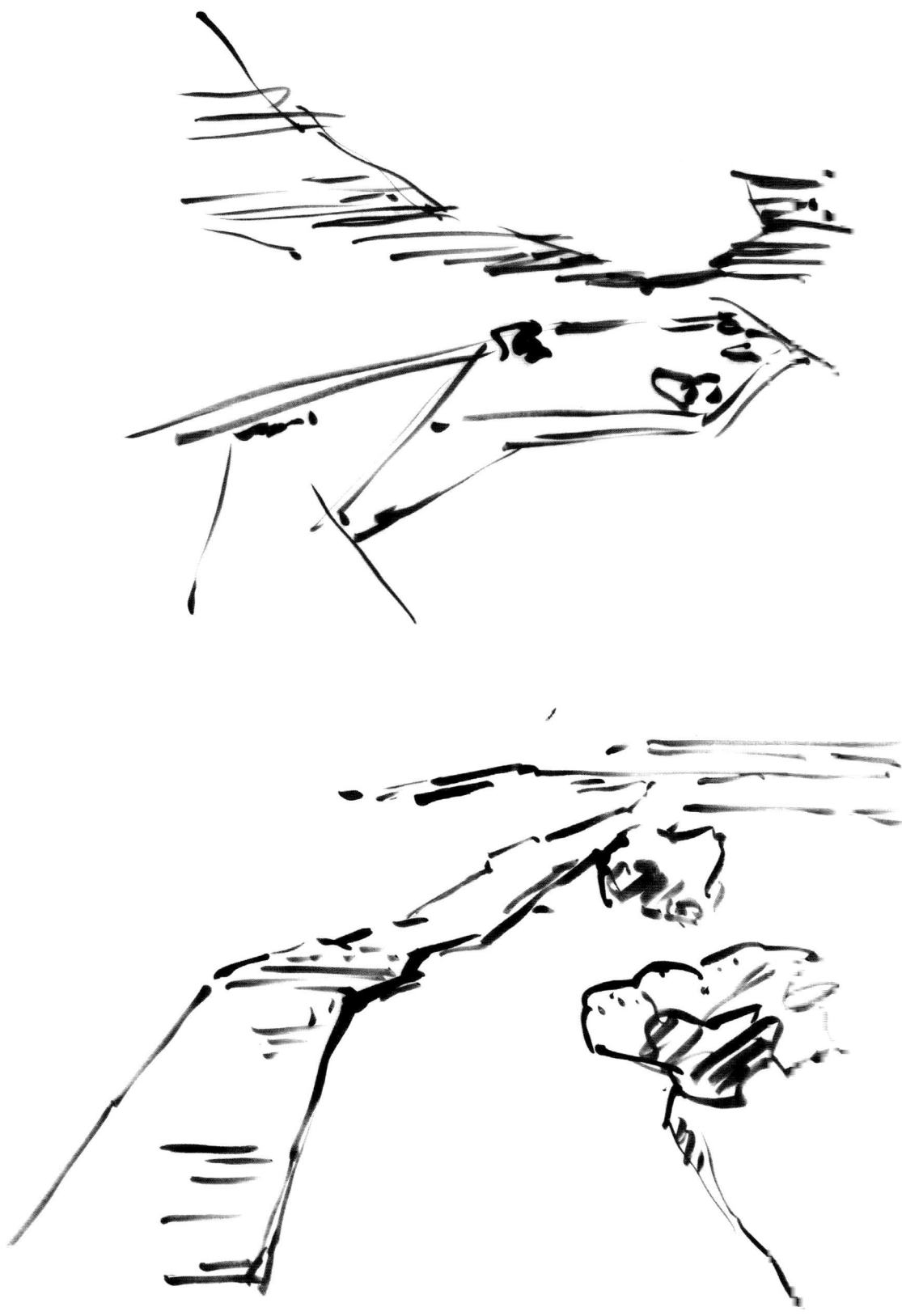

03. U-SHAPED HOUSE_

YANGPYEONG, KOREA, 2002

Cho feels he sees too many buildings that cast visual boundaries, cutting off the people within from the nature just outside their walls. The U-shaped House was Cho's experiment in restoring these broken relationships and celebrating the organic entwinement of man and his environment. But even beyond that, Cho wanted the peculiarities of a specific individual to contribute to this organic entity.

Since his thoughts on and intentions for the house were complicated from the beginning, and morphed several times before he settled on the final iteration, Cho realized it was essential that the building itself should be simple, leaving the structure and landscape to develop a rich and expressive dialogue. The building opens to the south, revealing an untouched landscape while obscuring the banalities of a busy street to the east and residences to the west. Cho extended the horizon by keeping the house's lines low. Looking

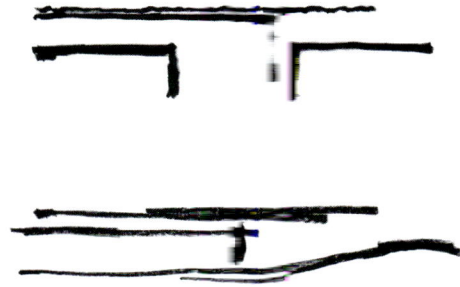

off into the distance, visitors may have the impression that the earth holds the building in its grasp, keeping it close to its bosom.

Two walls, one placed along the street and the other defining interior and exterior space, establish the resting place for two roofs. The walls extend beyond them, stretching into the neighbourhood. The roofs, made of two thin planes, float lightly above the building and harbour spaces where the building's discrete elements overlap. Cho placed dirt on the west side of the house, creating an artificial mound that undulates like the hills seen to the south. Between this mound is the entry courtyard composed of two masses, a contemporary take on the traditional Korean courtyard that establishes a relationship between all of the rooms in the house. The walls, flooring and mounds have a no-nonsense finish and avoid any appearance of slickness. The metal roofs are Galvalume corrugated steel plates, while the foundation was created by tying two 0.6 x 2.4 m (2 x 8 ft) composite beams, welded to steel plates cast in concrete. The external walls were finished in a black-stained red pine chosen for its contrast to the metal roof and concrete walls.

OPPOSITE_ *The view of the house from the street.*

ABOVE, CLOCKWISE FROM LEFT_ *Looking towards the street, sketches showing the relationship of the roof, the earth and the space in between and the entrance to the low house.*

PROJECT TEAM: Seung-hyun Kim

LOCATION: Bockpo-ri, Seo-myeon, Yangpyeong-gun, Gyeonggi-do, Korea

USE: Residential

GROSS FLOOR AREA: 151.4 m² (1,629.6 ft²)

STRUCTURE: Reinforced concrete, 2 x 4 wood frame

OPPOSITE_ *The view of the deck from the courtyard.*

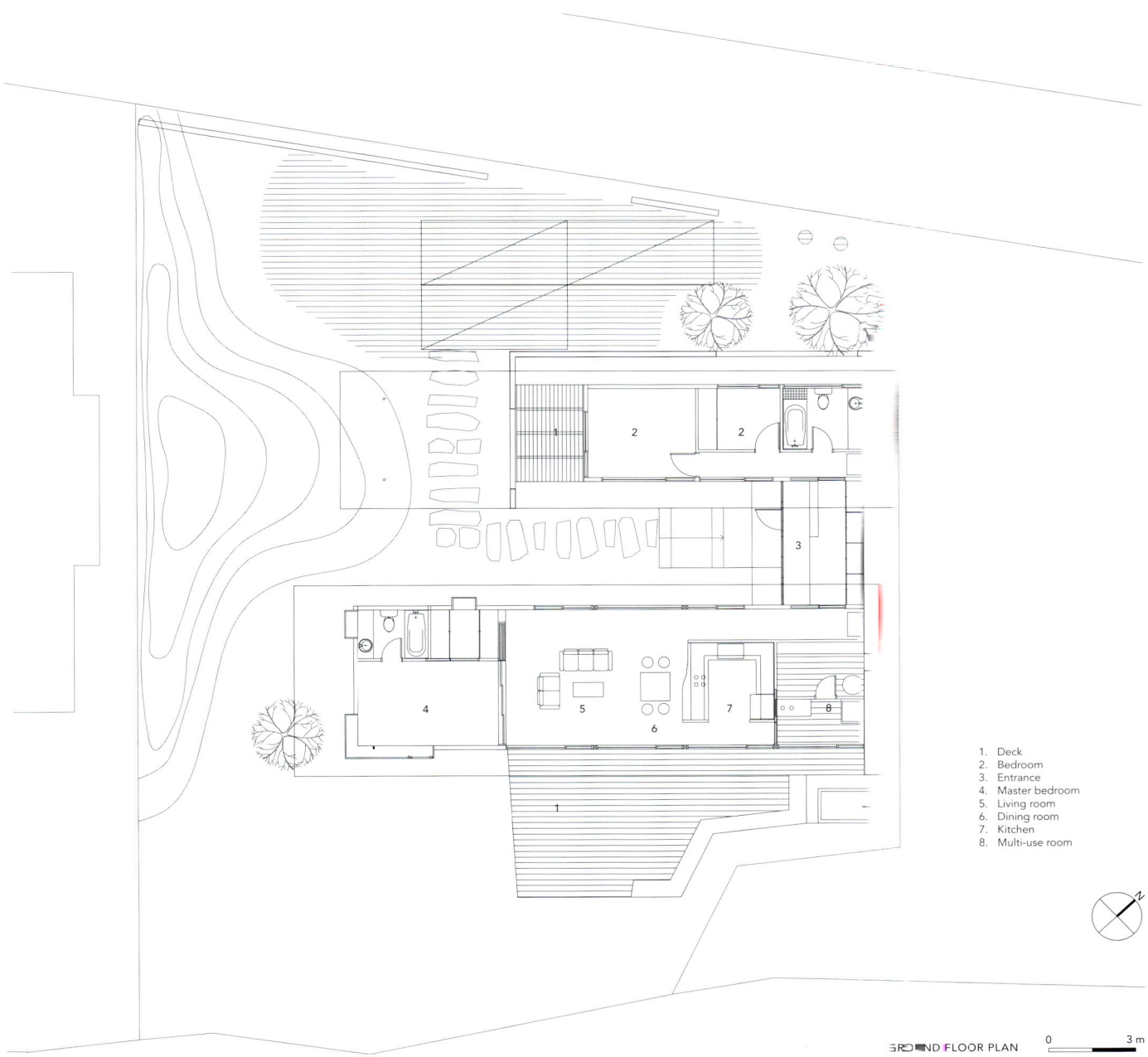

1. Deck
2. Bedroom
3. Entrance
4. Master bedroom
5. Living room
6. Dining room
7. Kitchen
8. Multi-use room

GROUND FLOOR PLAN

0   3 m

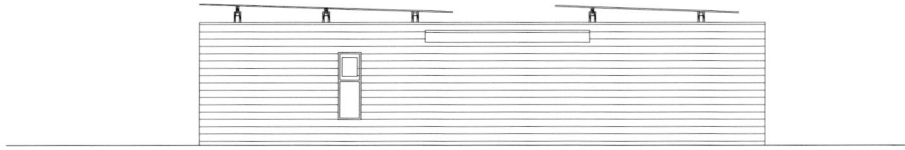

EAST ELEVATION

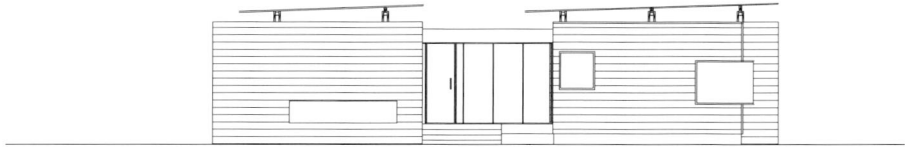

0   3 m

WEST ELEVATION

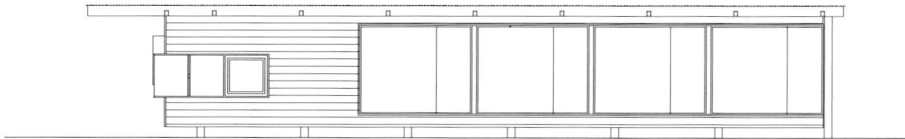

0   3 m

SOUTH ELEVATION

0   3 m

NORTH ELEVATION

0   3 m

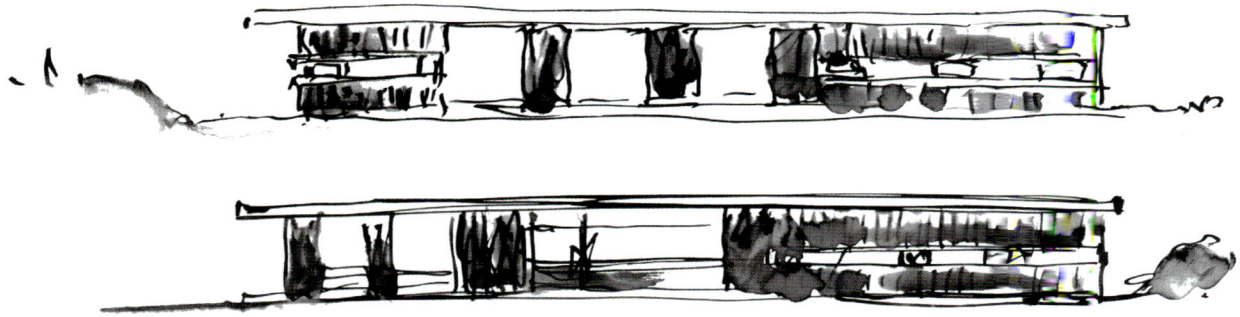

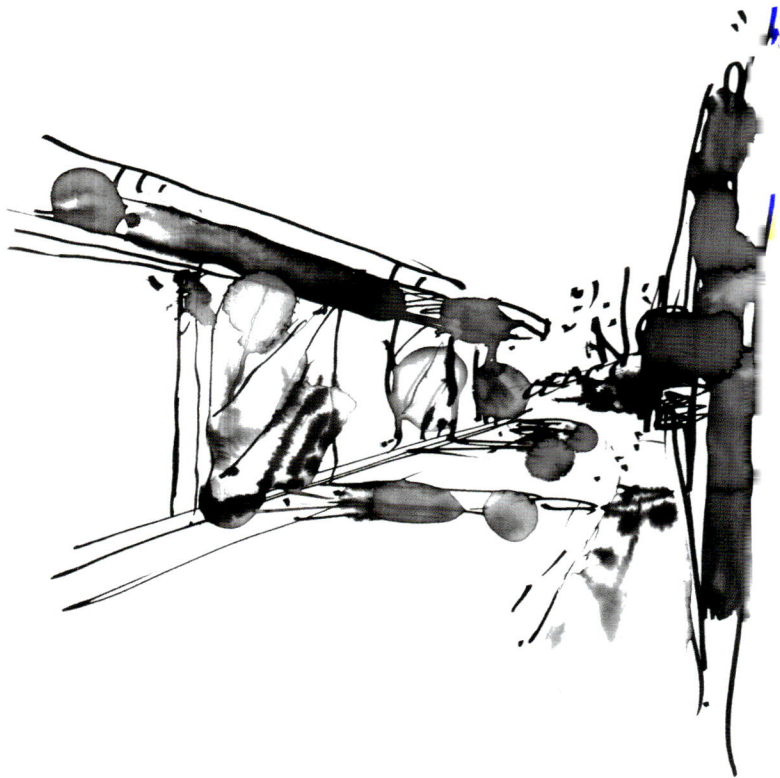

TOP AND ABOVE_ *Early sketches showing the elevations and the entrance looking towards the garden.*

04. CAMERATA MUSIC STUDIO_

HEYRI ART VALLEY, PAJU,
KOREA, 2003

Heyri Art Valley, in Paju, 20 miles northwest of Seoul, is a town built by artists and cultural activists to promote the culture of a united Korean community. Named after an old folk song, it is less than three miles from the demilitarized zone between North and South Korea, the most heavily fortified border in the world. In a terrain pocked by abandoned bunkers from the Korean Conflict, the people of South Korea have established a living, thriving shrine to peace and cooperation through art.

Commissioned by In-Young Hwang, a now retired beloved anchor on national television, the Camerata Music Studio, Gallery and Residence, one of about 150 buildings in Heyri, was designed to serve two distinct functions: as Hwang's residence and also a library and listening space for his vast collection of vinyl records. He listens to them on antique 1930s gramophones. The listening studio is open to the general public – in the client's words, to "whoever loves music".

Camerata bridges the urban and natural environment, triggering a meaningful conversation between the two. Cho intended for the building to operate as a single organism, supporting the intense

OPPOSITE, FROM LEFT TO RIGHT_ *Camerata Music Studio: the bay windows are on the second level. The external steel wire screen adds a rustic feel.*

BELOW_ *The view from the south.*

memories and emotions, experience and perception related to an individual's relationship to music.

Partly in response to the site – Camerata is built into the side of a sloping hill – the design started as a box, with minimal formal expression on the exterior and a deceptively simple-looking interior. In order to preserve the view, a defining feature of the site, Cho split the box into two parts along its north–south axis and placed a water garden and a floating, cantilevered steel staircase in the divide, creating a visual connection between the hill and the street. This split mass also manifests visually the separation of the residence's two functions. The gap between the two halves not only drives circulation through the middle of the building on the north–south axis, but also brings to light what Cho calls a "void space" that frames the landscape behind. The result is serene, contemplative and poetic, an enlightened setting that sets the visitor up for a transformative experience through music.

Cho's biggest concern for the interior was to maintain an ambience of simplicity and harmony with nature. He pushed all building functions to the periphery of the site, creating a column-free central atrium that serves a vital acoustic purpose. This primitive space was kept as spare as possible and sunlight streams through windows in the entrance, which offer vistas of the surrounding hills.

The void areas of the south wall on the second level were finished in a stainless steel wire mesh, adding a rustic feel to reference the village's modest beginnings. Cho collaborated with a manufacturer of wire for conveyor belts to develop a screen with a wide surface that could reflect light in unexpected ways. The horizontal windows on the second level were manufactured by attaching steel plates to the aluminium windows. Situated to the west, a long concrete formwork wall emphasizes the joints of the pinewood used in the casting process, its textures further highlighted when caught by sunlight. Lastly, the music studio is suspended in air. It is made of timber hung on thick wire, creating a space inside a space and aiding sound absorption. When all of these elements are put together, it is easy to see how Camerata may be the world's most intimate and personal music hall.

PROJECT TEAM: Moon-hyeon Jo
LOCATION: G-18, Heyri Art Valley, Beopheung-ri, Tanhyun-myeon,
Paju, Gyeonggi-do, Korea
USE: Residential and music café
GROSS FLOOR AREA: 917.5 m² (9,875.8 ft²)
STRUCTURE: Reinforced concrete, wooden slab

CLOCKWISE FROM TOP_ *Sketch of the east view with the sloped earth.*
Study of the metal screen on the second level and a study of the metal
screen, from the front.

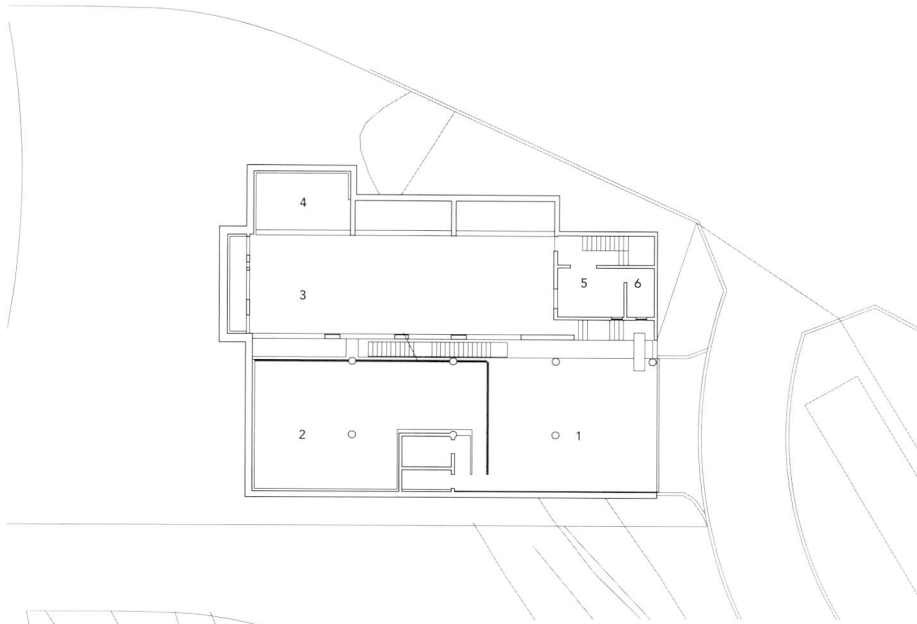

GROUND FLOOR PLAN

1. Parking
2. Exhibition gallery
3. Music studio
4. Dl room
5. Kitchen
6. Storage

C____5 m

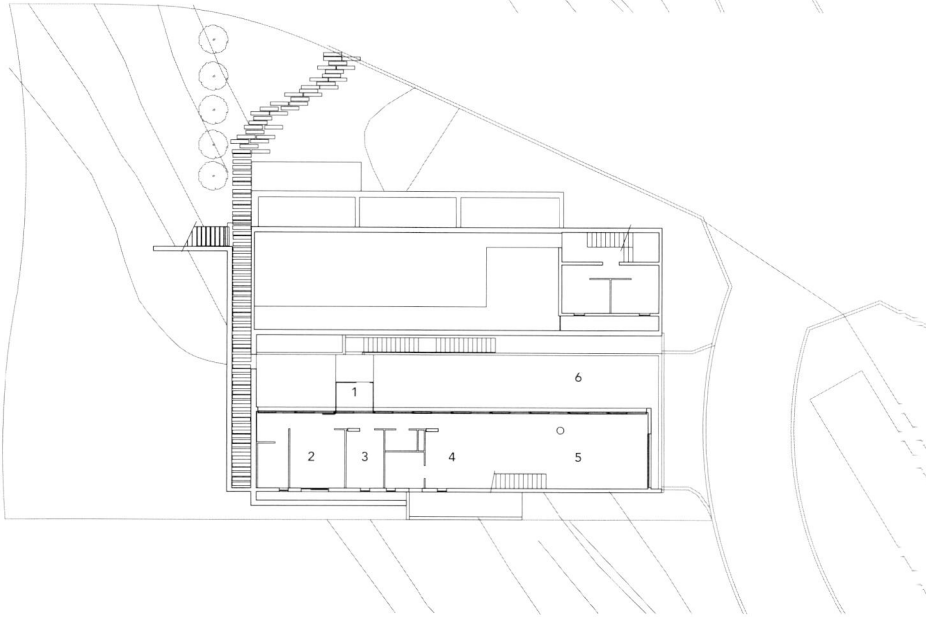

FIRST FLOOR PLAN

1. Glassed entrance foyer
2. Master bedroom
3. Bedroom
4. Kitchen
5. Living room
6. Courtyard

C____5 m

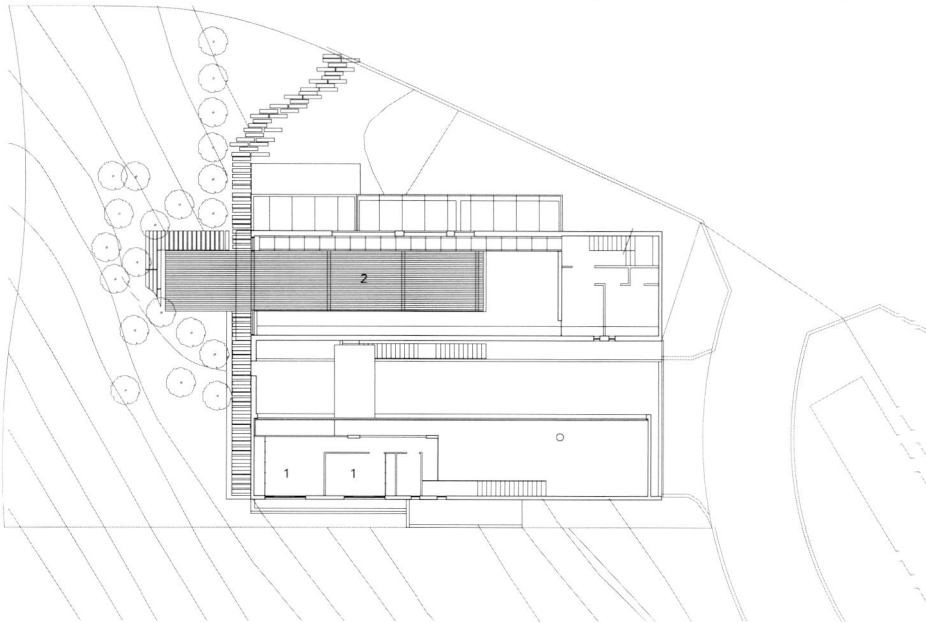

SECOND FLOOR PLAN

1. Bedroom
2. Cafe (mezzanine of music space)

C____5 m

CLOCKWISE FROM TOP_ *The music hall seen from the east. The music hall with a hanging upper wooden floor suspended using steel wire.*

OPPOSITE_ *Suspended timber plates in the music hall that act as the structure, the appearance and sound-absorbing insulation.*

1. ST PL. T=16
2. 25 mm dia. pin
3. ST. clevis
4. 12 mm dia. S.S. tension wire
5. Turnbuckle
6. ST PL. T=16
7. D* mm dia. T= steel tension wire
8. D* mm dia. T= ST PL. 40 mm dia. nut;
   D* mm dia. tie
9. Laminated 2 x 10 mm pinewood
10. 12 mm clear safety glass

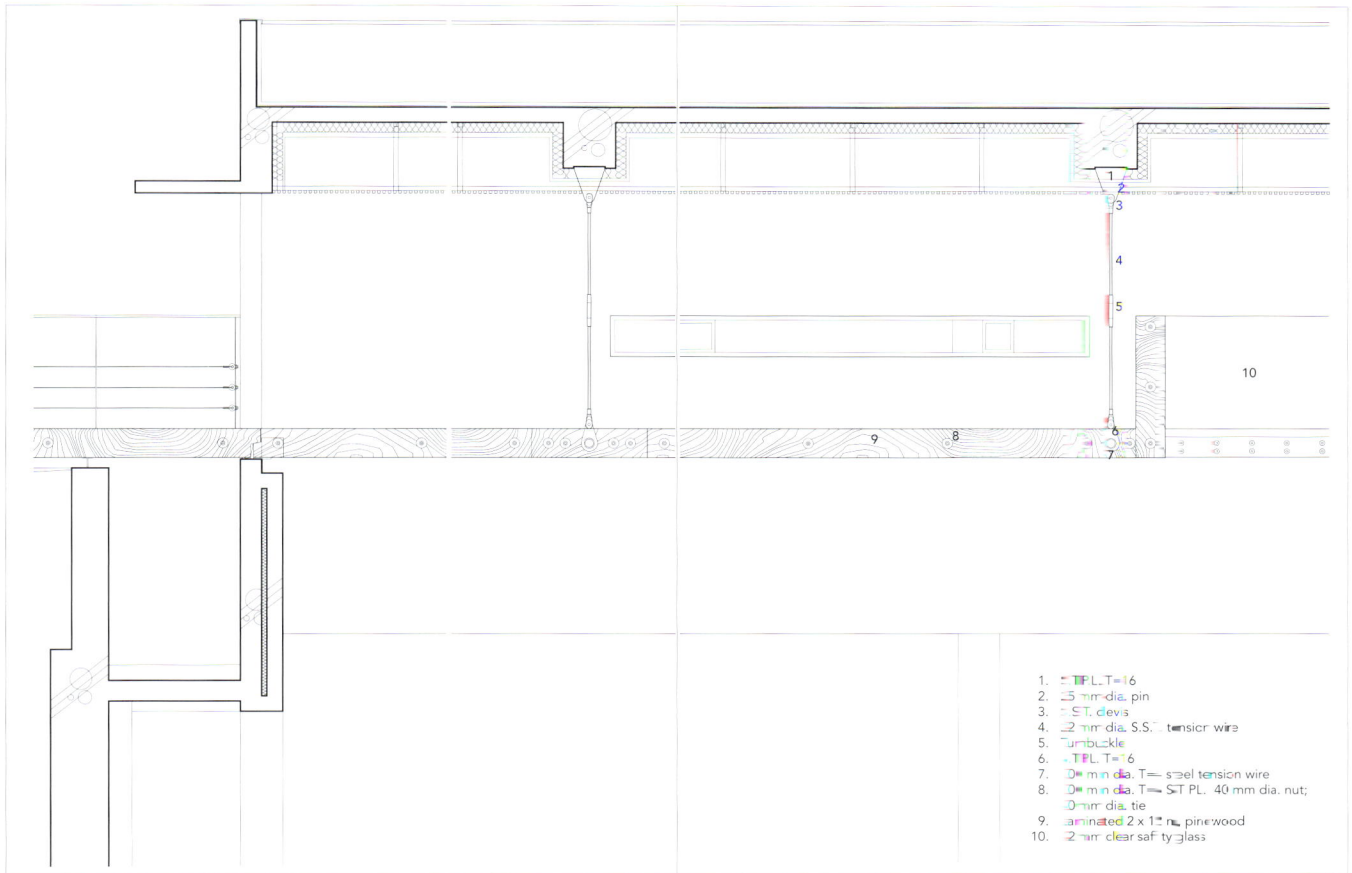

WOODEN STRUCTURE DETAIL
Section AA
Scale 1 : 50

05. THREE-BOX HOUSE_

HEYRI ART VALLEY, PAJU, KOREA, 2004

As with many of Cho's works, the Three-box House is driven by three dichotomies: the public and the private, the urban and the natural, the open and the bound. Responding to the specific site's characteristics, Cho composed the house as three concrete boxes, positioned in order to exploit changes in levels while providing separation from their busy surroundings. Each box interacts uniquely, both vertically and horizontally, with the other boxes and with the neighbourhood. Each assumes different functions, while linking the low courtyard and high driveway.

Cho secured two of the boxes into the earth, setting one further down to protect the privacy of the middle box. The smallest box of the group is delicately raised upon slender steel columns, giving the impression that it floats. It houses the living room and two thin columns emphasize this feeling of delicacy as they are placed diagonally to support the load efficiently. The middle box adopts a columnless interior to emphasize the long horizontal openings; this is achieved by using bars hidden in the walls, rather than columns, to support the load. The louvres are made of Merbau timber connected

to steel plates that are firmly fixed to the building by round steel bars. A stainless steel wire screen was installed on the east side, allowing natural light and views from the living room.

A horizontal timber louvre unifies the fragmented boxes visually and creates transitional spaces in between the units. The three boxes overlap, and their simplicity and modesty help carry the eye through them out to the world beyond, lending the house a feeling of spaciousness. Despite the three separate units, the building achieves completeness, a single entity in relation to nature and to its inhabitants.

OPPOSITE, CLOCKWISE FROM TOP LEFT_ *Three-box House as seen from the street, upper level concrete box supported by a metal structure, horizontal wooden screen wall with metal columns and space below, and a view of the lower level.*

단면 개념

사진에 세로 들어오는
"옥상정원 · 하늘"

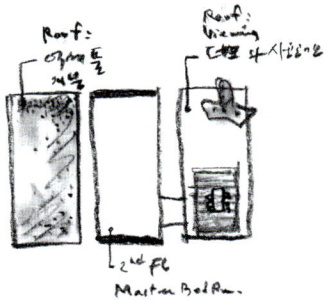

Roof:
옥상테
라스

Roof:
Viewing
대지 사산기념

2nd Fl
Master Bed Rm.

- 두개의 다른개념
사산기념, 바깥바닥기념

2층
옥상개념 :
지붕 2층 Master bed Rm.

Car   Kit   Liv.

Green
Wall
East

Ground Level
옥상개념 : Car, Kit, Liv의 방향

Garden

East Section

Frontal / Care Taken Section

Underground Level
옥상개념

OPPOSITE, CLOCKWISE FROM TOP LEFT_ *The garden as seen through the stairs, the entrance to the house, looking down onto the outdoor space below and the exterior of the house.*

ABOVE_ *The sketches show the relationship between the boxes and the earth.*

PROJECT TEAM: Yoon-heui Kim, Gi-hyeon Park and Young-jin Kang
LOCATION: 1652-420, Beopheung-ri, Tanhyun-myeon, Paju, Gyeonggi-do, Korea
USE: Residential
GROSS FLOOR AREA: 231 m² (2,486 ft²)
STRUCTURE: Reinforced concrete

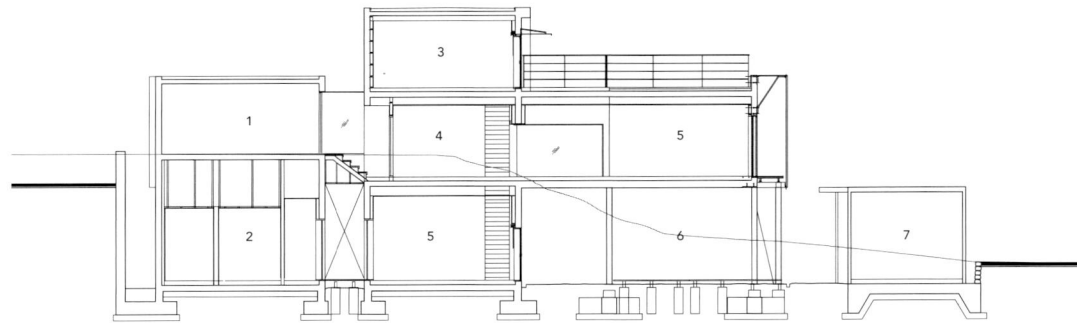

SECTION A 0 ___ 5 m

1. Master bedroom
2. Bathroom
3. Bedroom
4. Kitchen
5. Living room
6. Deck
7. Studio

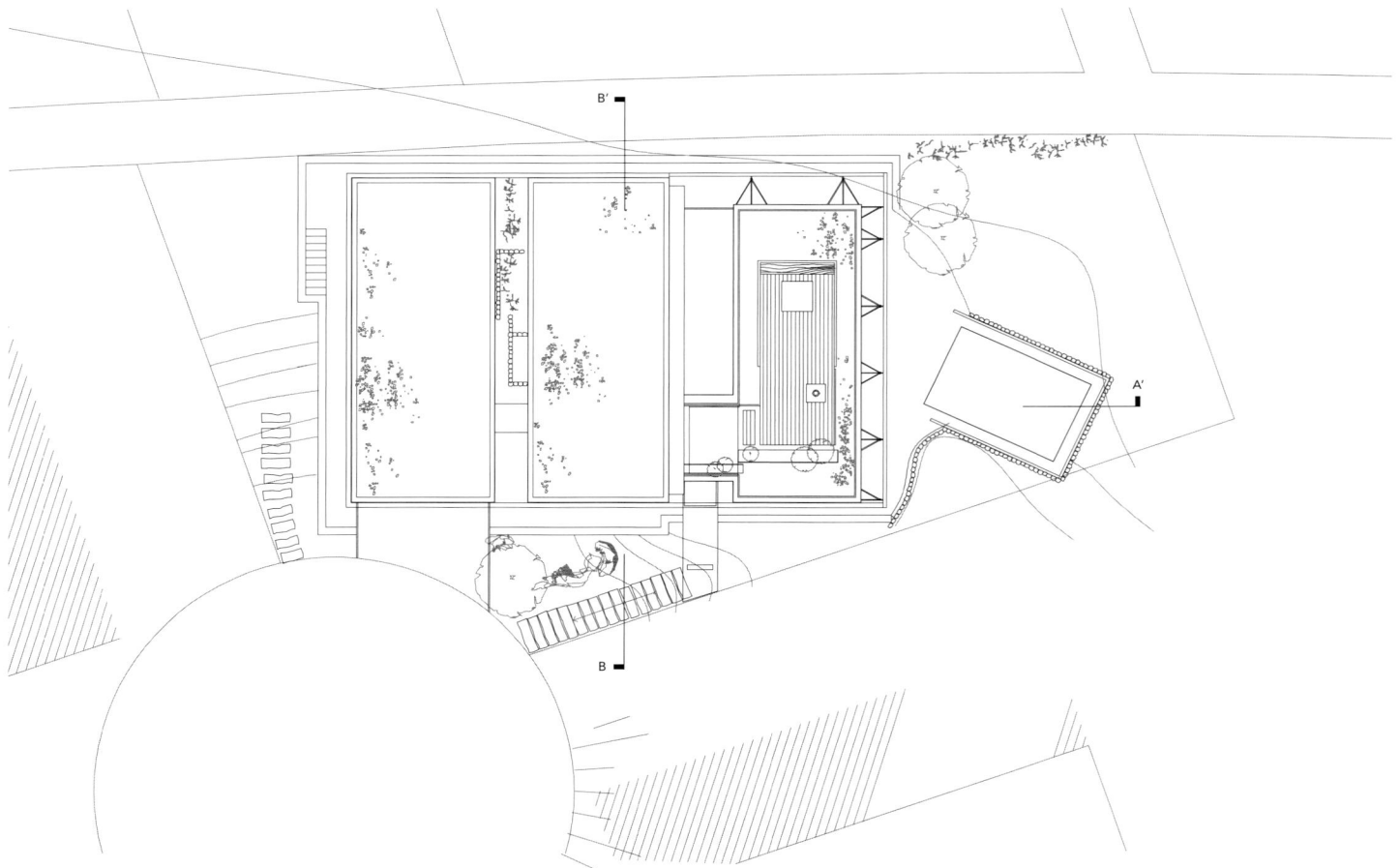

B'

A'

B

N

SITE PLAN 0 ___ 5 m

THREE-BOX HOUSE_

BYOUNG CHO_

64 //

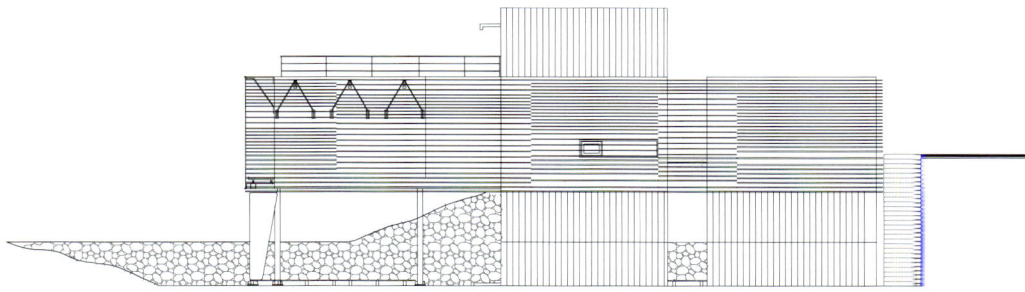

NORTH ELEVATION

0   5 m

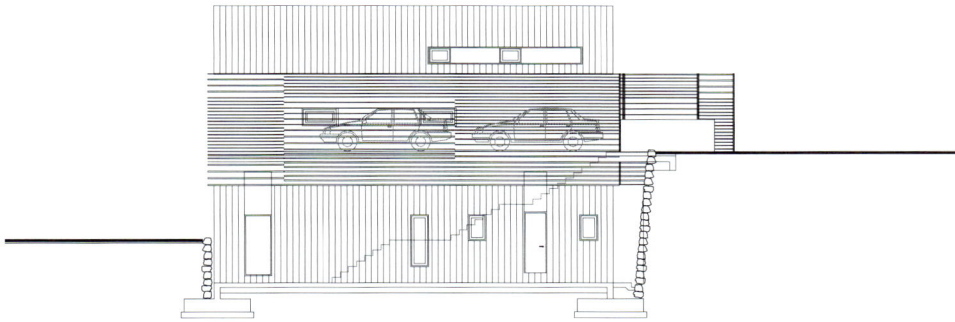

WEST ELEVATION

0   5 m

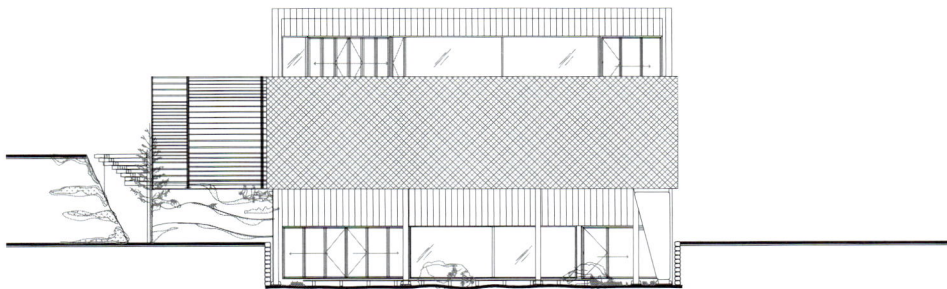

EAST ELEVATION

0   5 m

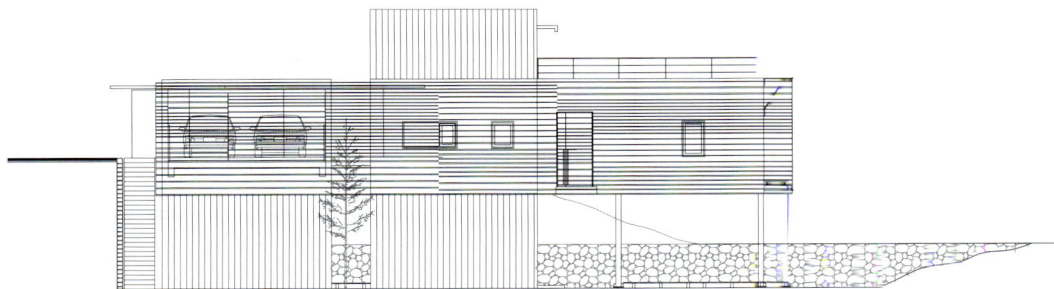

SOUTH ELEVATION

0   5 m

06. RAMP BUILDING_

SEOUL, KOREA, 2004

"Buildings often have an awkward relationship with the surrounding city, resulting in a banal and anxious association, lacking scale and sensibility," says Cho. His Ramp Building, on a busy intersection in Seoul's upscale Gangnam District, addresses this tension by bringing the street into the building. Cho conceived a ramp that creates an intriguing and enticing transition from the street into the cave-like lower portion of the structure, a seamless corridor from the public into the private. The ramp's sensuous lines are reiterated in unexpected ways throughout the building, resulting in a visually rich, inviting presence that adds a distinctive building to its neighbourhood.

The Ramp Building occupies a site sloping from the south to the west: the ramp exploits the existing change in the street level, penetrating the structure. This primitive yet poetic space offers interesting views out of a long, low window. A gently curving wire screen envelops and defines one corner, along the exact boundary of the site. This highly sculptural installation on the periphery, which Cho calls a "non-space", is a symbolic gesture, allowing the visitor to experience the space and materiality differently, inside and out.

Cho designed a wine bar on the lower level, a moody and appealing room with a window looking onto a waterfall in a deep crevasse. This void is intended to create an interesting opportunity to explore the boundaries of the site. The main cubic mass of the building is intentionally lifted from the chaotic ground floor and kept as pure as possible with a column-less interior. The pure abstraction is juxtaposed by punctuations using different materials and the organic ground floor creates an interesting transitional space contrasted by materiality changes. Emphasis was made on how visitors would experience the in-between spaces as they passed through the building. It was designed so that one would experience natural air circulation and unique light movements as well as interesting visual relationships.

OPPOSITE_ *The north side of the Ramp Building, showing the main stairs.*

CLOCKWISE FROM TOP_ *Second-floor interior with a ramp, a public passage and a view of the wire screen from below.*

OPPOSITE_ *The exterior as seen from the southern corner.*

OPPOSITE, CLOCKWISE FROM TOP LEFT_ *The building as seen from the south, the ramp penetrating the building, the wire screen façade from the south and an interior view of the ramp.*

ABOVE_ *Early studies showing the roof and the ramps.*

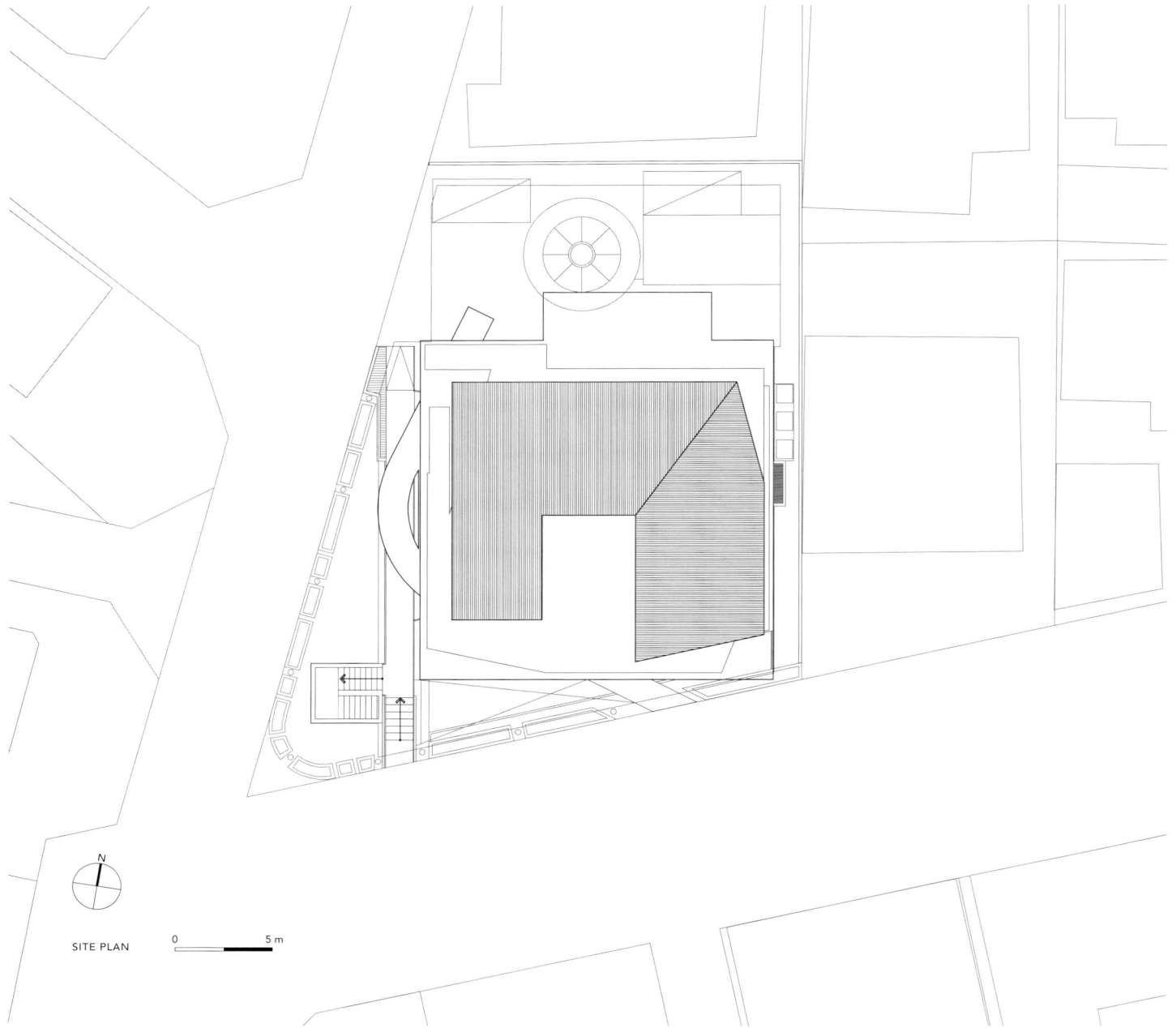

N

SITE PLAN   0   5 m

PROJECT TEAM: Dong-hyun Go, Yong-joon Jo,
In-ae Kang and Greg Jonason
LOCATION: 626-78, Sinsa-dong, Gangnam-gu,
Seoul, Korea
USE: Neighbourhood facility
GROSS FLOOR AREA: 396.5 m² (4,267.8 ft²)
STRUCTURE: Reinforced concrete, steel concrete

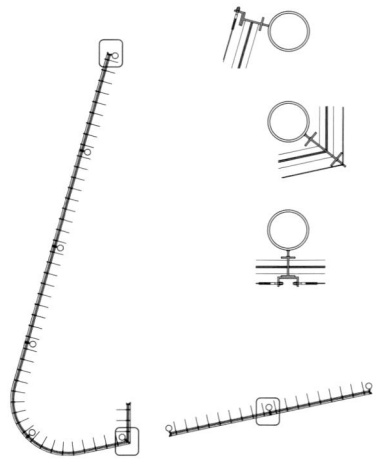

WIRE SCREEN HORIZONTAL DETAIL   WIRE SCREEN VERTICAL DETAIL

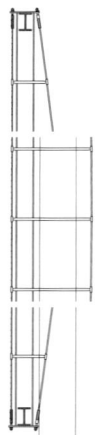

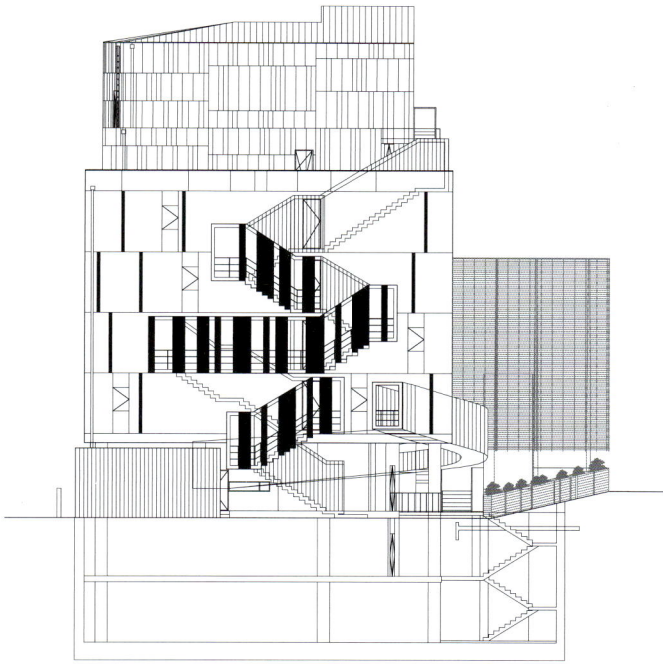

NORTH ELEVATION   0   5 m

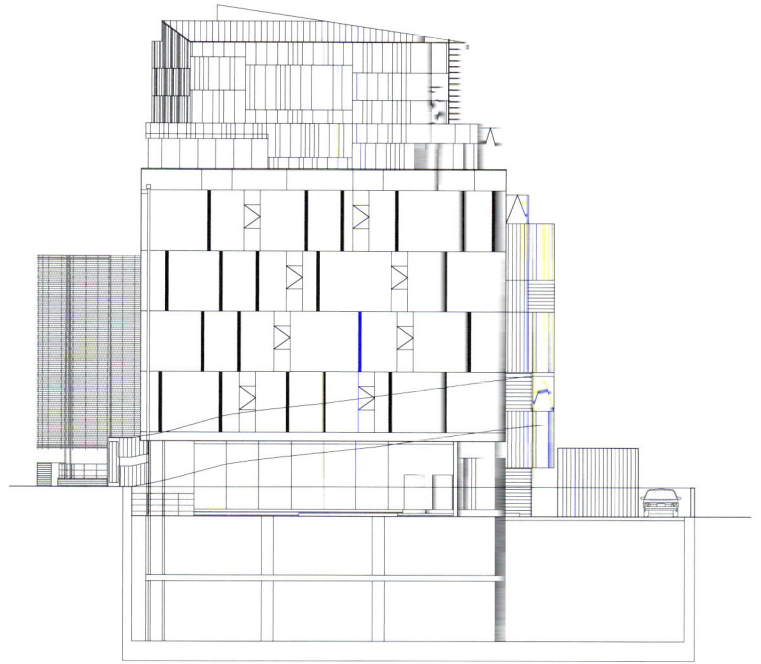

EAST ELEVATION   5 m

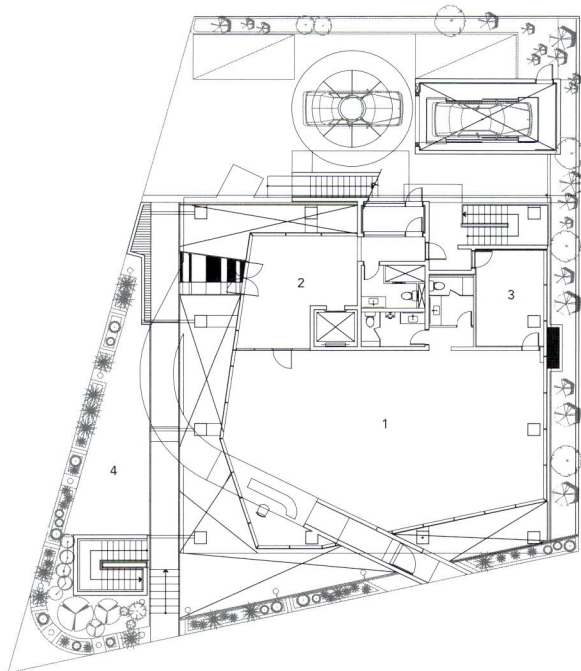

GROUND FLOOR PLAN   0   5 m

1. Retail
2. Lobby
3. Office
4. Patio

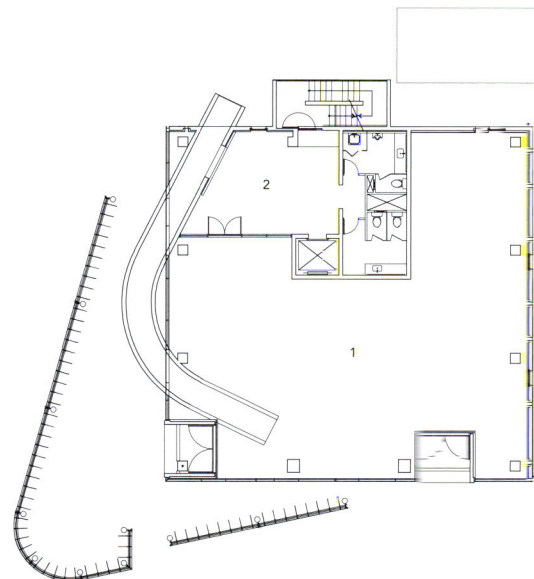

FIRST FLOOR PLAN   5 m

N

1.
2.

07. STONE WALL HOUSE_

YANGPYEONG, KOREA, 2004

The acts of splitting and dividing in architecture can produce dramatic effects; they can induce stronger relationships, reveal points of focus, and create new spaces. These effects can be further heightened by a classical use of juxtapositions. Stone Wall House implements these architectonic ideas, introducing, with boldness, a play between solid and void, heavy and light, and smooth and rough and, in doing so, a stronger connection between dwelling and landscape is created. With contrasting opposites the perception of phenomena can be more dramatically experienced.

Sitting in a rocklike landscape, the house becomes coupled to its surroundings by a stone façade constructed from reclaimed rocks from the site. This volume is split into two in order to create a dramatic connection that serves as a void to enter the home. With unobstructed views over a beautiful valley, the home is composed of five interconnected masses, each positioned in relation to one another to form distinct spatial relationships.

Two south-facing masses are linked on the ground floor by a hollow box that forms an overhang and an extended floor slab. Additionally, the box also acts as a transitional space, paradoxically becoming a place that is open to nature and yet has an aura of intimacy. A broken mass is orientated on the first floor longitudinally, with a view towards the east, juxtaposing the south-facing ground-floor mass. A diverse assortment of materials has been used in the construction of the house – zinc, concrete, stone, timber and glass combined together to make a unique collage of rich textures and patterns.

OPPOSITE, FROM LEFT TO RIGHT_ *The front of Stone Wall House: the structure is predominantly reinforced concrete that is purposefully exposed or concealed and the front of the house seen from the hill.*

ABOVE, CLOCKWISE FROM TOP LEFT_ *The garden is visible from the bedroom window, the exterior seen from the south, the view from the living room, looking south, and an exterior shot of the ground floor.*

땅의 움과 돌담, 1동의 산띠에 배치
2동, 건물, 톤백녀,

ABOVE AND OPPOSITE_ *Sketches of the relationship of the stone wall to its surroundings and the relationship of the building to the rock hill behind.*

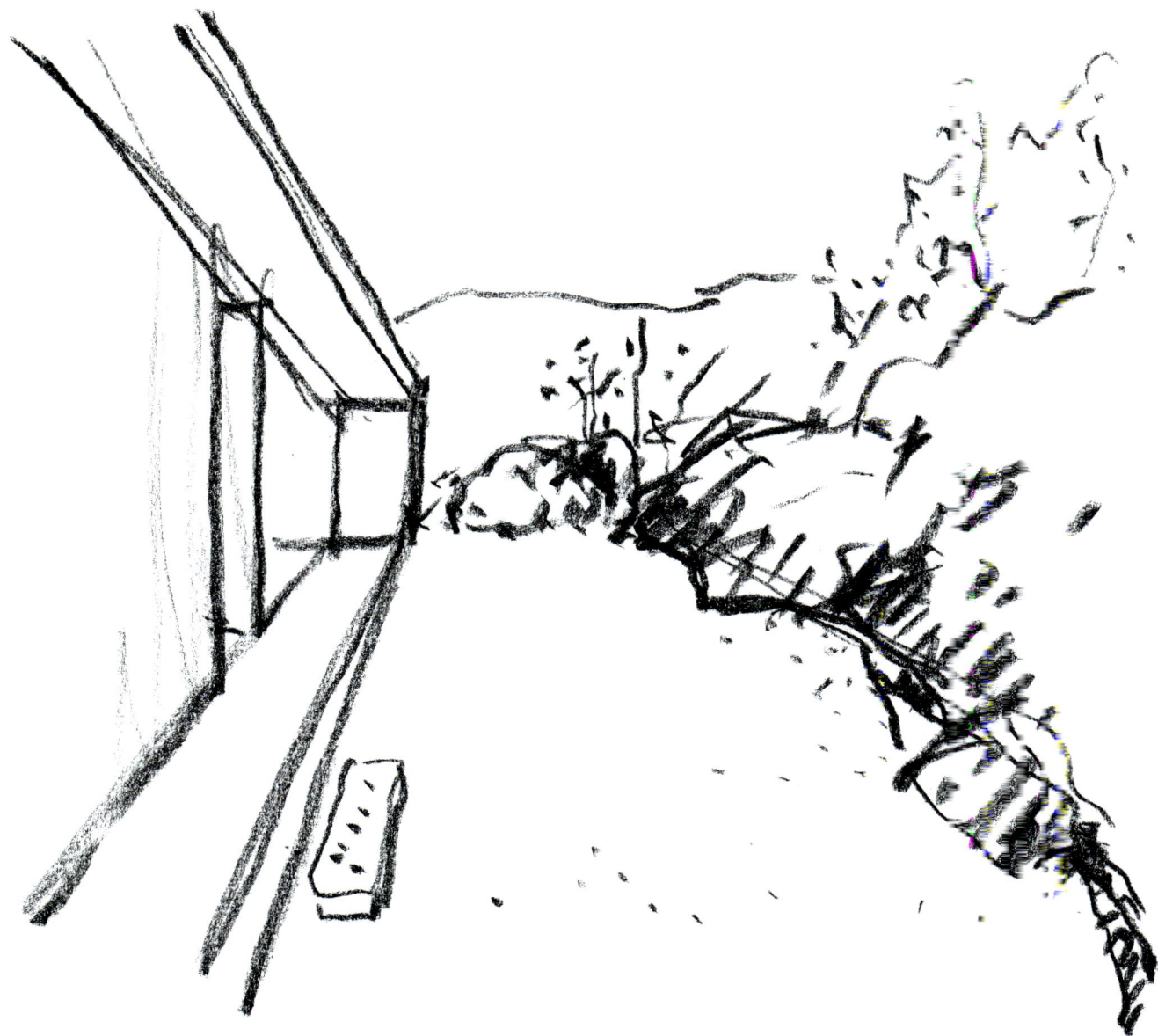

버려졌던 뒷뜰과 돌축대,
돌, 샘물 땅방

PROJECT TEAM: Yong-joon Jo
LOCATION: 898, Songhak-ri, Gangsang-myeon,
Yangpyeong-gun, Gyeonggi-do, Korea
USE: Residential
GROSS FLOOR AREA: 155 m² (1,668.4 ft²)
STRUCTURE: Reinforced concrete

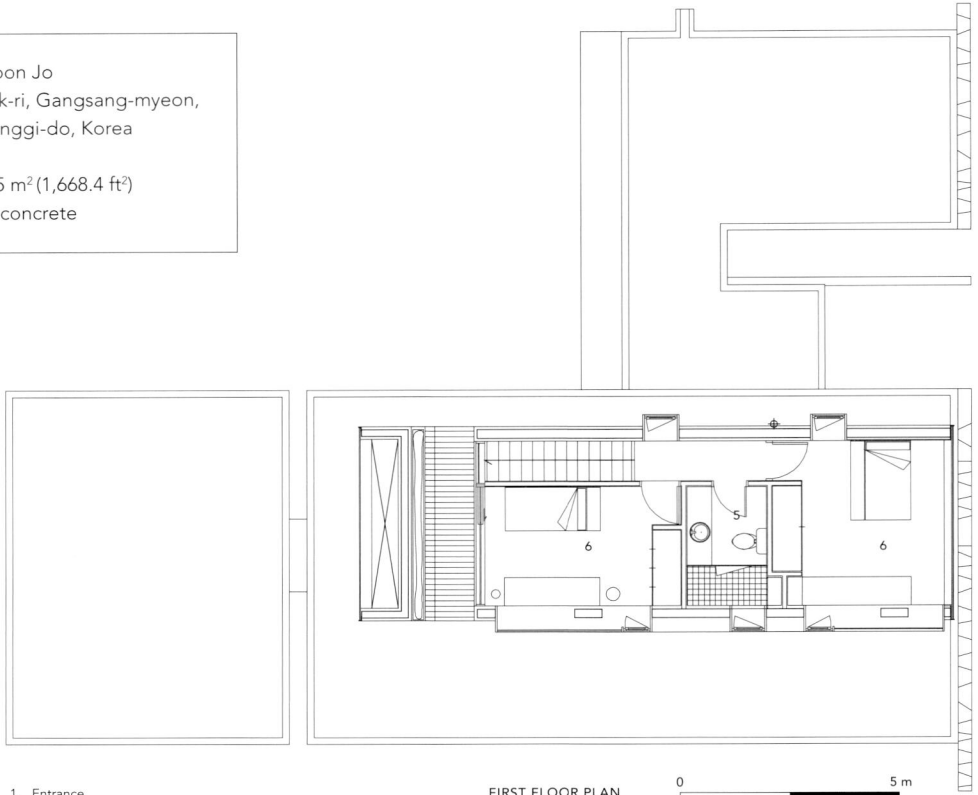

1. Entrance
2. Storage
3. Kitchen
4. Living room
5. Rest room
6. Bedroom
7. Library

FIRST FLOOR PLAN

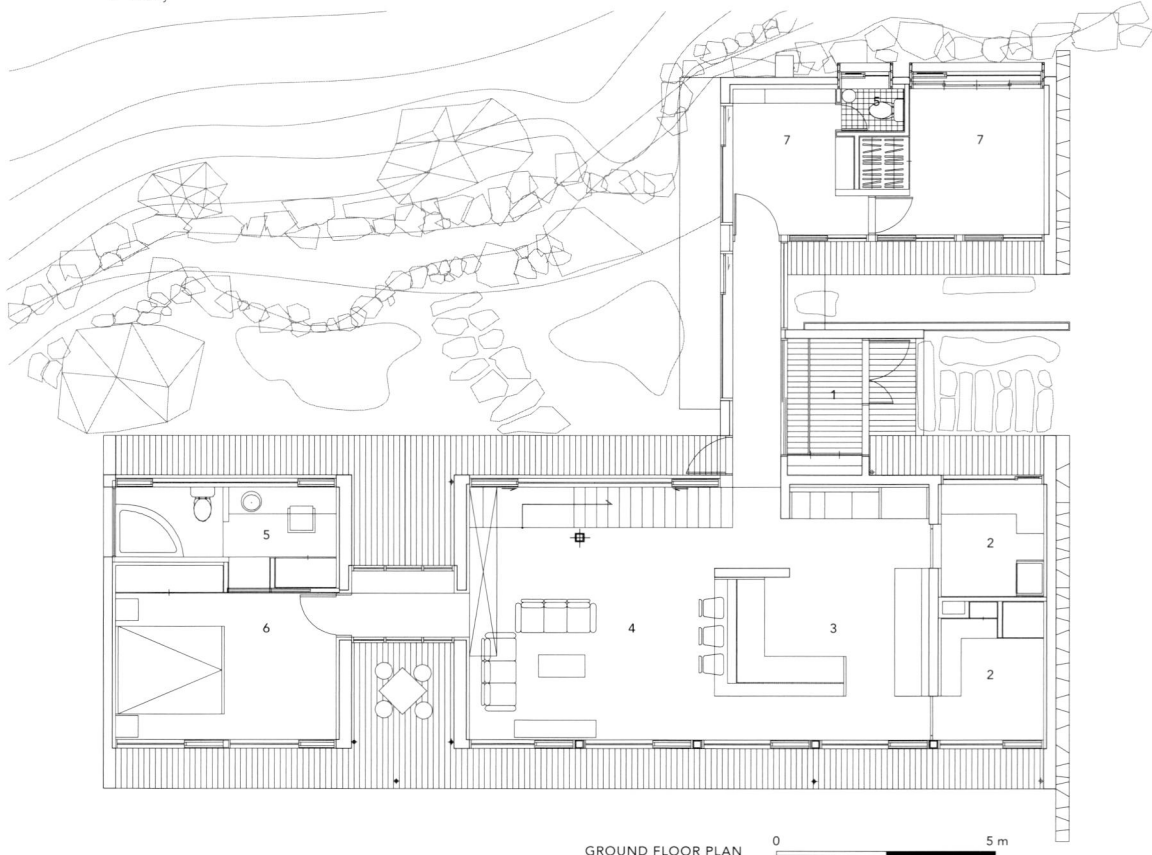

0   5 m

GROUND FLOOR PLAN

0   5 m

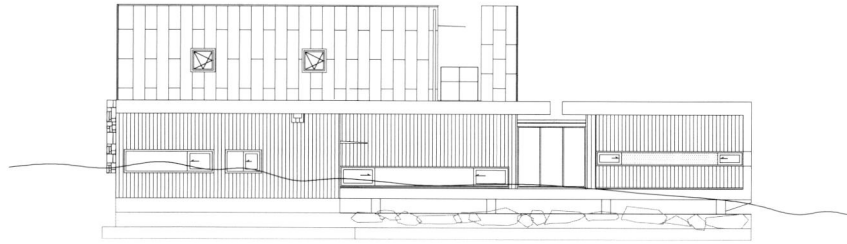

NORTH ELEVATION

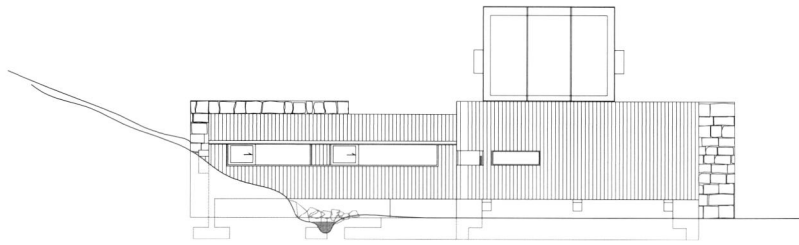

0   5 m

WEST ELEVATION

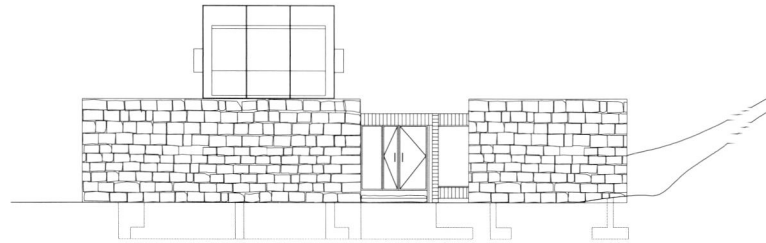

0   5 m

EAST ELEVATION

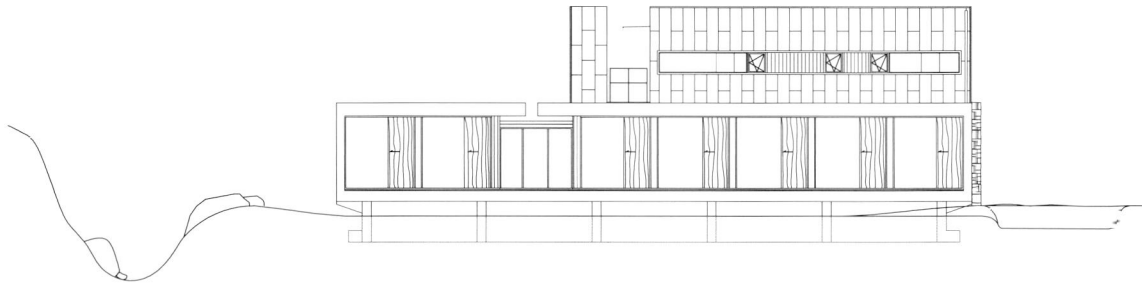

0   5 m

SOUTH ELEVATION

0   5 m

08. TWO-BOX HOUSE_

HEYRI ART VALLEY, PAJU, KOREA, 2005

Two-box House draws heavily on the theme of splitting and dividing that Cho explored in Stone Wall House. It is in this act of splitting that a tension is created: it can become spatially powerful, offering solidity to the human forces that both bind and separate the inhabitants. Thus, by creating a tension in architecture the perception of phenomena can become dramatically experienced.

This residence and studio in Heyri Art Valley consists of two buildings, separated by an elongated courtyard, 2.1 m (7 ft) in width. The house reacts to the existing site conditions by following the given site plan, while also fitting into the existing terrain in section. The result is a fluid link between the level changes with the roof level corresponding to the top of the hill. The courtyard and a short bridge visually connect these two parts of the house while inducing a strong relationship between these elements. Programmatically, it also separates the kitchen and dining room from the living and studio quarters situated in the largest section.

An interaction with nature is sought by placing a serene garden in the void: all the rooms have a view, while the smallest building is punctuated at roof level to embrace the natural hillside, facilitating a space for the inhabitants to watch the seasons change. This is formed by a staircase and a parapet intended to be below eye level when sitting on the roof.

The exterior aesthetic can be defined by the earth red steel that contrasts with the exposed concrete giving the building a certain industrial appearance, while being both rustic and vernacular. Laminated skylights with no frames continue the premise of a rustic aesthetic. This is further heightened by leaving the reinforced concrete structure exposed showing the humanistic quality of the construction process.

OPPOSITE, CLOCKWISE FROM TOP LEFT_ *Detail of the skylight, the entrance, the dry garden, the kitchen seen through a window and the view from the south.*

Dir / Kit

studio

steel plate 거 기
불과 마감

CL

5 × 0.6 = 3.0 m

Steel + Part (6T)
(placed before Pond)

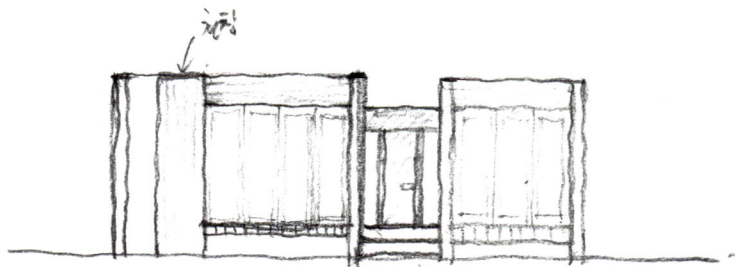

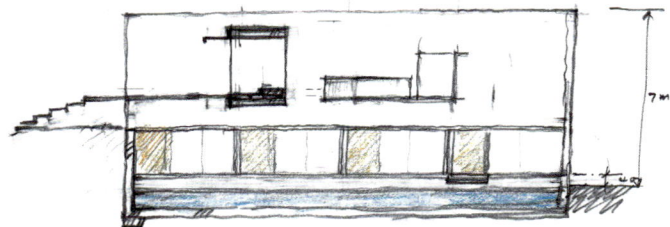

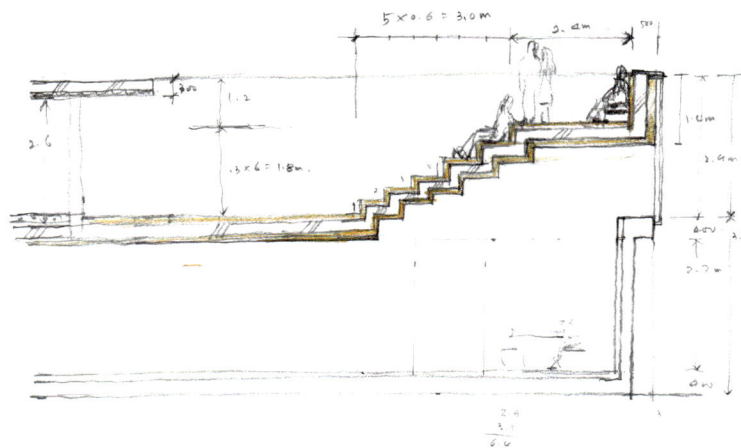

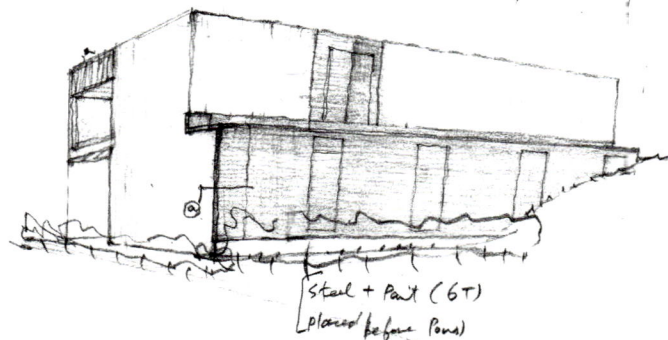

PROJECT TEAM: Ho-jung Kim and Gi-hyeon Park
LOCATION: C 1–7, Heyri Art Valley, Beopheung-ri, Tanhyun-myeon, Paju, Gyeonggi-do, Korea
USE: Residential
GROSS FLOOR AREA: 213.5 m² (2,298 ft²)
STRUCTURE: Reinforced concrete

ABOVE_ *Early studies.*

OPPOSITE, CLOCKWISE FROM TOP LEFT_ *The living room, the outdoor theatre and seating space, the living room and the dry garden.*

N

B'

A' ——————————— A

B

ROOF PLAN   0 ——— 5 m

FIRST FLOOR PLAN   0 ——— 5 m

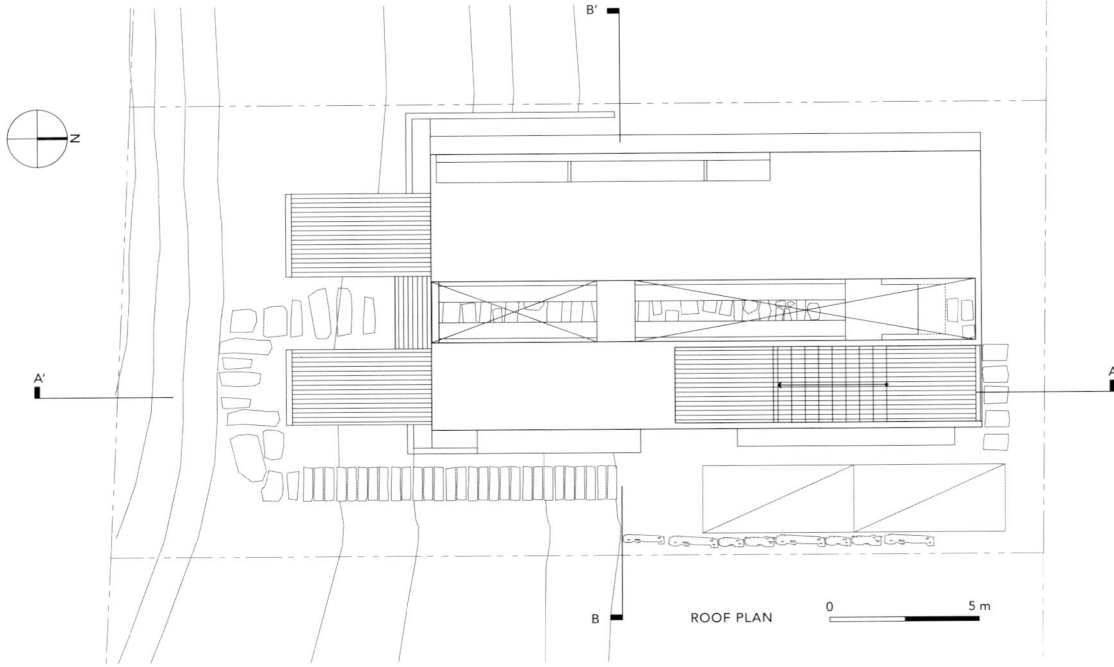

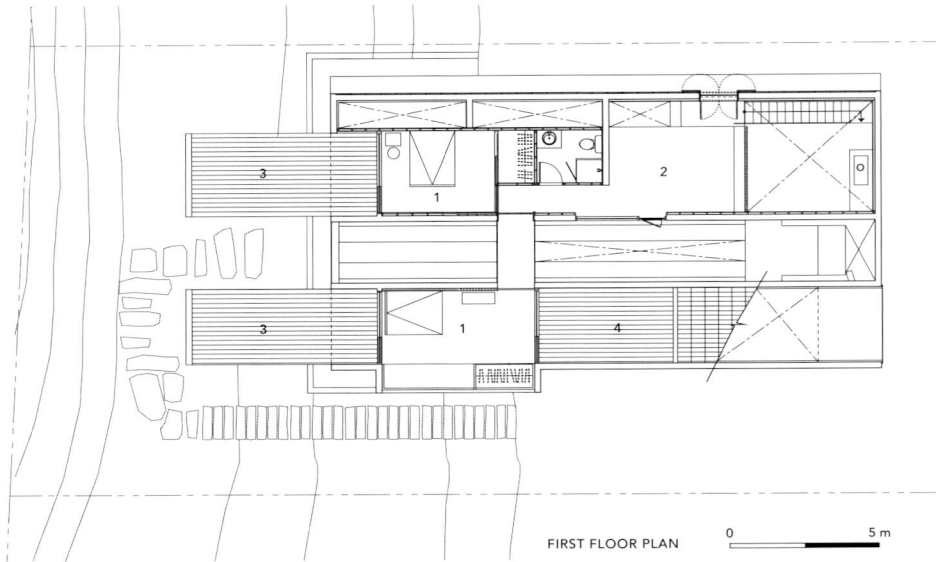

1. Bedroom
2. Studio
3. Terrace
4. Sky space

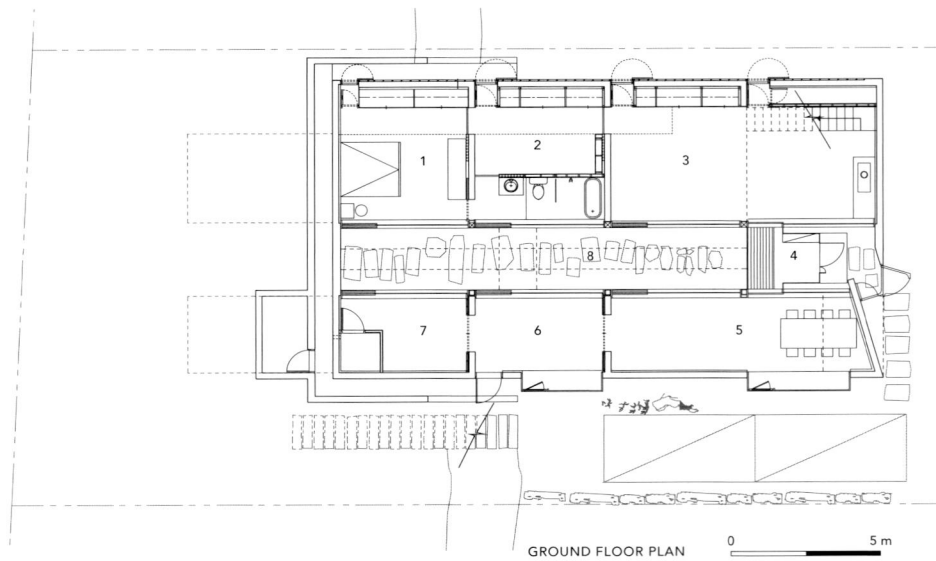

GROUND FLOOR PLAN   0 ——— 5 m

1. Master bedroom
2. Dressing room
3. Living room
4. Entrance
5. Dining room
6. Kitchen
7. Multi-use room
8. Courtyard

1. Bedroom
2. Bridge
3. Kitchen
4. Courtyard
5. Bathroom
6. Dance room

SECTION B

0   5 m

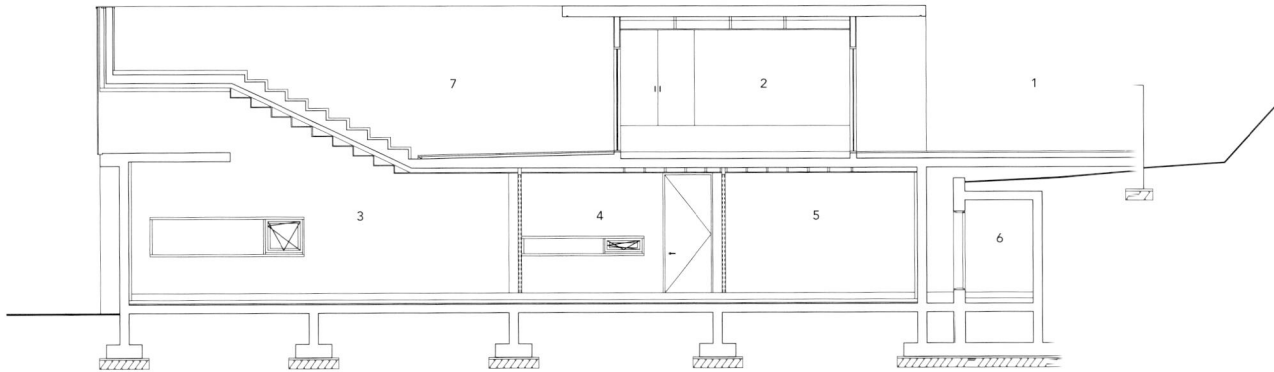

1. Terrace
2. Bedroom
3. Dining room
4. Kitchen
5. Multi-use room
6. Storage
7. Sky space

SECTION A

0

09. OISOO LEE HOUSE WITH WRITING SCHOOL_

HWACHEON, KOREA, 2006

Western tradition has historically acquired a hierarchical relationship with the natural. Man has always reigned, continually trying to control and tame the natural environment. In stark contrast, East Asian sensibilities have seen man as a part of the natural environment, forming an organic phenomenon – noticeably evident in landscape painting where there is a particular emphasis on the harmonious relationship between architecture and landscape. This fish-shaped house follows, and is shaped by energy flowing down a beautiful valley; it is to this extent that it becomes a harmonious fixture of the landscape, evoking a scene from a traditional painting.

Situated in the lush and scenic natural surroundings of Hwacheon, Gangwon-do Province, this house was designed for Oisoo Lee, a renowned writer and Zen painter. Crystal-clear water meanders through the long valley along the east–west axis, surrounded by low hills in this truly rich and picturesque landscape. An emphasis was placed on retaining these unique elements and designing a house that could sufficiently absorb the unspoiled natural environment. In order to

reflect Lee's maturity and sensitive image as a novelist and painter, the simple and natural elements have been emphasized as much as possible, creating a space where he can work in harmony with nature. The space used by Lee and his wife predominantly for writing and painting is divided into living and studio/working quarters. The public and semi-public areas are separated by using two adjoining buildings. Inspired by Lee's passion for the moon and his deep regard for nature, his living space in the basement receives natural light through voids planted with small gardens; they are also a vantage point for the couple to look at the ever-changing skies.

In keeping with the rest of the building, the flat roof was designed in a simple manner. The parapet was eliminated and the roof plate has been treated using a steel trowel. This was finished on the stem several times without the need for a waterproof agent or mortar. The windows were kept as simple as possible, completely concealed except from the steel plates.

OPPOSITE, FROM LEFT TO RIGHT_ *The views of the house from the north and the view from the west.*

ABOVE_ *View from the west, looking toward the writing school and the residence.*

PROJECT TEAM: Dong-hyun Go, Yong-joon Jo and In-ae Kang
LOCATION: 799, Damok-ri, Sangseo-myeon, Hwacheon,
Gangwon-do, Korea
USE: Residential
GROSS FLOOR AREA: 273.3 m² (2,941.8 ft²)
STRUCTURE: Reinforced concrete

Writing school

House

1. Guest room
2. Room
3. Picture archive
4. Small kitchen
5. Studio
6. Stone garden
7. Study
8. Office
9. Kitchen
10. Dining room
11. Entrance
12. Living room
13. Master bedroom
14. Dressing room
15. Tea room

GROUND FLOOR PLAN

0   5 m

N

SITE PLAN

1. Back garden
2. Hand garden
3. Pond
4. Spring
5. Dry stream
6. Office
7. House

0

OPPOSITE, CLOCKWISE FROM TOP LEFT_ *View of the dry garden from the living room, the studio and the stone garden between the writing school and the residence.*

ABOVE_ *Sketches showing how people experience nature at the site.*

10. OISOO GALLERY_

Oisoo Lee is one of Korea's most revered and popular writers and has written over thirty books. He has the distinction of having the largest number of followers on Twitter of any Korean celebrity. A professed eccentric, he claims to have endured sub-zero temperatures for months while consuming nothing but frozen rice water. On his widely acclaimed radio show, he relates stories about his experiments with personal seclusion, transformations of his mind through meditation, and his philosophical musings, all striking in their detail and content. He is also an artist whose ink drawings and paintings have been lauded for their simplicity and essential character.

The Oisoo Gallery, Cho's second project for Lee, was commissioned by the city of Hwacheon. Located directly downstream from the writer's residence, it hosts temporary and permanent exhibitions on Lee's work and life. Oddly futuristic yet remarkably in tune with its pristine surroundings, the austere subterranean gallery is tucked into a rocky

slope. Its shape and angles – first conceived using a piece of folded paper with an irregular shape cut out of the centre – allow the building to nestle into a mountain valley. The gallery's flat, faceted roof blends into the rock-lined site and appears to merge with the existing hillside. A circular path leads to a small theatre used for writing workshops, film screenings and discussions; a kiosk for internet users; a display of a collection of the writer's personal belongings and used brushes; an office; and a reception desk at the entrance. Small pods around the gallery allow visitors to rest and spend more time in front of the artwork and displays. Video projections of Lee's interviews and lectures can be seen on pull-down screens.

OPPOSITE_ *View of the gallery's roof and the gallery courtyard.*

ABOVE_ *The western hill towards the northeast.*

CLOCKWISE FROM TOP_ *View from the courtyard, the courtyard, the exhibition space and the entrance.*

OPPOSITE_ *Sketches of the site.*

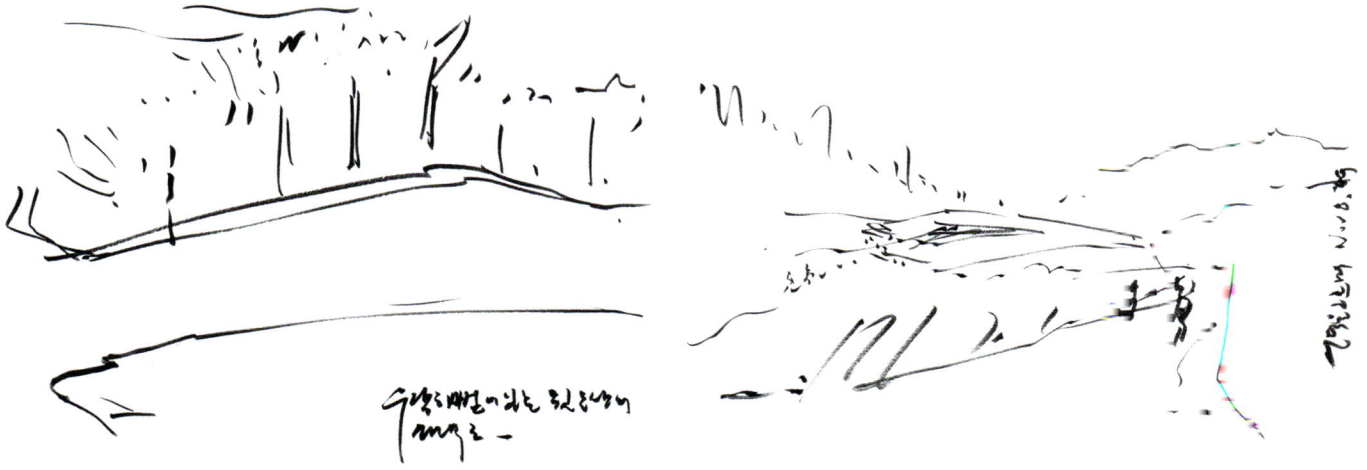

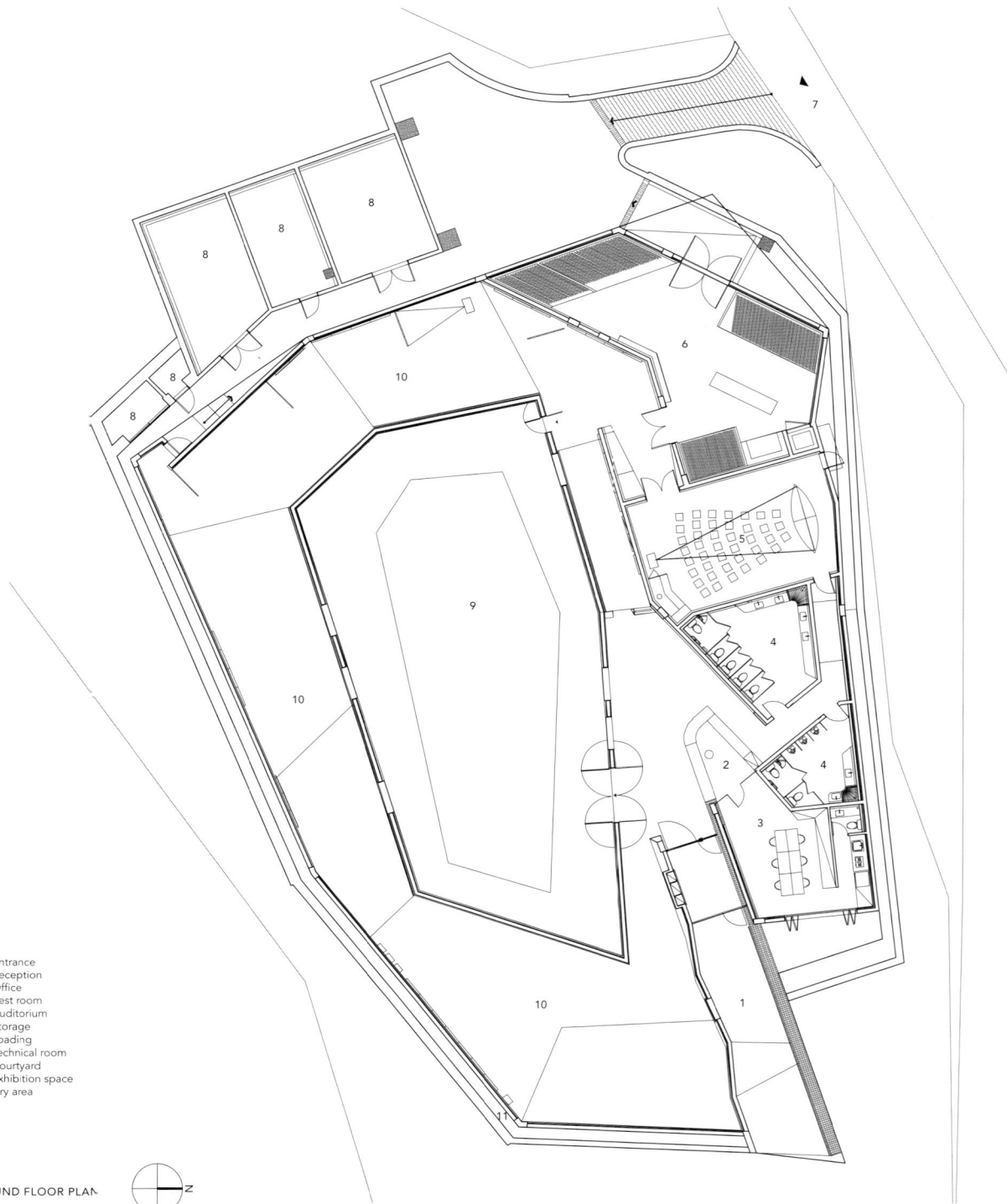

1. Entrance
2. Reception
3. Office
4. Rest room
5. Auditorium
6. Storage
7. Loading
8. Technical room
9. Courtyard
10. Exhibition space
11. Dry area

GROUND FLOOR PLAN

0   5 m

PROJECT TEAM: Yong-eun Bae, Kyu-young Kim,
Steven Clarke and Sun-yong Choi
LOCATION: 792, Damong-ri, Sangseo-myeon,
Hwacheon-gun, Gangwon-do, Korea
USE: Exhibition hall
GROSS FLOOR AREA: 850 m² (9,149 ft²)
STRUCTURE: Reinforced concrete

EAST ELEVATION

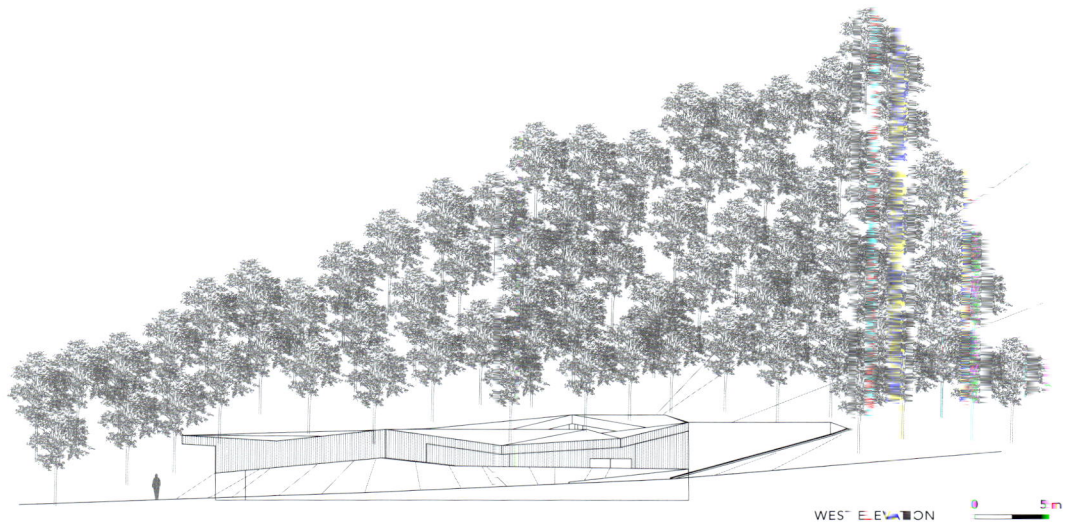

WEST ELEVATION

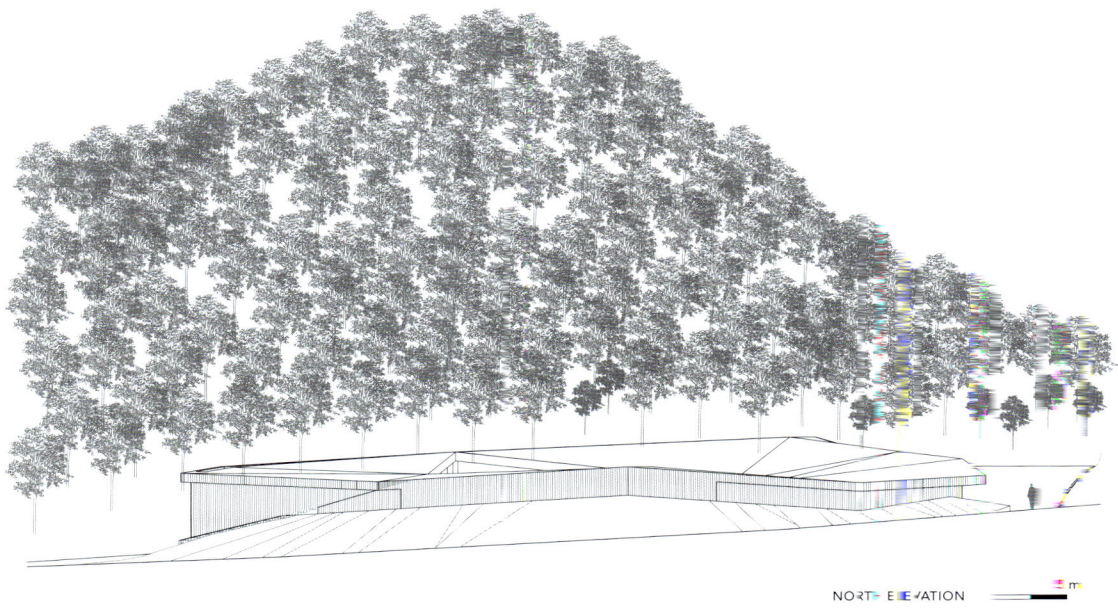

NORTH ELEVATION

11. AREOMSOL KINDERGARTEN_

YANGJU, KOREA, 2007

From a young age, we begin to perceive through the experience of sensations and emotions, and this continually shapes our human consciousness and is fundamental to our growth. The process that creates and presents these phenomena is the architecture Areomsol Kindergarten seeks to realize, creating an environment that would enable rather than constrain education.

Situated on a greenbelt, Areomsol Kindergarten teaches traditional Korean songs and dance to children. The clients, two living national treasures in the field of Korean traditional performance, hold a deep passion for Korean culture evidently shown in their choice of site that features ample natural flows and views.

The peaks of Mount Obong and Mount Bukhan are seen in the distance, casting shade over the site. However, in the early afternoon there is still too much sunlight for the pupils to be comfortably cool. Considering the topographical and physical conditions of the site, the initial idea was to create a cubic space where children could gather in a circle to enjoy music and dance. This was intended to be a space where sunshine and wind would pierce through the open ceiling, granting the opportunity for the children to experience and study nature. These early ideas were manifested by inserting a simple, yet efficient concrete box into the gentle surroundings. A main courtyard was created where children could learn the virtues of Korean society based on sharing, while singing and dancing. The geometric roof, which is flat, was designed for use as a productive garden, a space where the children could learn planting skills while studying nature. As a venue to "experience and appreciate" nature, it was important the children gained first-hand experience of the flow of the mountains and the beautiful skies that change behind them. This was further developed by the use of a bent glass wall, which reflected and distorted the natural surroundings in an interesting way, becoming another element for the children to explore.

The horizontal plane is emphasized in Areomsol Kindergarten with a columnless interior, so a structural system was developed that used flat slabs. Thin steel bars 3 mm (¼ in.) in width replaced beams at 200 mm (8 in.) intervals, securing long spans. Internally, a rammed earth wall was erected from mud excavated from the site, and a skylight was installed to allow the children to get a feel for the texture. The only vertical element in the space is a large timber column.

The external earth wall is alternated with glass, creating a dramatic connection between the heavy and light materials. In order to heighten this connection, all the frames were concealed in the rammed earth wall, creating a clean effect that emphasized the juxtaposition of the materials.

In collaboration with a sandwich panel company, the hall was built as simply as possible, mainly due to budgetary constraints. Towards the south, 16 mm (½ in.) polycarbonate panels were fixed on to a wooden frame, while the decked areas were finished with prefabricated 12T ash wood.

OPPOSITE, CLOCKWISE FROM TOP_ *The main courtyard seen from the entrance, the courtyard with the roof garden above, the view from the entrance and the approach to the kindergarten.*

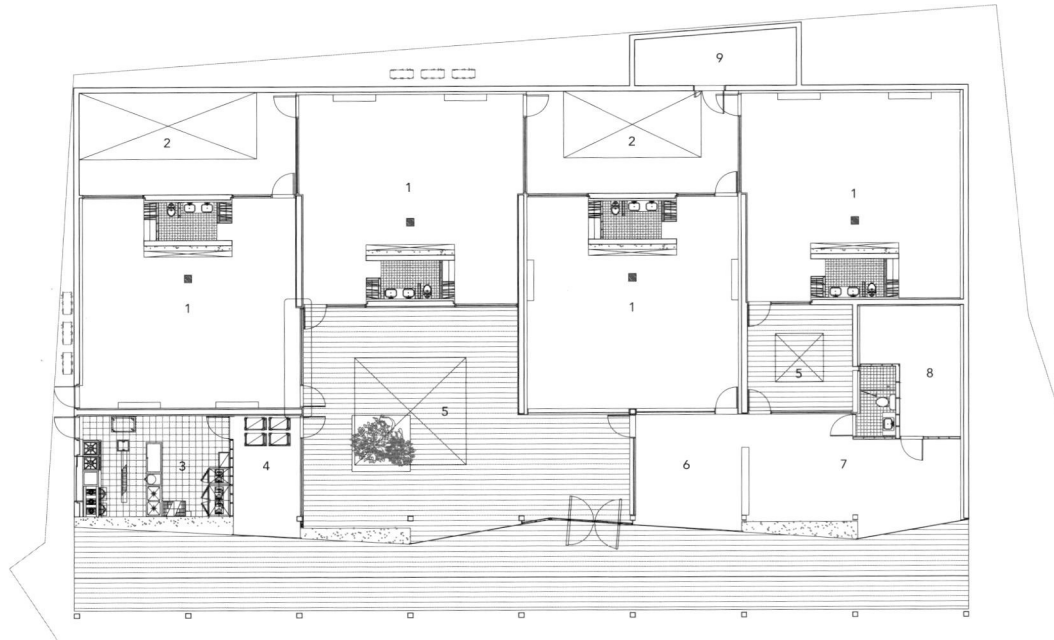

GROUND FLOOR PLAN   0 ___ 5 m

1. Class room 2. Exterior class room 3. Kitchen 4. Cafeteria 5. Courtyard 6. Waiting room
7. Administration office 8. Library 9. Machinery room

ABOVE_ *Early sketches of the site.*

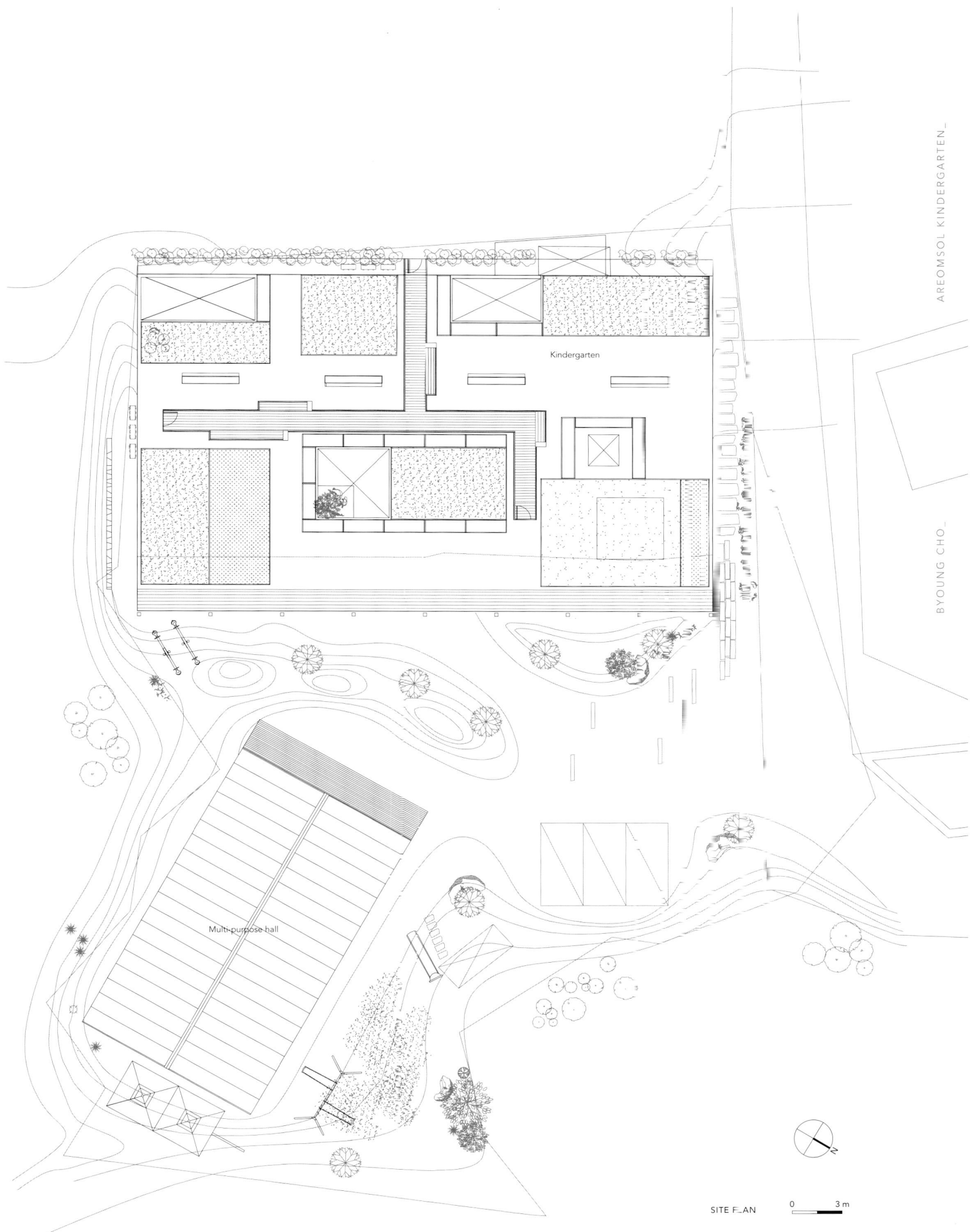

Kindergarten

Multi-purpose hall

SITE PLAN

0 ———— 3 m

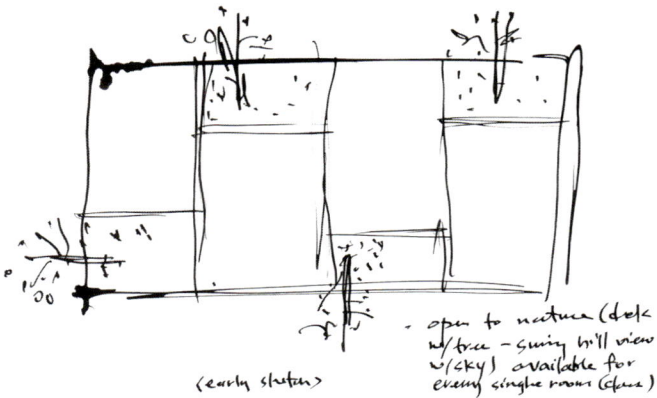

BYOUNG CHO_

PROJECT TEAM: Joon-seok Seo and Ho-joong Kim
LOCATION: 180–11, Gyohyeon-ri, Jangheung-myeon,
Yangju, Gyeonggi-do, Korea
USE: Kindergarten
GROSS FLOOR AREA: 722.6 m² (7,778 ft²)
STRUCTURE: Reinforced concrete, flat slab,
wood column

TOP_ *The interior.*

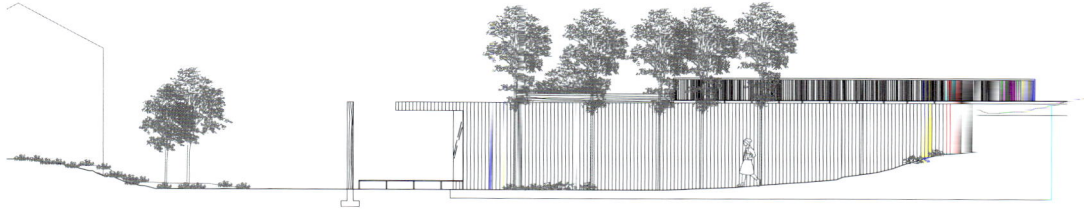

WEST ELEVATION 3 m

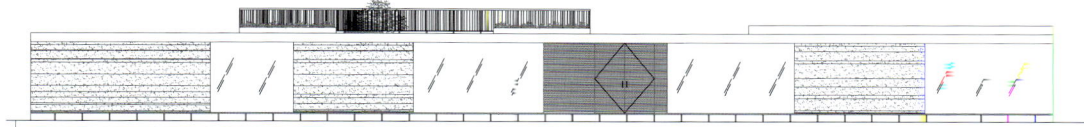

NORTH ELEVATION 3 m

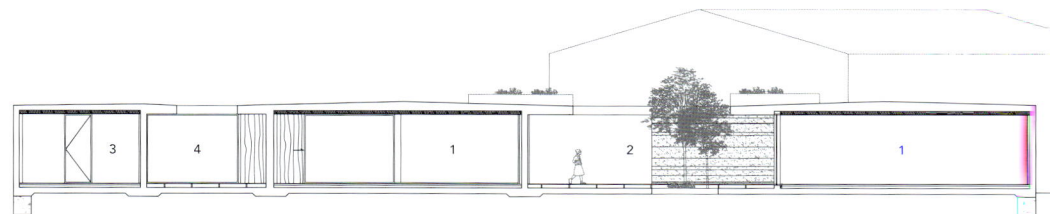

SECTION A 3 m

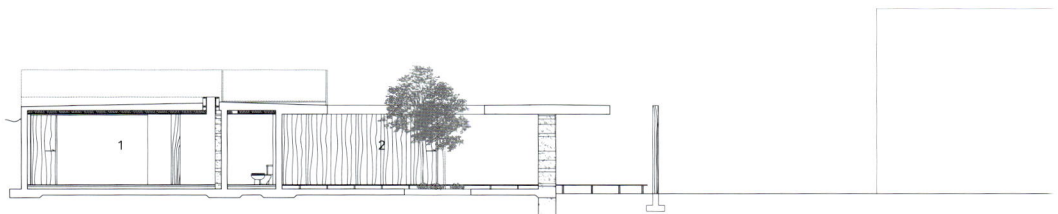

SECTION B 3 r

1. Class room
2. Play room
3. Library
4. Guidance

12. FOUR-BOX HOUSE_

SEOUL, KOREA, 2007

Built in the attractive residential neighbourhood of Pyeongchang-dong, Seoul, and spread over a hardy mountain, this house provides a peaceful retreat in the bustling city. The simple concept of four overlapping boxes arranged around a central courtyard responds specifically to the particular constraints of the site while expanding on elements of traditional Korean architecture.

To maximize the sun's penetration into the house, the boxes are extruded two storeys high and hollowed at the edges, which allows for larger windows and thus creates a bright, fresh interior. These wood-framed windows capture the light and the views without revealing the neighbouring buildings – heightening the impression of isolation from the city.

The open-air courtyard is a key spatial element of the design, a space for reflection and relaxation maintained by an air of simplicity. The courtyard also holds a functional use as it improves air circulation, while in summer the glass doors can be opened on all sides to host soirees, seamlessly blending the transition between interior and exterior.

Another significant space presents itself as a small tea room situated on the second floor. Constructed of timber, glass and paper, this contemplative space pays homage to traditional Korean tea rooms and is basked in sunlight during the morning.

The structure of Four-box House is predominantly concrete formwork, intentionally left exposed in particular elevations to reveal the texture from the construction process. Recycled Indonesian timber boards are used vertically as cladding, the repetition broken horizontally by zinc brackets. This creates a human scale to the house's exterior and produces a soft addition to the often brutal Seoul cityscape. These design considerations are followed through into the house interior where themes of repetition, texture and scale are present throughout. The palette of materials is expanded internally with some walls dressed in fine white paper or an assortment of exposed concrete and wood.

OPPOSITE_ *A partial view from the north side the street and the dining room seen from the courtyard.*

ABOVE_ *The central courtyard and the light staircase.*

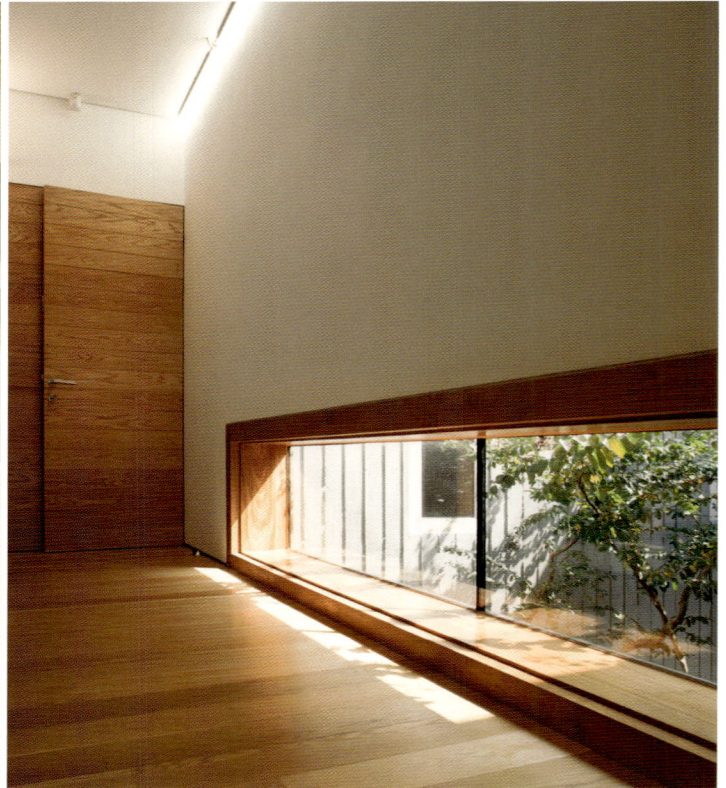

CLOCKWISE FROM TOP_ *A tree growing in the courtyard, light streaming in the lower wooden window, the tea room with paper-covered walls and the living room.*

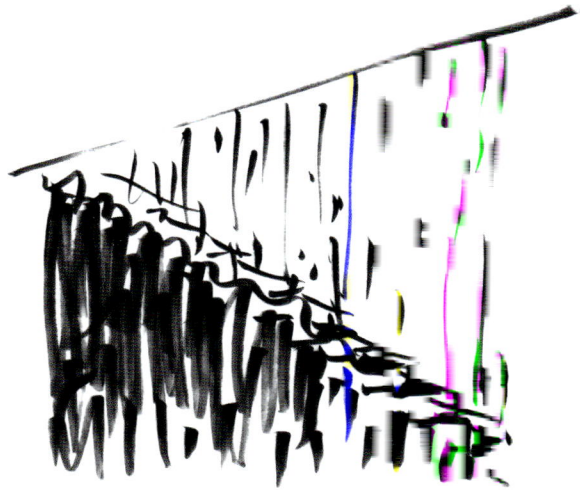

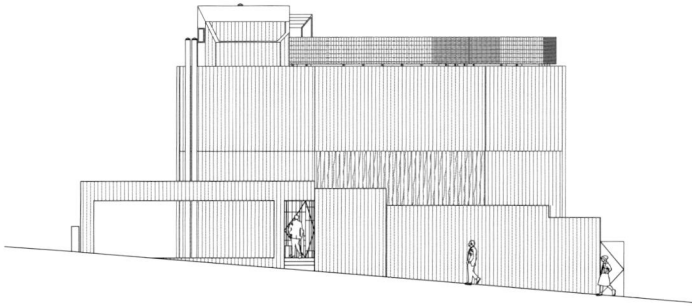

NORTH ELEVATION 0   5 m

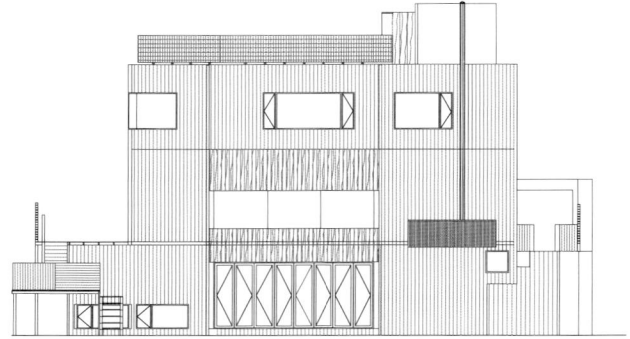

SOUTH ELEVATION 0   5 m

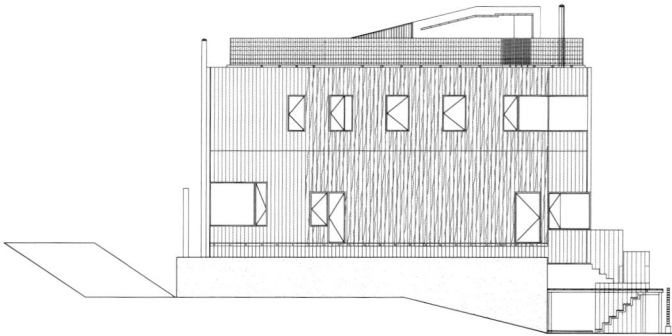

WEST ELEVATION 0   5 m

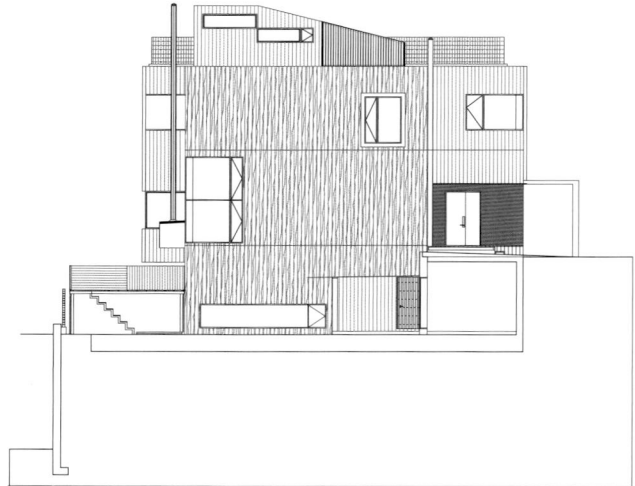

EAST ELEVATION 0   5 m

PROJECT TEAM: Joo-hyeon Park and Su-yeong Jeong
LOCATION: 438-11, Pyeongchang-dong, Jongno-gu,
Seoul, Korea
USE: Residential
GROSS FLOOR AREA: 480 m² (5,167 ft²)
STRUCTURE: Post-tension system, reinforced concrete,
hanging wire type

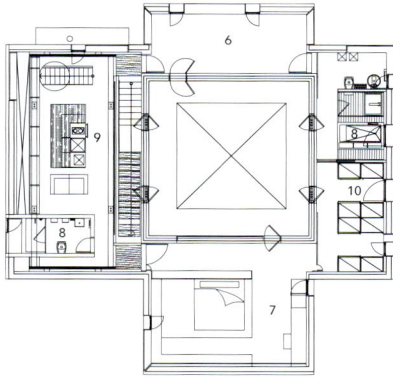

FIRST FLOOR PLAN   0   5 m

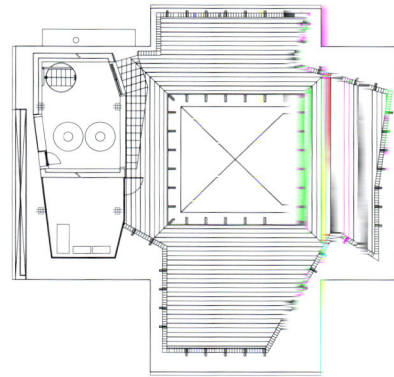

ROOF PLAN   0   5 m

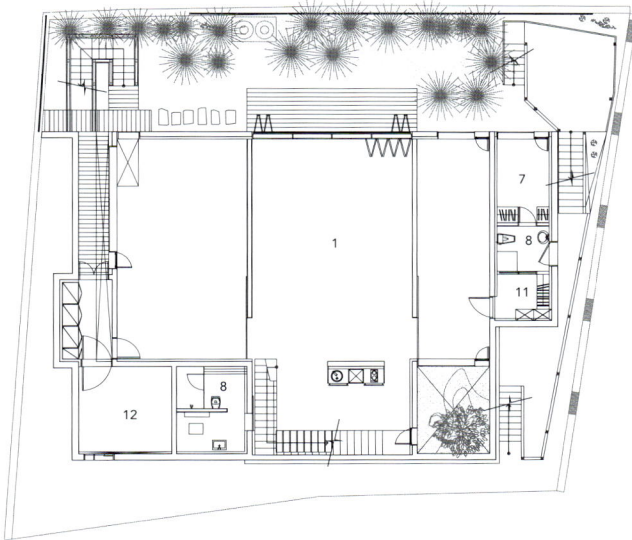

BASEMENT PLAN   0   5 m

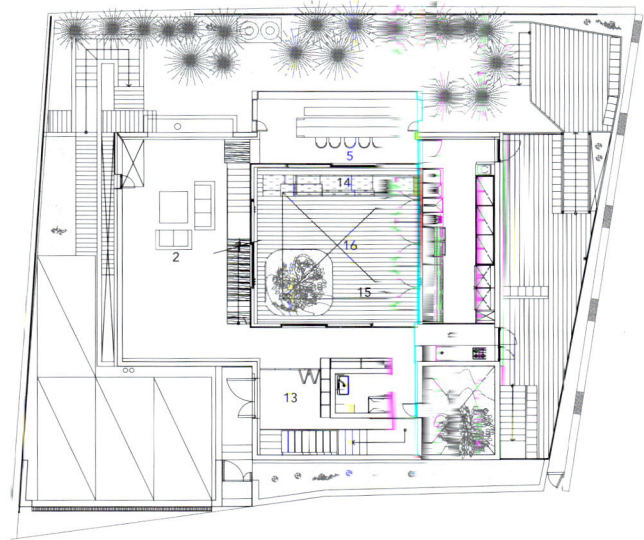

GROUND FLOOR PLAN   0   5 m

1. Exhibition hall 2. Living room 3. Kitchen 4. Kitchen 5. Dining room 6. Korean-type room
7. Bedroom 8. Rest room 9. Library 10. Dressing room 11. Storage 12. Boiler 13. Entrance
14. Corridor 15. Water garden 16. Courtyard

13. E-SHAPED HOUSE_

SEOUL, KOREA, 2008

As its name indicates, this house takes the form of an E in plan, allowing it to create a dialogue with the existing site conditions. The elongated section of the house becomes hard and closed, creating a barrier between the house and a busy road to the north. The southern façade gently opens to and greets the landscape, forming a holistic relationship between the two. Cho heightened this effect by minimizing work on any existing elements and by keeping the site's slope and natural features intact.

Cho devised a simple floor plan that allows the building to become easily divided, with clear viewing lines and circulation throughout the home. *Madang* spaces pay homage to traditional Korean architecture, providing areas to pause and reflect as well as breaking up the building mass. The house's two courtyards are, according to Cho, a "water garden and earth garden that allow the users to transition from the dwelling to landscape" open to the south. The earth garden, filled with moss and aspen trees, was intended as a natural habitat in which the inhabitants could observe the changing of the seasons.

The north end of the E-shaped House is a simple box meant for a family room oriented towards Namsan Mountain. This room projects outward for enhanced views and provides a canopy above the entrance, presenting itself as the main architectural feature of the façade. A canopy protects the south-facing elevation from the high summer sun, yet in winter allows sunlight to penetrate the building. These overhangs are the most striking visual elements of the façade, and in the rainy season also act as a rain screen.

Structurally, the E-shaped House is composed of solid reinforced concrete, juxtaposed internally by the use of light materials to create a tension. A mezzanine floor in the main living room is suspended by 30 mm (1 in.) columns and braced internally to take the lateral load. This creates a light, delicate addition to the space that leaves the room's beautiful views of the surrounding landscape intact. Pre-cast concrete in the living room is contrasted with light gypsum walls, the effect being a rich textural experience. Bespoke furniture was created for the living room, including a table made of six large segments of timber and fragmented partition walls that can be used to reconfigure the room to suit a variety of needs.

OPPOSITE, CLOCKWISE FROM TOP LEFT_ *The water garden, the edges of the structure in solid reinforced concrete and the view from the south.*

GROUND FLOOR PLAN   0   5 m

FIRST FLOOR PLAN   0   5 m

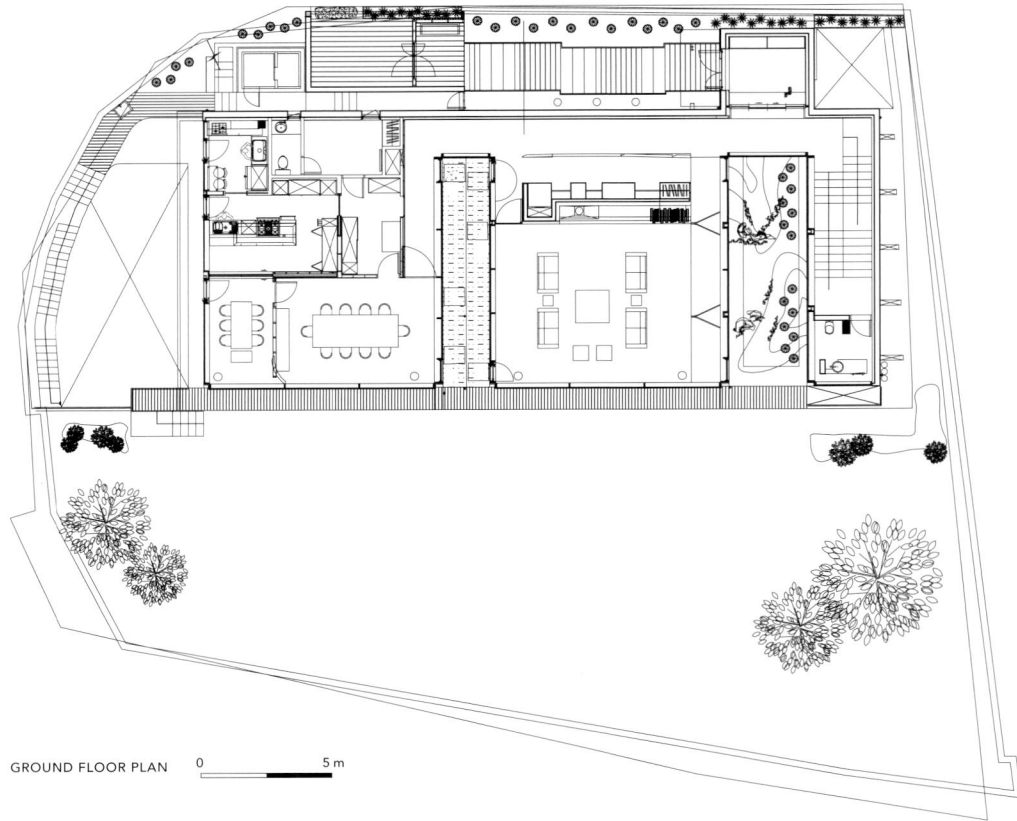

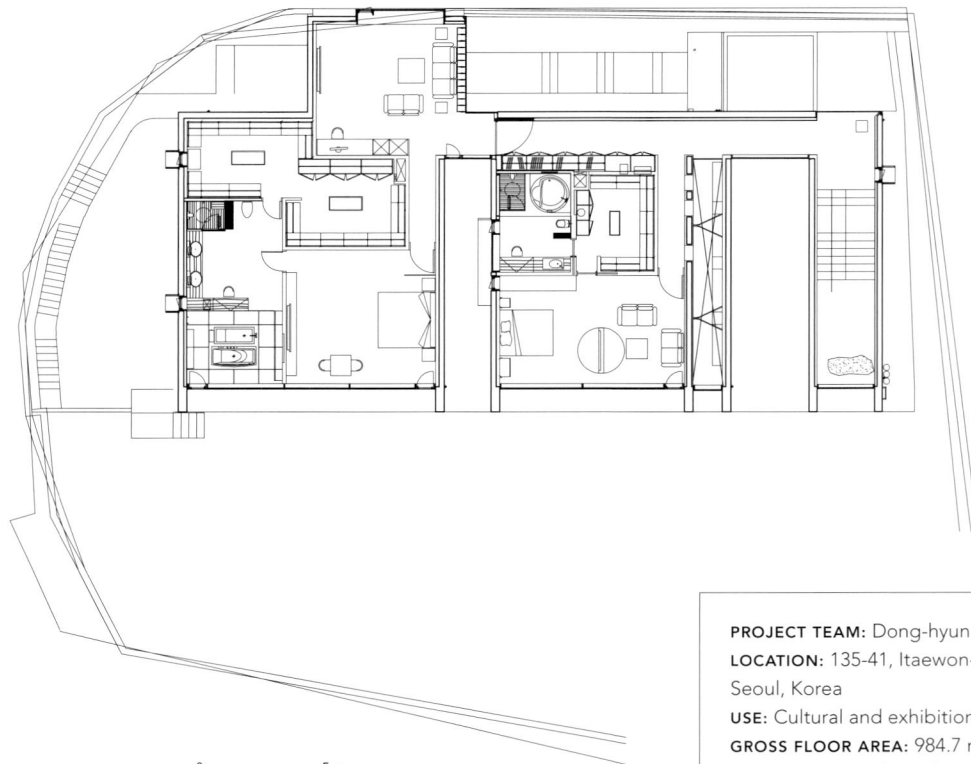

PROJECT TEAM: Dong-hyun Go and Young-jin Kang
LOCATION: 135-41, Itaewon-dong, Yongsan-gu, Seoul, Korea
USE: Cultural and exhibition centre, residential
GROSS FLOOR AREA: 984.7 m² (10,599 ft²)
STRUCTURE: Reinforced concrete

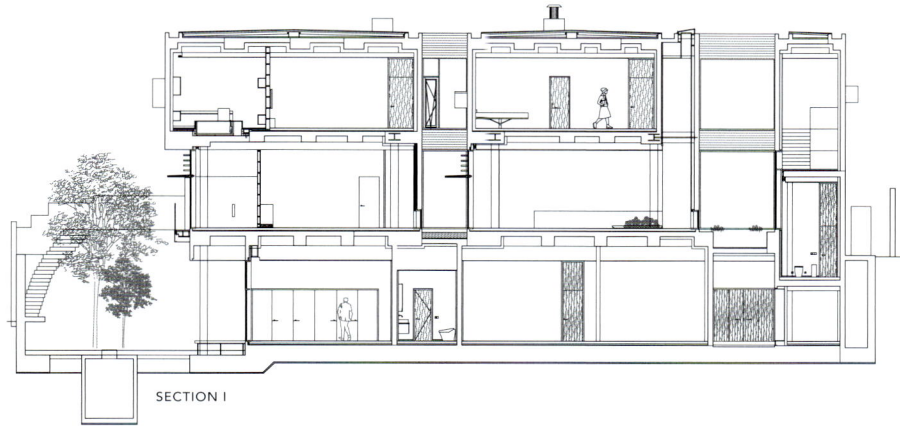

SECTION I

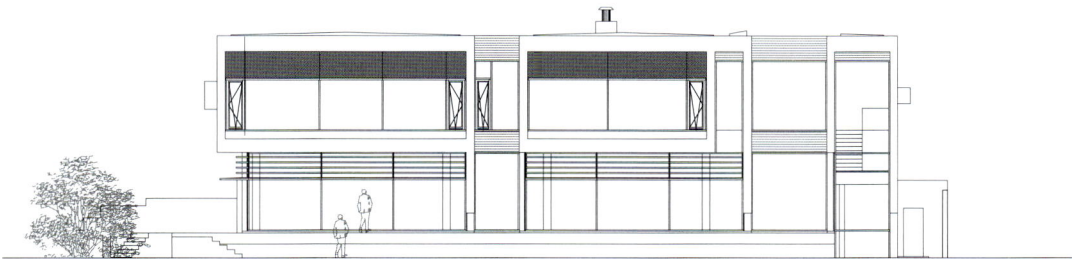

SOUTH ELEVATION

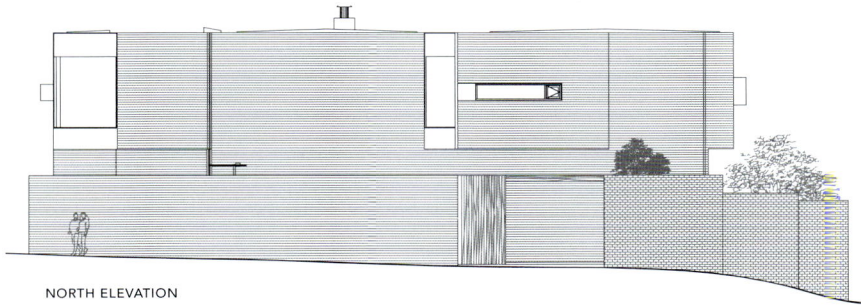

NORTH ELEVATION

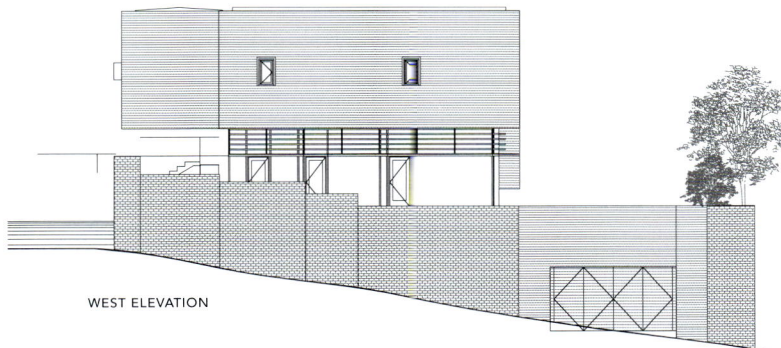

WEST ELEVATION

0   5 m

OPPOSITE, CLOCKWISE FROM TOP_ The grass corner of the building
seen from the garden below, the living room, the entrance and the corridor.

CLOCKWISE FROM TOP LEFT_ *Dining room buffet table, living room side table and dining room buffet table, all designed by Byoung Cho.*

OPPOSITE, CLOCKWISE FROM TOP LEFT_ *Living room table and dining room table, designed by Byoung Cho.*

14. CONCRETE BOX HOUSE_

YANGPYEONG, KOREA, 2004

Cho designed the Concrete Box House to serve as his family's vacation home, a retreat from the busy, noisy life of the city. Located on a quiet, tranquil hill overlooking the rice fields of Yangpyeong, the house takes the shape of a primitive and limited form. Cho started with a 14 x 14 m (46 x 46 ft) square box and placed a 5 x 5 m (16 x 16 ft) hole in the centre. He aimed to evoke the "primitive", removing ornament and peeling away superfluous layers. The structure holds a sense of mystery and lets the visitor experience the subtle changes in nature.

Cho states, "For this project, I wanted the presence of the moon and moonlight to be very strong in the interior. I designed it to be a space in which to contemplate the moon – a moon-watching space. All of the details are very simple, rough, and clean, and the overall structure is intended to appear industrial or storage-like. The design intent was to create a building that would appear quiet and unassuming on the outside, and offer elements to connect

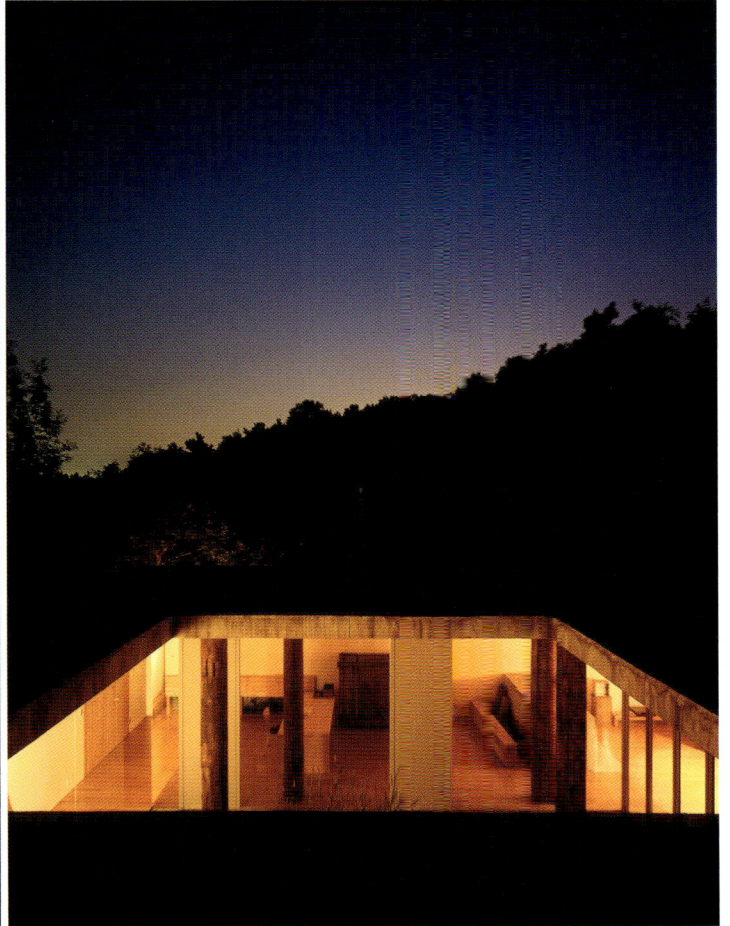

those inside with what is outside." For Cho, the desire to have nature enter and occupy the space was the foremost requirement of this experiment. Reminiscent of James Turrell's "skyspaces", the square opening in the ceiling frames the sky as if it were a work of art. Looking up at the heavens, the visitor experiences the sky as a minimalist trompe-l'oeil, the spell broken occasionally as a cloud or a bird or an aeroplane passes overhead. The skylight features 8 cm (3 in.) thick, nearly imperceptible glass set into the concrete.

Other details stand out in the house, such as steel doors and windows, which, when closed, seemingly disappear into the wall, giving the structure a clean, industrial feel. The roof, including the structure, finishing materials and insulation, is only one foot thick. Cho and his team altered the concrete curing process by using a metal trowel four times every four hours, creating a waterproof seal naturally and allowing the roof to have clean edges.

OPPOSITE_ *The house seen from the east.*

CLOCKWISE FROM TOP LEFT_ *The exterior of the house, looking down into the interior and the skylight with laminated glass.*

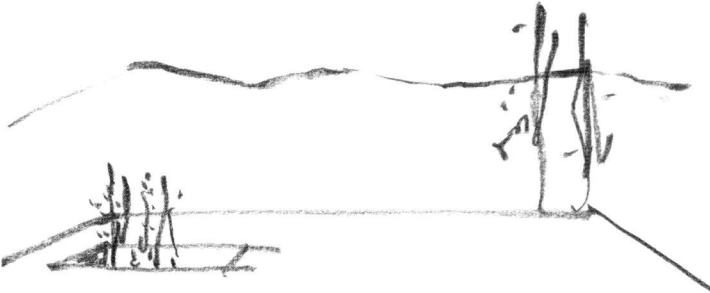

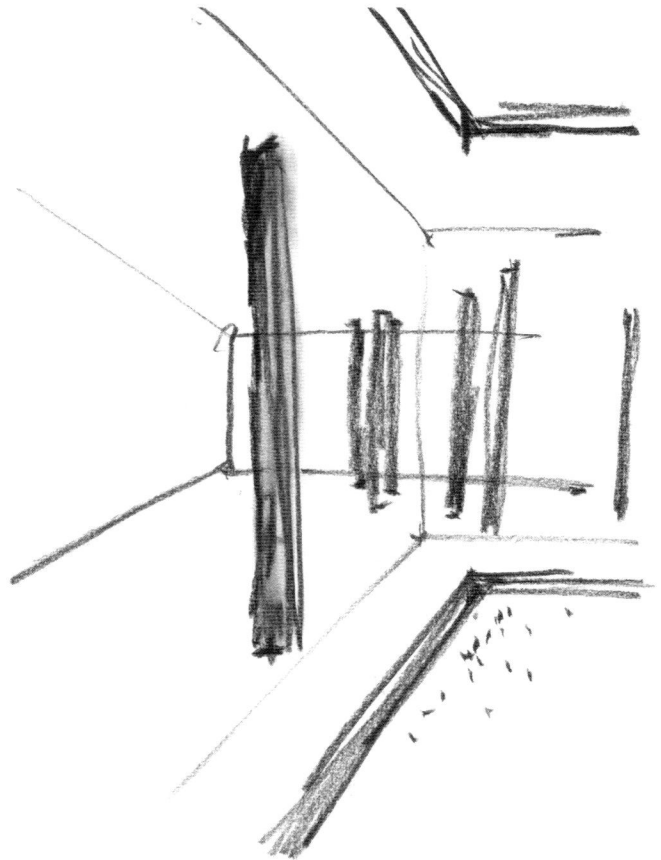

PROJECT TEAM: Yong-joon Jo
LOCATION: 789-3, Sugokri, Jije-myeon, Yangpyeong-gun,
Gyeonggi-do, Korea
USE: Studio
GROSS FLOOR AREA: 191 m² (2,056 ft²)
STRUCTURE: Reinforced concrete, wood

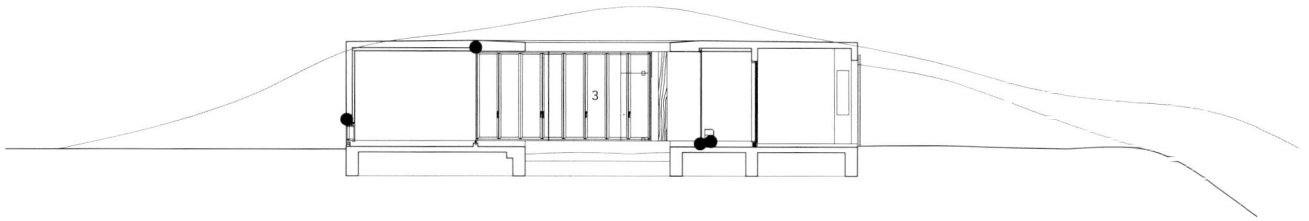

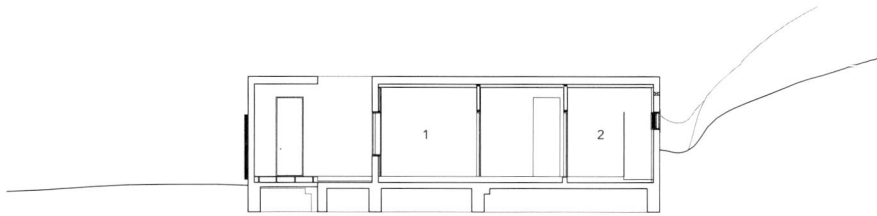

SECTION   0   5 m

1. Room   2. Rest room   3. Water garden

GROUND FLOOR PLAN

1. Entrance
2. Corridor
3. Master bedroom
4. Living room
5. Kitchen
6. Rest room
7. Storage
8. Water garden

0   5 m

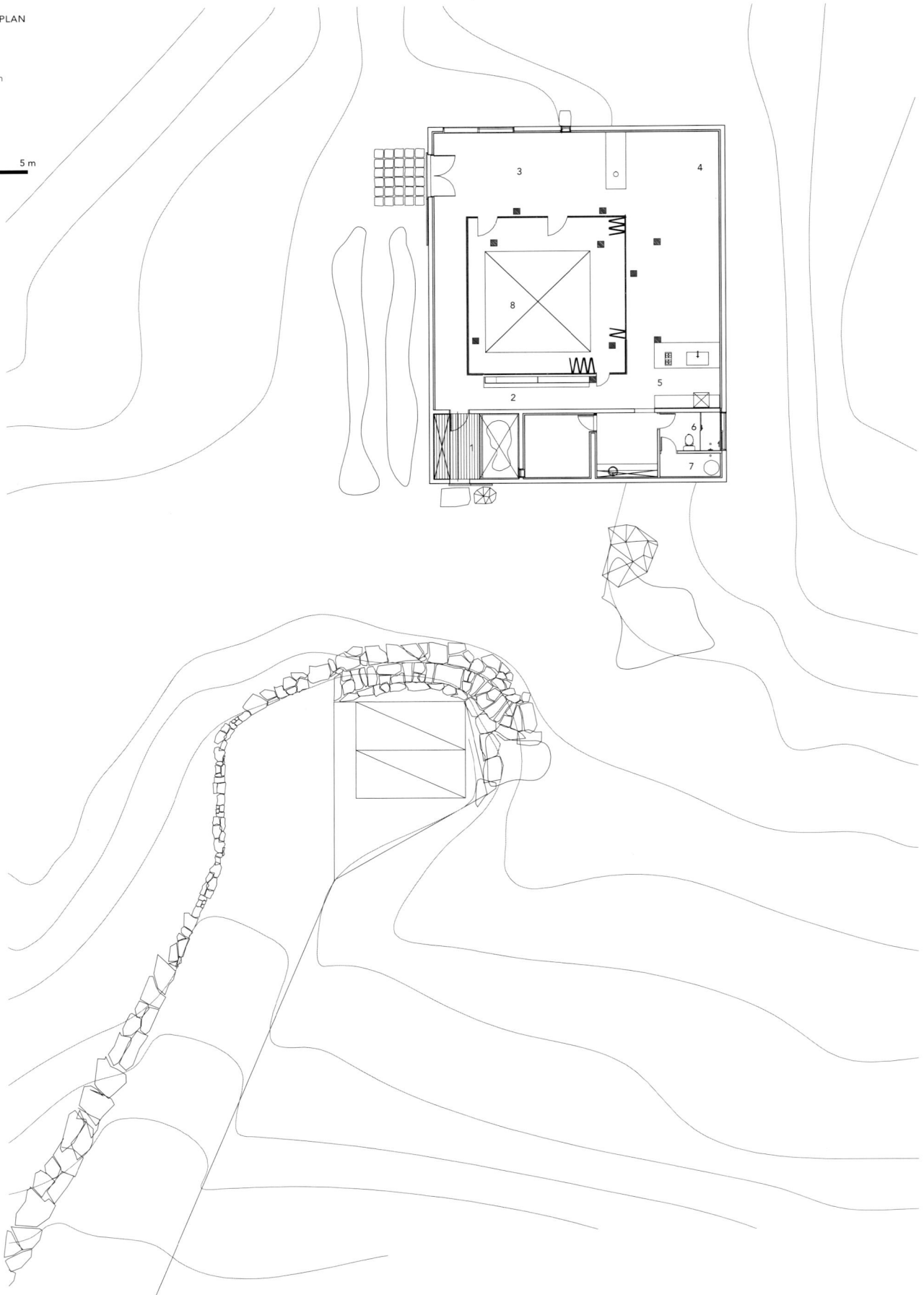

OPPOSITE, CLOCKWISE FROM TOP_ *The view from the southwest looking into the courtyard, a detail of the join between the concrete plate and an old wood column and the interior with old wood columns.*

15. COMMUNITY HOUSE_

YANGPYEONG, KOREA, 2008

Community House is a small-scale structure nestled into an idyllic setting of dense woodland in Yangpyeong, Korea. It is part of a series of buildings that place a strong emphasis on the interaction between nature and place. The structure uniquely reacts to the site by roughly following the outline of an artificial boundary, a road to the east, while becoming embedded in the natural topography of the landscape.

Geometrically following the topography of the site, the stepped roof becomes a significant feature of the design, visually linking lower and ground floors, while becoming an open circulation space at roof level. A concrete retaining wall acts as an extension of the building, cutting the landscape to the east, creating an open decked area and an entrance.

Internally, the building is open plan, split by a mezzanine floor that allows service spaces to be placed underneath. The stepped roof is exposed within and finished in plaster, creating a sculptural quality to the space, which is intensified by a poetic play on light filtered from openings in the roof. These rooflights are designed to conceal fixtures, producing a seamless connection between interior and exterior when viewed internally and consequently between the inhabitant and nature.

Homage is paid to the process of construction with the concrete formwork structure left bare to the elements. This gives Community House a ruggedness that is achieved through the imprint of timber grain onto the concrete and by leaving the construction ties hollow. Furthermore, by using concrete and inserting the house into the ground, a high thermal mass is attained, stabilizing temperatures in both winter and summer.

OPPOSITE, CLOCKWISE FROM TOP LEFT_ *The house seen from the west, detail of the glass layers in the skylight, the structure embedded in the landscape and the house from above at right*

PROJECT TEAM: Tae-hyun Nam
LOCATION: 789–40, Sugok2-ri, Jipyeong-myeon,
Yangpyeong-gun, Gyeonggi-do, Korea
USE: Studio
GROSS FLOOR AREA: 123.5 m² (1,329 ft²)
STRUCTURE: Reinforced concrete

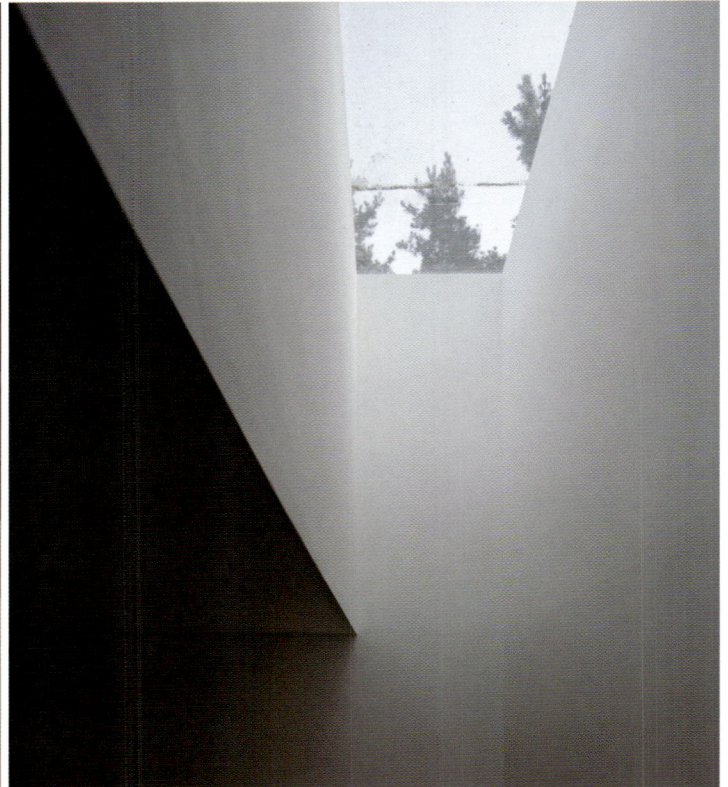

CLOCKWISE FROM TOP_ *Roof edge with concrete and laminated glass, light entering through the skylight and an interior view of the tilted space.*

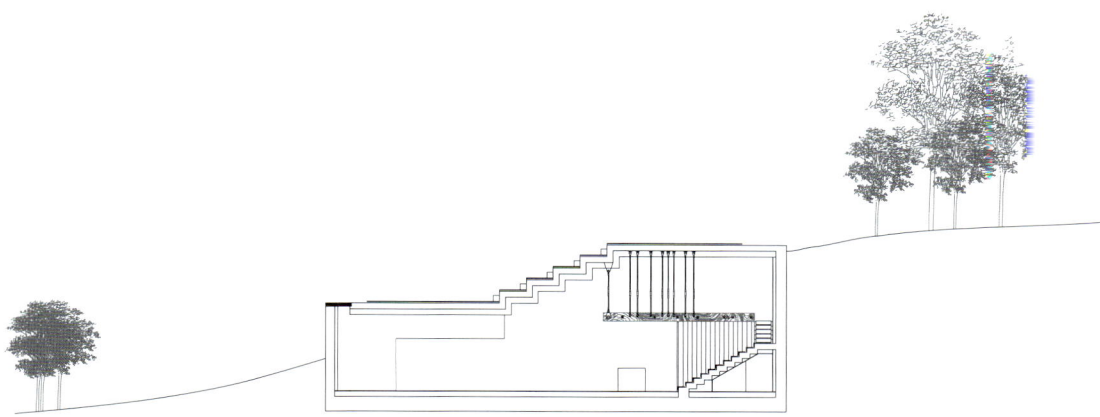

SECTION A   0   m

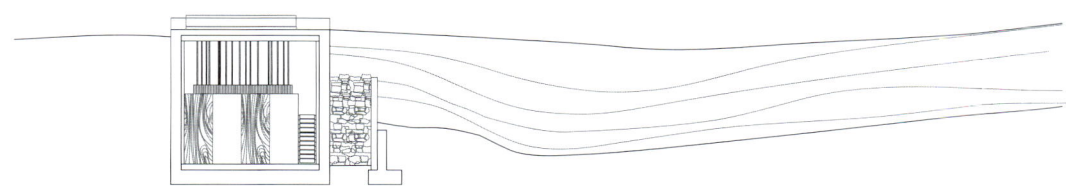

SECTION B   0   m

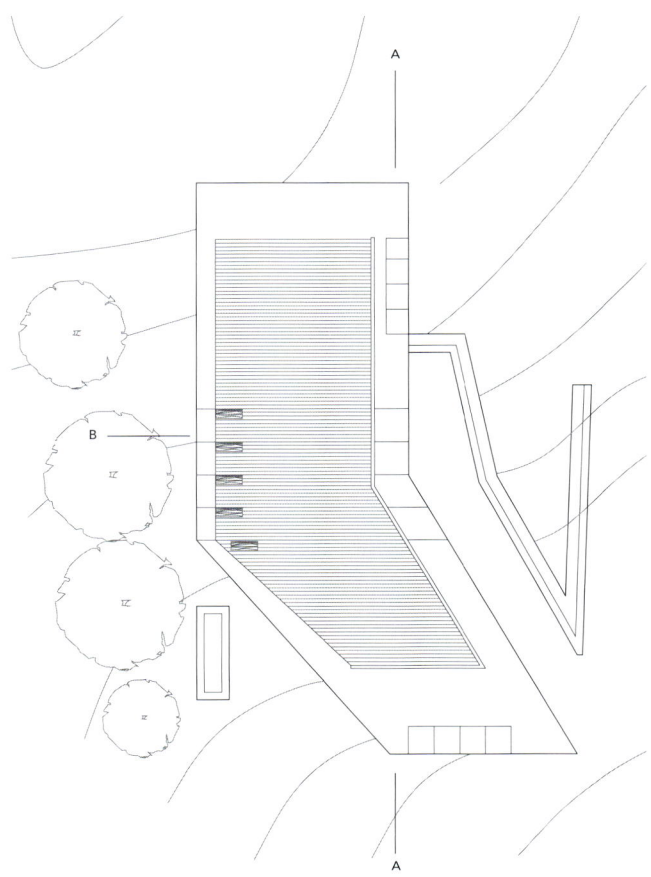

ROOF PLAN   0   5 m

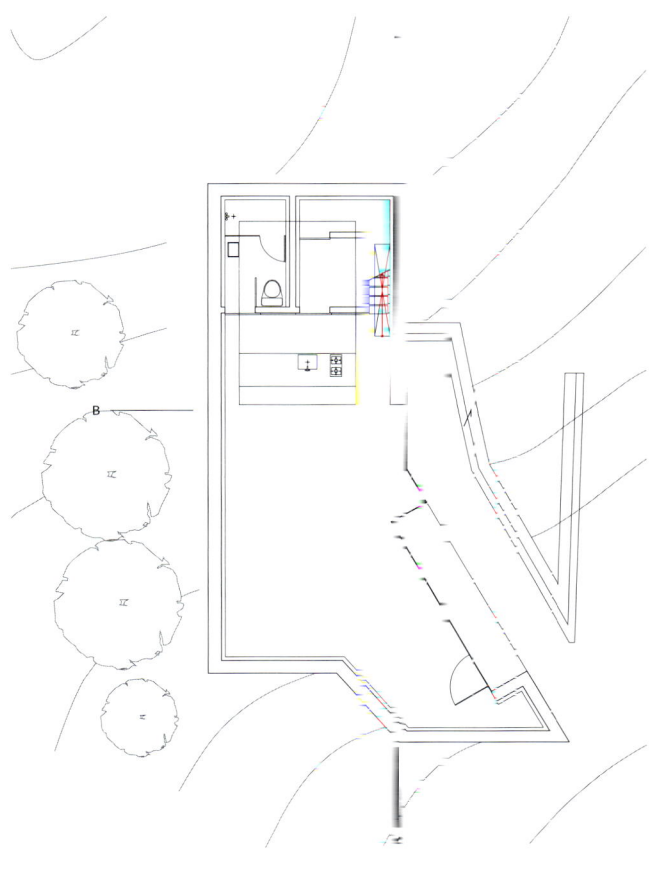

GROUND FLOOR PLAN   0   5 m

A great country is like a low land.
It is the meeting ground of the universe,
The mother of the universe.

The female overcomes the male with stillness,
The lying low is stillness.

– *Tao Te Ching*

16. EARTH HOUSE_

YANGPYEONG, KOREA, 2009

As with Cho's Concrete Box House, the Earth House explores how people relate to nature. When asked what prompted him to build houses in the earth, Cho replied, "The earth is our mother, the mother of all that lives and will be born. Being underground, one can experience nature more strongly and vividly, especially as the sky and the light change. Moreover, building into the earth can be very sustainable, as the ground maintains a stable temperature, allowing for temperature regulation with less energy."

The 14 x 7 m (46 x 23 ft) concrete box contains two earth-filled courtyards open to the sky, as well as a small kitchen, a library that doubles as a meditation room, two rest rooms, a bathroom with a wooden tub and toilet, and a wash room. The rooms are all adjacent to one another and open directly onto the courtyards. Connecting rooms can be joined to create a bigger room. The house doors are small, which means that to enter the house, one must "reduce one's shape", according to the architect.

Within the ground, the building resists lateral pressure from the earth on all four sides thanks to thick concrete retaining walls and a flat roof and base plate. A hidden steel column in the centre wall reinforces the structural plates. Rammed earth walls provide all the interior spatial divisions and the walls facing both courtyards. The earth used for the walls was excavated from the site. Minimal white cement and lime were used so the earth walls could later return to the soil. The house employs a geothermal cooling system and a radiant floor heating system under the rammed clay and concrete floor. Off-peak electricity is used at night to heat the small gravel under the floor. A combination of passive cooling and geothermal tubes buried in the earth around the buildings keeps the temperature cool in summer and warm in winter.

Cho sliced a pine tree cut down at the site into 80 mm (3½ in.) thick discs and then cast them in the walls of the courtyard so that as the house decays, new life will arise in time. The wooden canopy protecting the entrance into the small house uses 39 mm (1½ in.) tensile wires. Recycled lumber was cut into pieces 300 mm (12 in.) wide and 50 mm (2 in.) and joined with a flat steel bar, keeping the use of the material to a minimum. All of the interior furniture and closets are made of wood recycled from old Korean gates.

Cho built the Earth House in honour of Yun Dong-Ju (1917–45), a Korean poet who exalted the beauty of nature in his posthumous collection, *Sky, Wind, Star, and Poem* (1948). Through his poetry Yun, who was labelled a "thought criminal" by the Japanese and died in prison, expressed his hope for the future during times of great peril. For Cho, the house is a place to practise restraint, reflection and mindfulness.

OPPOSITE, CLOCKWISE FROM TOP_ *Earth House appears to be a concrete box buried in the ground, the house seen from the forest and the courtyard.*

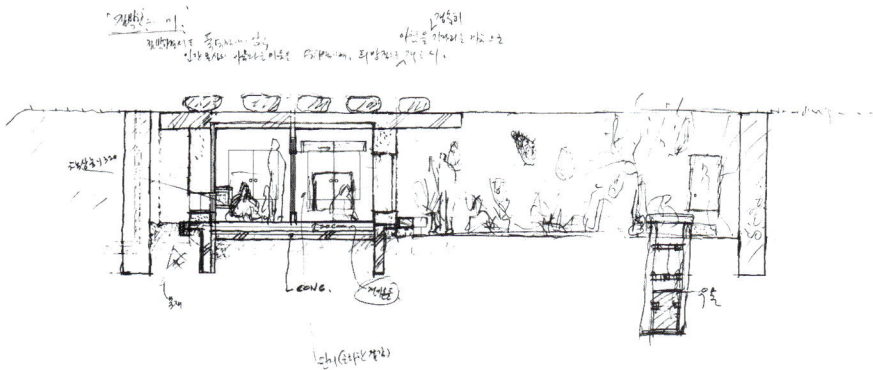

OPPOSITE, CLOCKWISE FROM TOP LEFT_ *The interior seen through
a small wooden door, a window in the rammed earth wall, view of the rammed
earth wall and door from the courtyard and a detail of the interior.*

ROOF PLAN   0   3 m

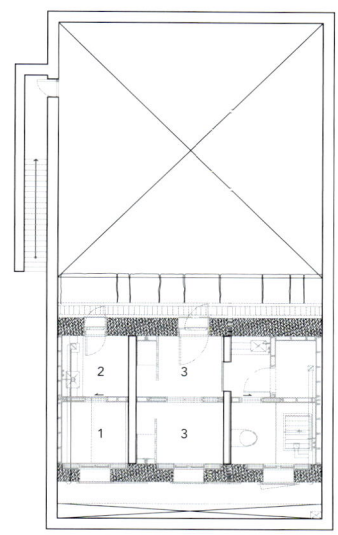

BASEMENT FLOOR PLAN   0   3 m

2
3
1
3

N

1. Library
2. Kitchen
3. Room

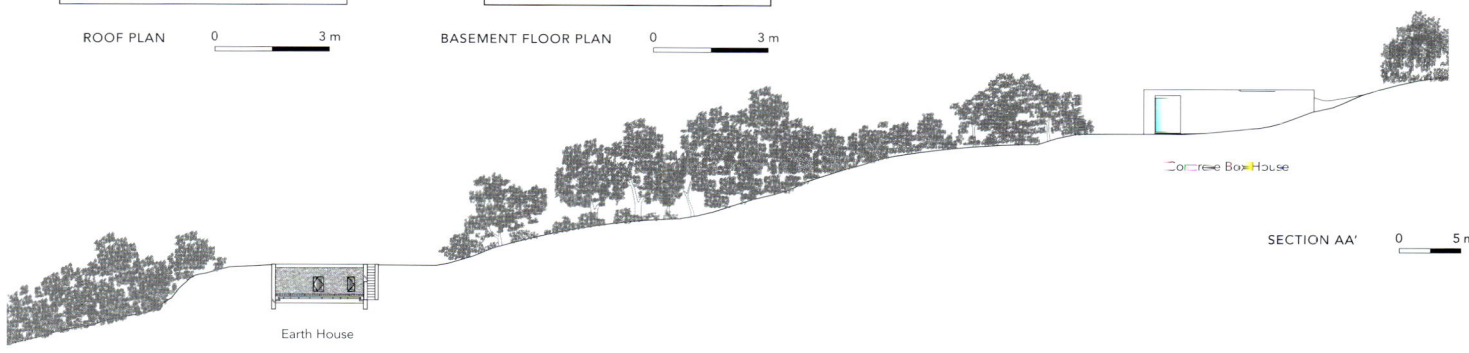

PROJECT TEAM: Hong-soon Yang, Woo-hyun Kang and Tae-hyun Nam
LOCATION: 789-55, Sugok2-ri, Jioyeong-myeon, Yangpyeong-gun Gyeonggi-do, Korea
USE: Library, meditation room
GROSS FLOOR AREA: 32.5 m² (350 ft²)
STRUCTURE: Recycled concrete, flat slab

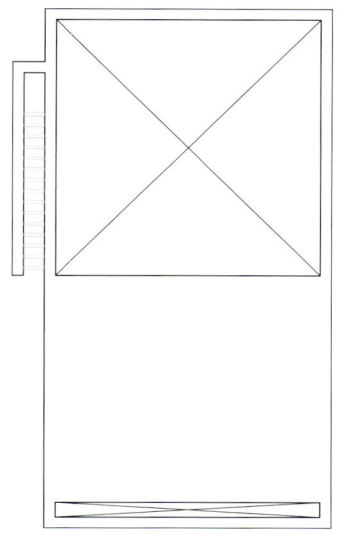

Concrete Box House

Earth House

SECTION AA'   0   5 m

A   A'

ROOF PLAN   0   5 m

OPPOSITE_ *Light streaming out through the linear opening and the courtyard at night.*

17. HANIL VISITORS' CENTRE AND GUEST HOUSE_

DANYANG KOREA, 2009

The Hanil Visitors' Centre project, part of the Hanil cement plant complex in Danyang, Korea, was conceived as a way to educate the public about the environmental benefits of recycling concrete. The making of cement, a primary component of concrete, generates enormous amounts of carbon dioxide and contributes greatly to global warming. Cho believes that it is imperative to reuse the concrete in buildings being torn down and replaced, thereby keeping concrete out of landfills and reducing the need to make more of it.

Cho practised what he preaches throughout this project. A gabion wall and fabric-encased concrete walls constitute the main façades of the Visitors' Centre. Concrete left over from building the façade was used to make gabion cages on the roof, which help insulate the building; and as landscape material on the streets surrounding the factory. Cho also recycled concrete waste generated while erecting the eastern wall to put up a new wall on the opposite side. The footing used for the fabric-formed wall was cut into pieces from 10 to 20 cm (4 to 8 in.) in size and put into gabion wire netting – to be recycled as exterior finishing material for the southern façade.

Recycling waste concrete not only has environmental and cost benefits, but also offers an antique feel, since dust and moss gather on the concrete as time passes. The fabric-formed concrete wall was developed in collaboration with C.A.S.T., based in Manitoba, Canada. Concrete moulds were created for the footing; the wall's forms were set using pipes; and high-strength fabric was stretched on top, like a mould. After connecting fittings were embedded, concrete was poured into the mould, producing a non-load-bearing concrete wall with convex and concave curves. Their undulating regularity evokes the trunks of trees in a dense forest.

The Visitors' Centre is located near the western end of the concrete factory, adjacent to Mount Sobaek National Park. Cho and his team brought a bit of nature back to the complex: earth was brought in to fill the courtyard between the two buildings. Cho incorporated the inner courtyard between the two structures, which houses the main lobby and the cafeteria, into the slope of the mountains in the west. In the spaces in between visitors can experience how the buildings shift around the central court. Four openings in the eastern wall and long vertical windows provide unexpected views. Through one window one can see how concrete is produced at the factory. Behind two larger openings the courtyard and the cafeteria appear, encircled by a water garden. In the Visitors' Centre, Cho recast used concrete into translucent and opaque tiles, made sample gabion walls, and created other revolving displays to induce visitors to look at this common material in a new light.

OPPOSITE, ABOVE_ *Rear view of the Visitors' Centre and guest house.*

OPPOSITE, BELOW_ *The front of the building with a fabric-formed concrete wall. The recycled concrete wall is also visible.*

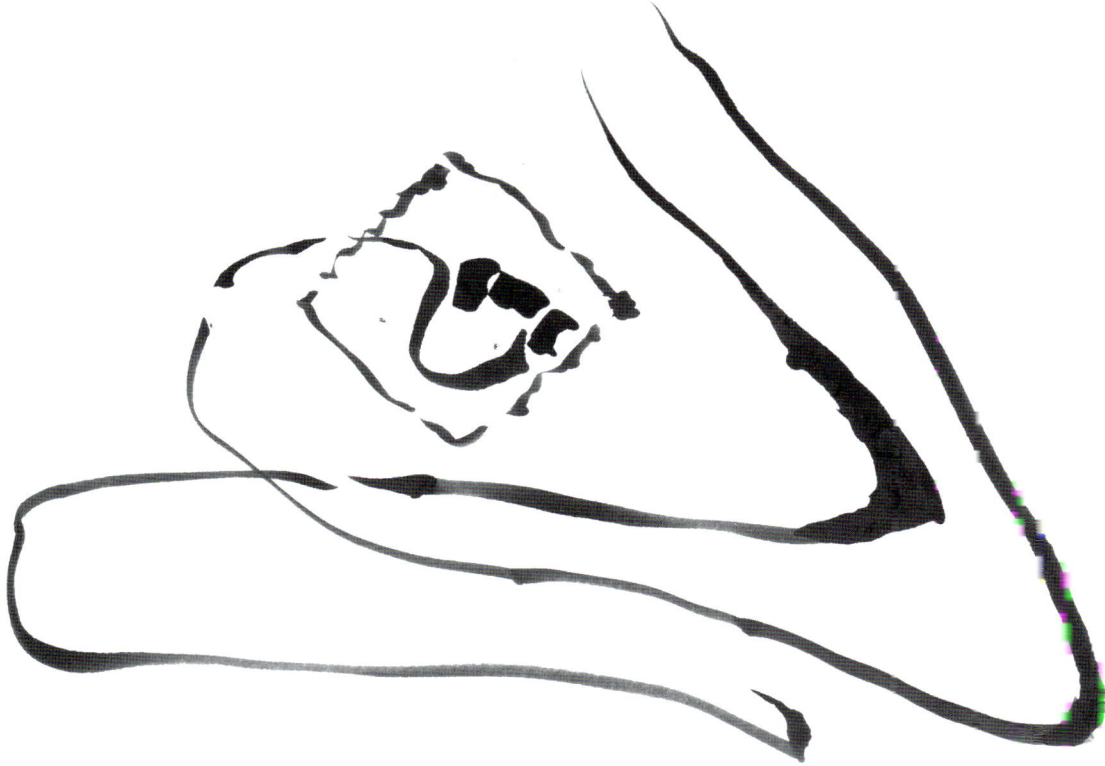

OPPOSITE_ *The central courtyard.*

ABOVE_ *A sketch of the light and shadow on the concrete wall and a study of the spaces in between the masses.*

OPPOSITE, CLOCKWISE FROM TOP_ *The interior of the visitors hall, the wire staircase, the dining room and the living quarters.*

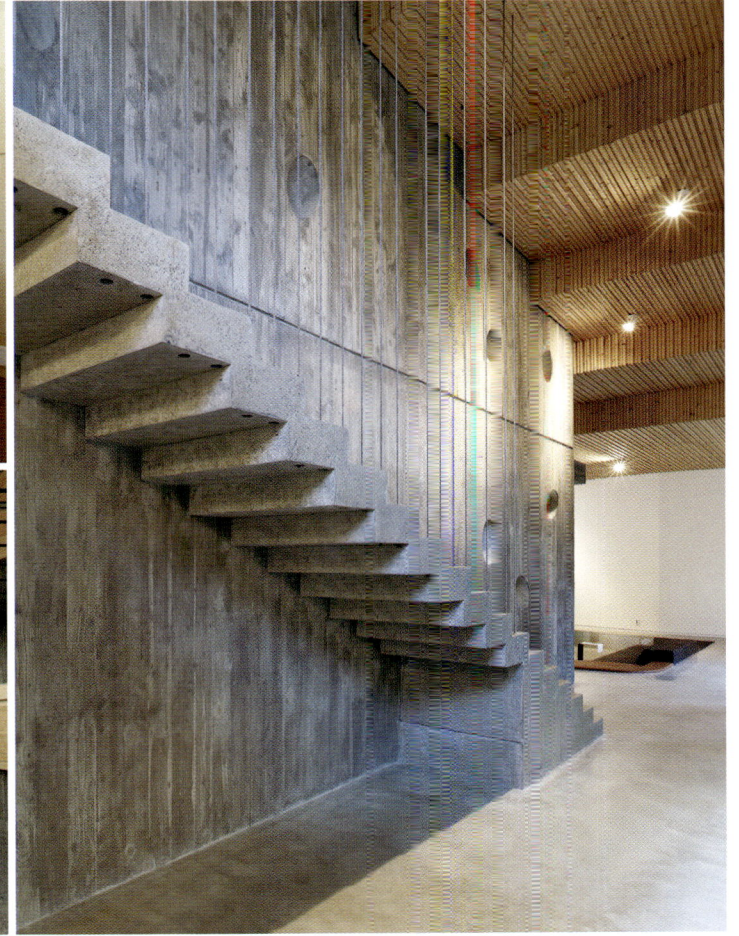

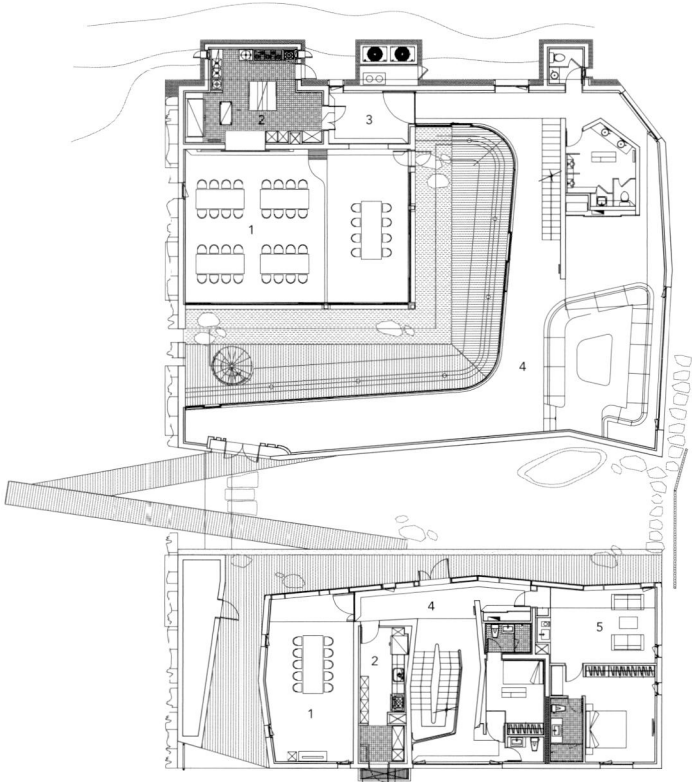

GROUND FLOOR PLAN 0 ___ 5 m

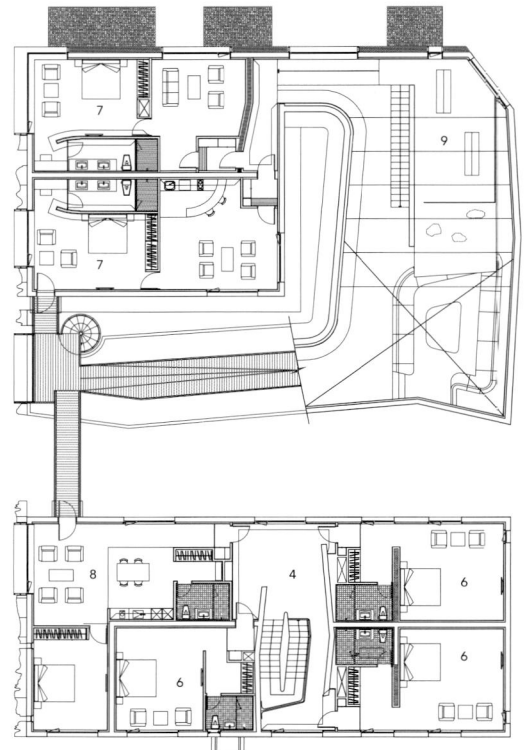

FIRST FLOOR PLAN 0 ___ 5 m

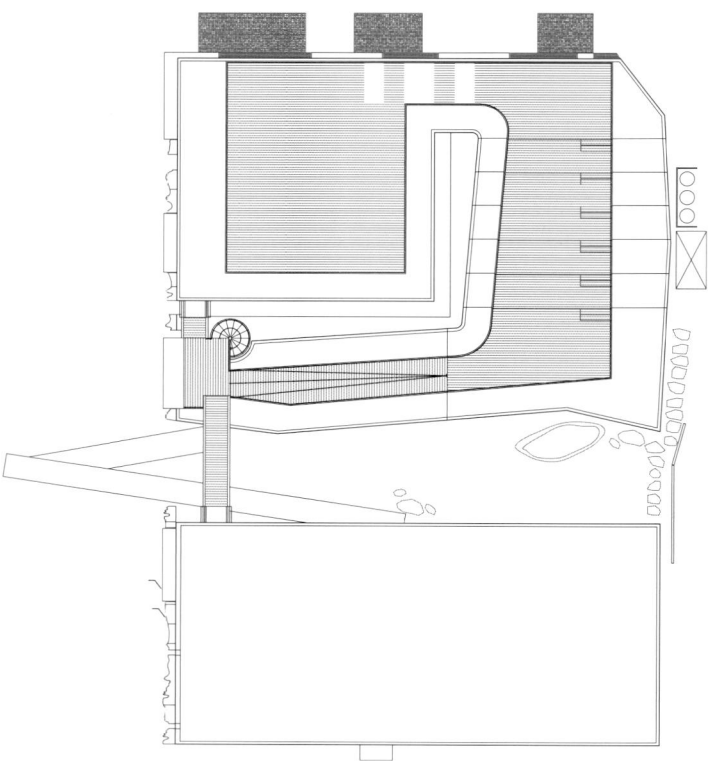

ROOF PLAN 0 ___ 5 m

1. Dining room
2. Kitchen
3. Reception hall
4. Hall
5. Assistant manager's room
6. Living quarters
7. VIP room
8. Manager's room
9. Lounge

PROJECT TEAM: Nick Locke, Young-jin Kang and Tae-hyun Nam
LOCATION: 77, Pyeongri, Maepo-eup, Danyang-gun, Chungbuk, Korea
USE: Visitors' centre and guest house
NET FLOOR AREA: 1,031 m² (11,098 ft²)
STRUCTURE: Reinforced concrete

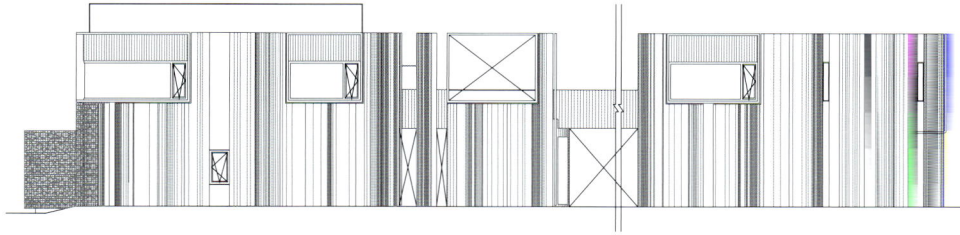

EAST ELEVATION   0   5 m

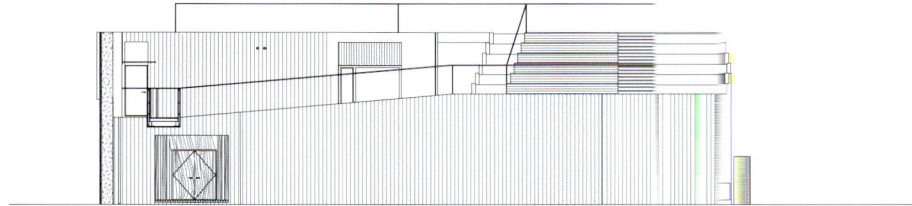

NORTH ELEVATION   0   5 m

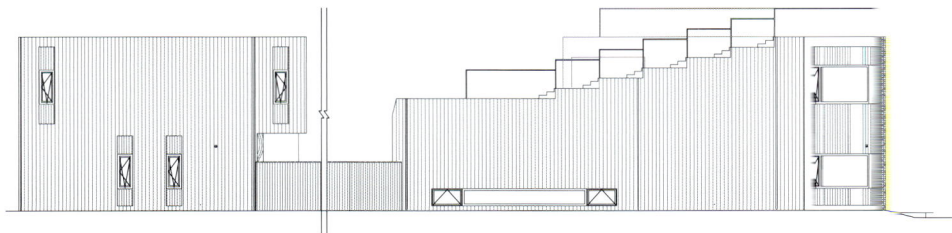

WEST ELEVATION   0   m

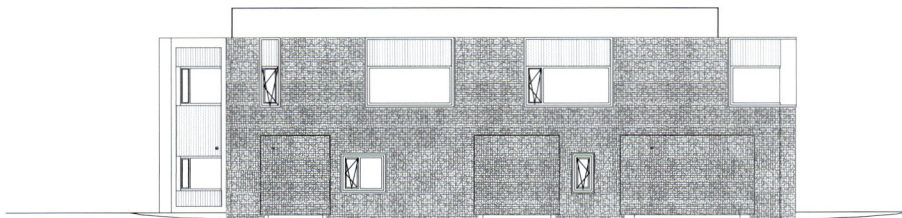

SOUTH ELEVATION   0   m

HANIL VISITORS' CENTRE AND GUEST HOUSE_

BYOUNG CHO_

18. HEYRI STUDIO HOUSE_

HEYRI ART VALLEY, PAJU, KOREA, 2009

This small structure is part of a series of arts-based commissions nestled in the Heyri Art Valley situated a short distance from Seoul. Initially an avant-garde arts community, due to the relentless drive of commercialism, the village has now become a major tourist destination. This has presented numerous problems: in particular, a distinct lack of privacy for the residents living and working there. Pertinent to this design is a rejection of the urban and the definition of the natural and so a resonance with the landscape is created.

Reacting to the unique site conditions and context, the design is akin to open arms, inviting to the west, and so creating an interaction with the landscape, while forming a hard boundary to the east, defining the street elevation. It draws on themes explored earlier in Community House. The client's intention was to relocate here in the future, so a second phase was planned that would create more rooms. One mass, embedded in the southern slope, represents the main living and studio space of Heyri Studio House. However, it is the subtle additions to this building that create a provocative composition, striking in its simplicity yet complex in its conviction. By using these architectural gestures to frame, border and define nature, the building becomes a vessel, creating a bond between the inhabitants and the natural.

The exterior is defined by a stepped roof intentionally left exposed to create a rugged addition to the landscape. This correspondingly means a double-height space internally that is used as an artist's studio; this stepped form becomes a functionalist device, trapping southern light as it ascends, thus providing a well-lit space for the artist.

Through an emphasis of low horizontal lines the courtyard creates an organic relationship with the terrain of the site while visually reinforcing the idea of the house belonging to the ground. Sliding doors blur the connection between interior and exterior, allowing the inhabitant to control air flows manually through the building. The exterior is typified by the exposed concrete finish juxtaposed by red steel for fenestration and doors, paying respect to the industrial vernacular of the area.

OPPOSITE, CLOCKWISE FROM TOP_ *According to Cho, the mass of the Heyri Studio House "creates a bond between the personal and the natural", the stepped roof seen from the street, the entrance, which juxtaposes an exposed concrete finish with red steel, and the view towards the west, showing the building's interaction with the landscape.*

CLOCKWISE FROM TOP_ *The stepped ceiling and the southern light, light entering through a window and the studio interior.*

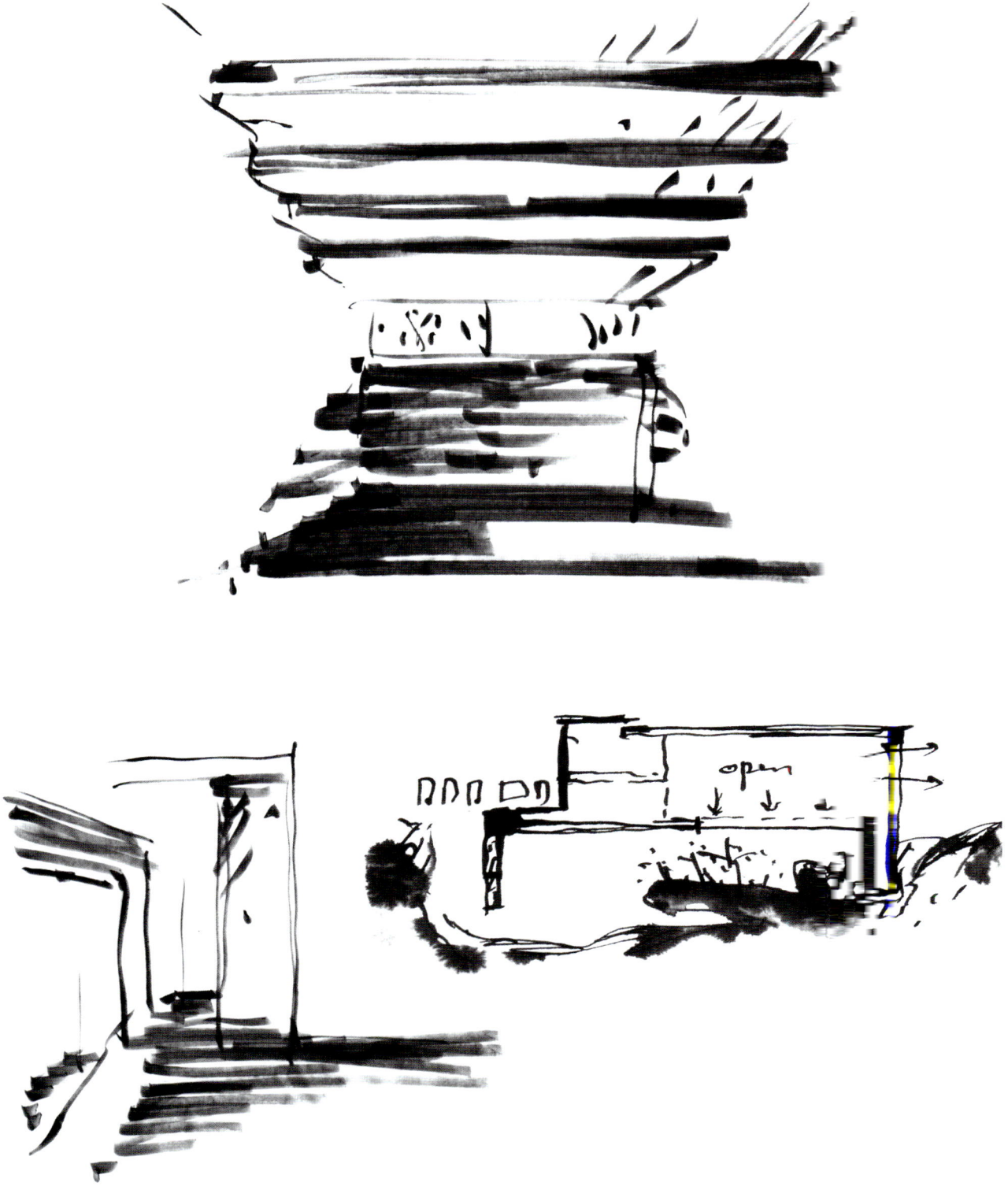

OPPOSITE_ *The view from the west and the wooden ceiling.*

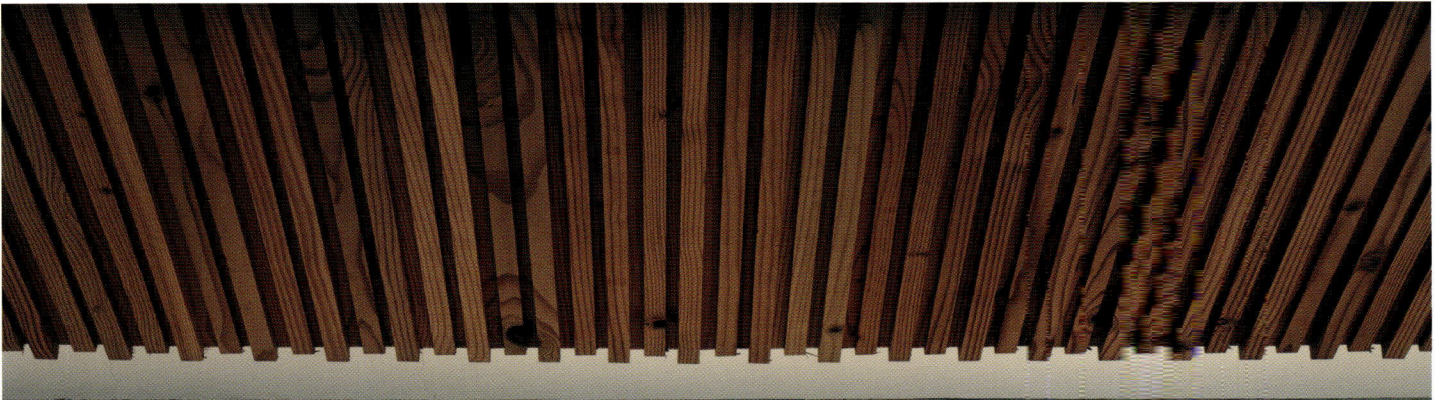

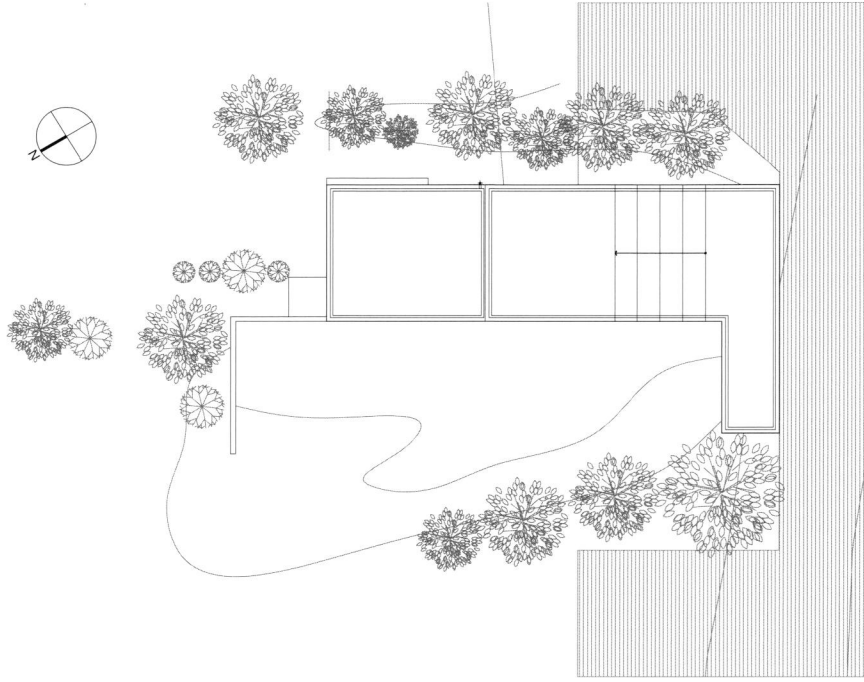

ROOF PLAN   0   5 m

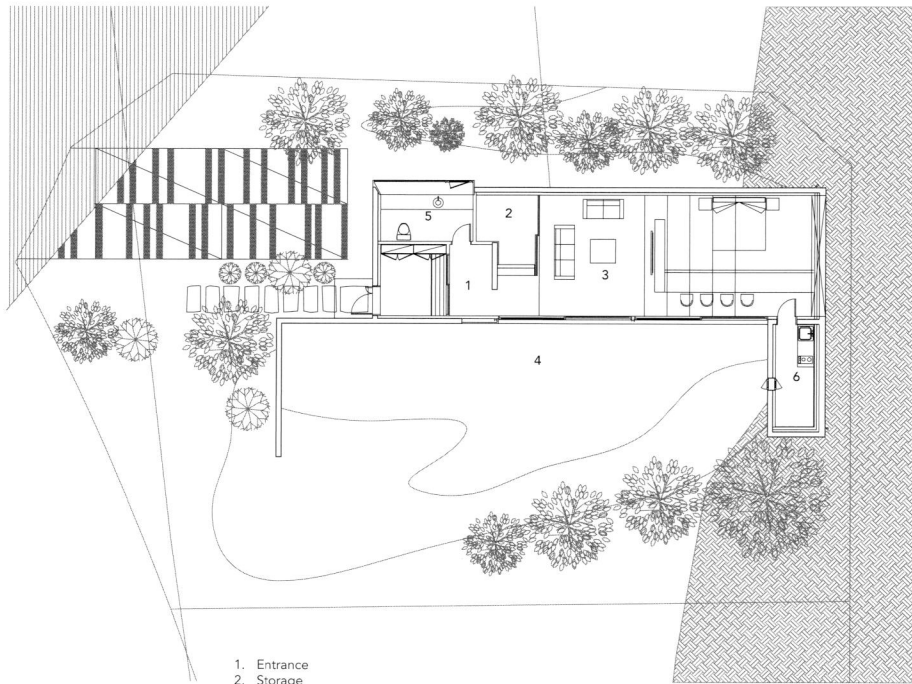

1. Entrance
2. Storage
3. Studio
4. Courtyard
5. Rest room
6. Kitchen

GROUND FLOOR PLAN   0   5 m

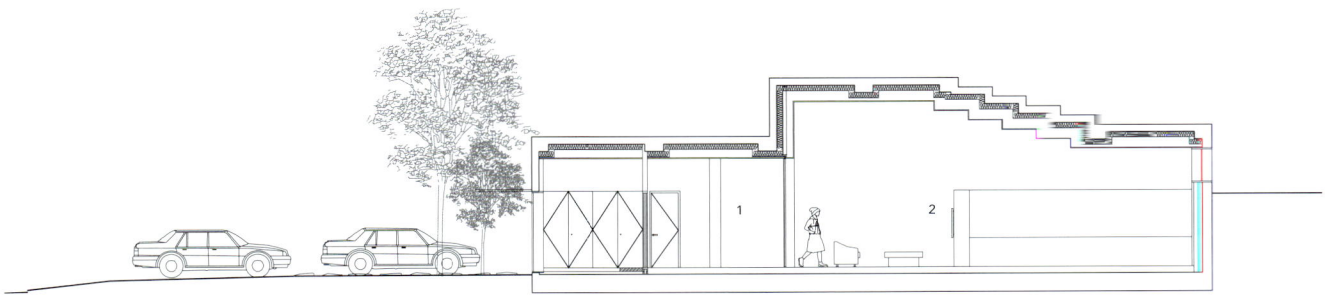

SECTION A

0   5 m

1. Entrance 2. Studio

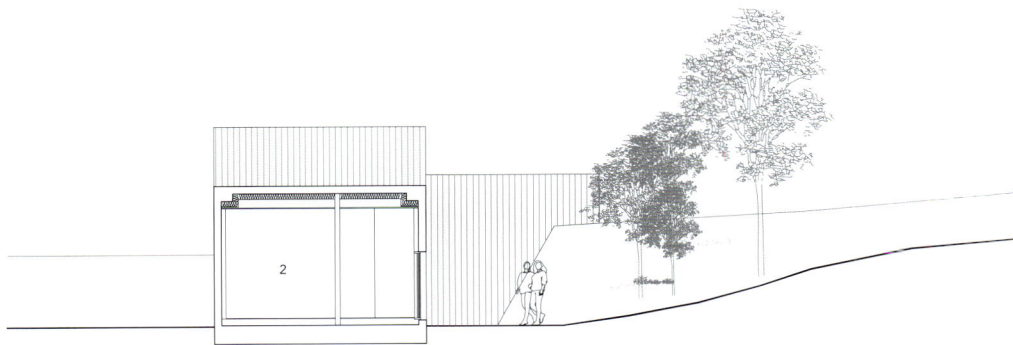

SECTION B

0   5 m

PROJECT TEAM: Woo-hyu Lee
LOCATION: Heyri Art Valley 3 Beobheung-ri
Tanhyun-myeon, Paju, Gyeonggi-do, Korea
USE: Studio
GROSS FLOOR AREA: 103 m² (1102 ft²)
STRUCTURE: Reinforced concrete, flat slab

19. JEDONG RANCH_

JEJU ISLAND, KOREA, 2010

Located on the tranquil Jeju Island, Jedong Ranch comprises three distinct structures arranged linearly across the top of the site, allowing unrestricted panoramic views. A dining pavilion and meditation space are clustered together and orientated in the same direction, while a guesthouse lies on its own 175 m (574 ft) away.

PROJECT TEAM: Hye-eun Choi, Jun-ho Ann and Jeon-am Kim
LOCATION: 16, Gyoraeri, Jocheon-eup, Jeju-si, Jeju-do, Korea
USES: Performance hall (596.4 m², 6,419.5 ft²); guest house (510.5 m², 5,494.9 ft²); meditation space (60 m², 645.8 ft²)
STRUCTURE: Reinforced concrete

DINING PAVILION

The main building, the largest of the three, is the dining pavilion, which presents itself as a multi-functional, adaptable structure with the potential to become completely closed or open depending on the occupants' desires. When closed, the building takes on a distinctly organic form, defined horizontally by the jagged lines of the floor and roof slabs and vertically by white steel shutters. Supported by a steel sub-structure, these shutters allow the exterior to become fully closed or neatly opened (the shutters slide open), revealing a terrace and the unimposing pavilion behind. Concealed footings and a raised floor slab give the building an appearance of delicately sitting in the natural landscape.

In plan, the pavilion is composed of four simple rectangles arranged longitudinally. To the south, these spaces become light and airy and are predominantly glazed. In contrast, to the north, where additional privacy and thermal efficiency are required, the spaces are somewhat heavier.

Internally, the theme of adaptability is continued with colourful patchwork partitions breaking up the main space, allowing multiple configurations and greater flexibility to the building. Sliding full-height glass windows provide an opportunity to gain unobstructed views of the surrounding landscape, while instantaneously blurring the boundary between interior and exterior.

OPPOSITE_ *The dining pavilion in the ranch.*

ABOVE, CLOCKWISE FROM TOP LEFT_ *View from the east, looking at the folding door from the north and the pavilion in the north.*

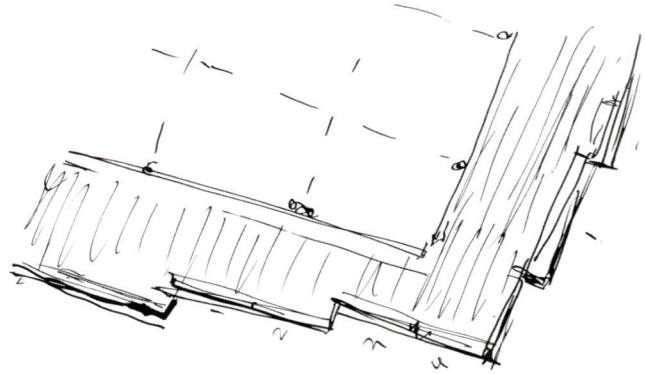

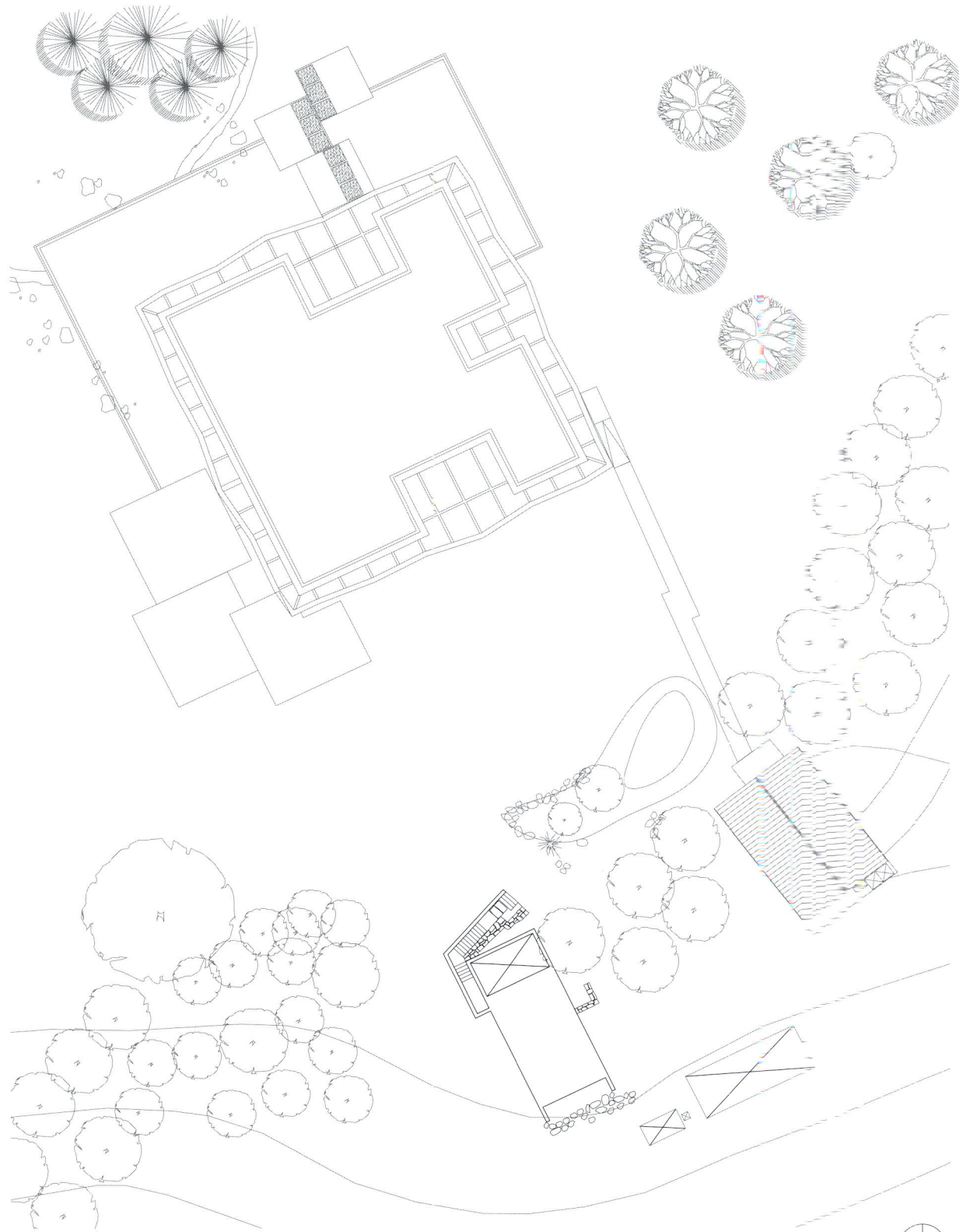

SITE

0   5 m

ROOF PLAN   0   5 m

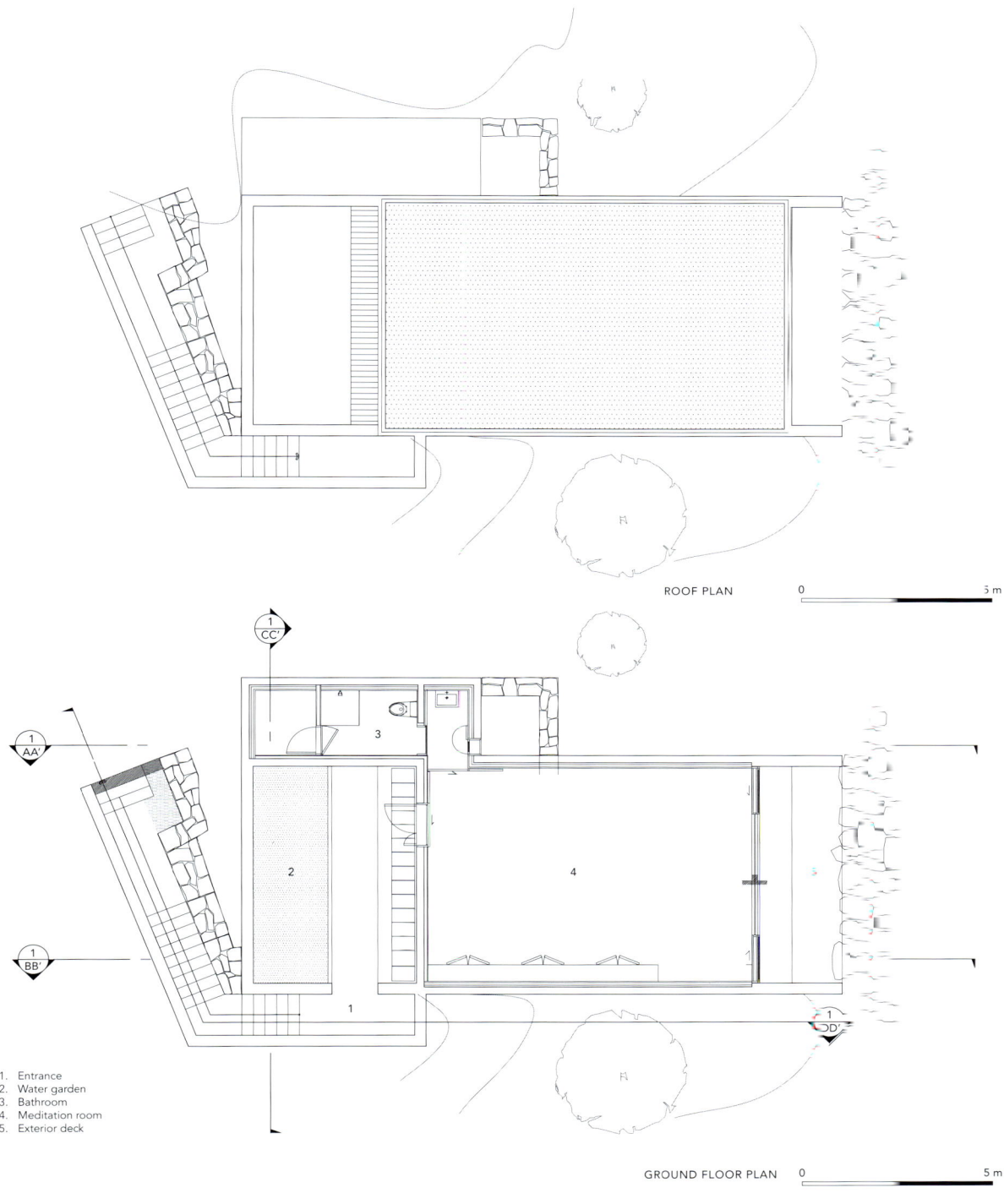

1. Entrance
2. Water garden
3. Bathroom
4. Meditation room
5. Exterior deck

GROUND FLOOR PLAN   0   5 m

MEDITATION SPACE

In stark contrast to the dining pavilion, seemingly floating in the landscape, the meditation space is deeply embedded in the ground, profoundly coupled with nature.

The approach to the space is intentionally prolonged, heightening the sense of anticipation, while becoming a powerful metaphor as one is quite literally submerged into the site. This is realized by a long staircase that gradually steps down while revealing more of the exposed concrete retaining wall. A courtyard opens the building to the sky, its exposed concrete walls becoming the main aesthetic throughout the exterior.

Oriented towards a canopy of trees, the meditation space celebrates man's interaction with nature, creating a certain dialogue. Interior finishes are kept clear and unpretentious. Timber sliding doors and a continuation of the ground out into the tree canopy grant the occupant intimacy and isolation, all against a backdrop of unspoilt nature.

OPPOSITE, CLOCKWISE FROM TOP_ *The meditation space seen from the west, a meditation room, looking out to the corner the staircase that leads to the entrance and the view from the east with the ranch in the background.*

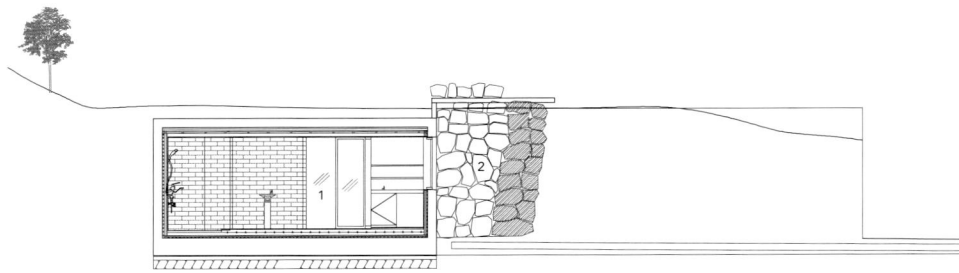

1. Bathroom 2. Exterior deck   SECTION A   0   5 m

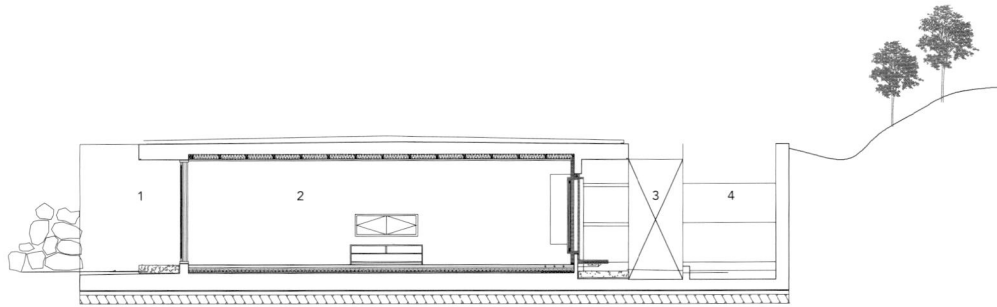

1. Exterior deck 2. Meditation room 3. Entrance 4. Water garden   SECTION B   0   5 m

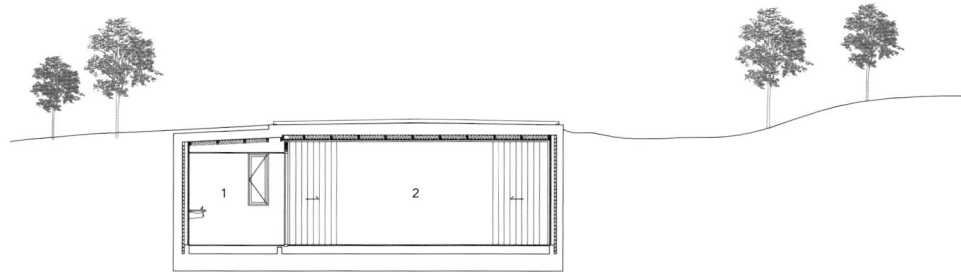

1. Bathroom 2. Meditation room   SECTION C   0   5 m

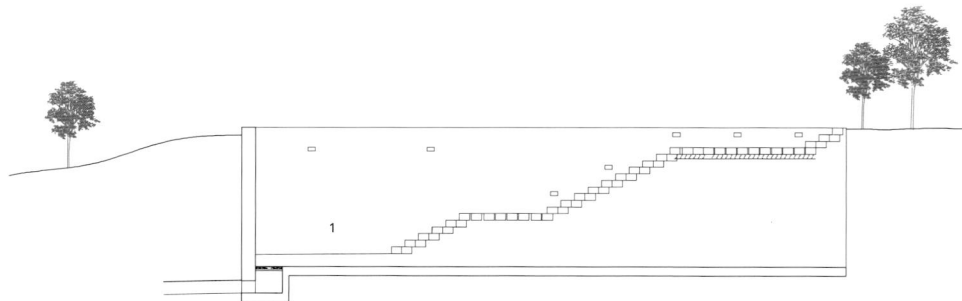

1. Entrance   SECTION D   0   5 m

GUEST HOUSE

The guest house sits on a gentle slope slightly raised off the ground. It is composed of two geometric buildings, the largest forming the ground floor, while a second, considerably smaller, sits on top, orientated at a slight angle. Similar to the dining pavilion, the exterior is formed of two integral parts, an inner and an outer skin. The outer skin is composed of a series of static and moveable timber shutters, while the inside is predominantly a glass box. The timber shutters constitute the main element of the façade, broken up by large white horizontal fascias.

Internally, the cubic floor plan deviates from the building's outline with the use of an elongated courtyard acting as a lightwell that filters light into the centre of the structure. An architectural feature is made of the main staircase connecting the two areas. It is cantilevered off a load-bearing concrete wall, apparently floating, while the glass balustrade conceals its fittings to create a simple yet bold element to the staircase. The master bedroom has a soft, yet effective, colour palette heightened by a powerful use of light diffused by paper screens to create a particular radiance. Unrestricted views are available from the roof. The roof can be reached from the master bedroom via a terrace.

OPPOSITE, CLOCKWISE FROM TOP_ *The guest house at the top of the gentle slope, the moveable timber shutters, the terrace with Hanra Mountain in the background and the two geometric masses.*

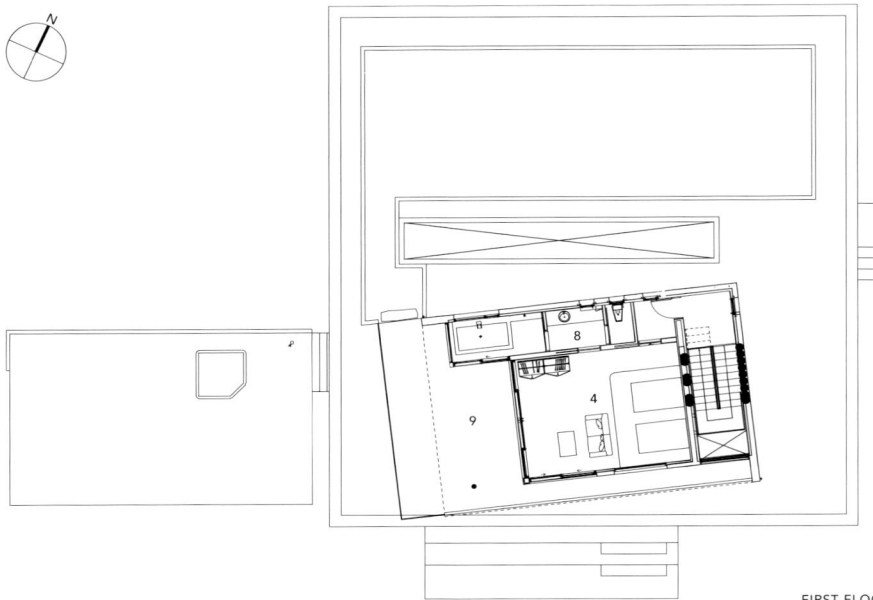

FIRST FLOOR PLAN   0 _____ 5 m

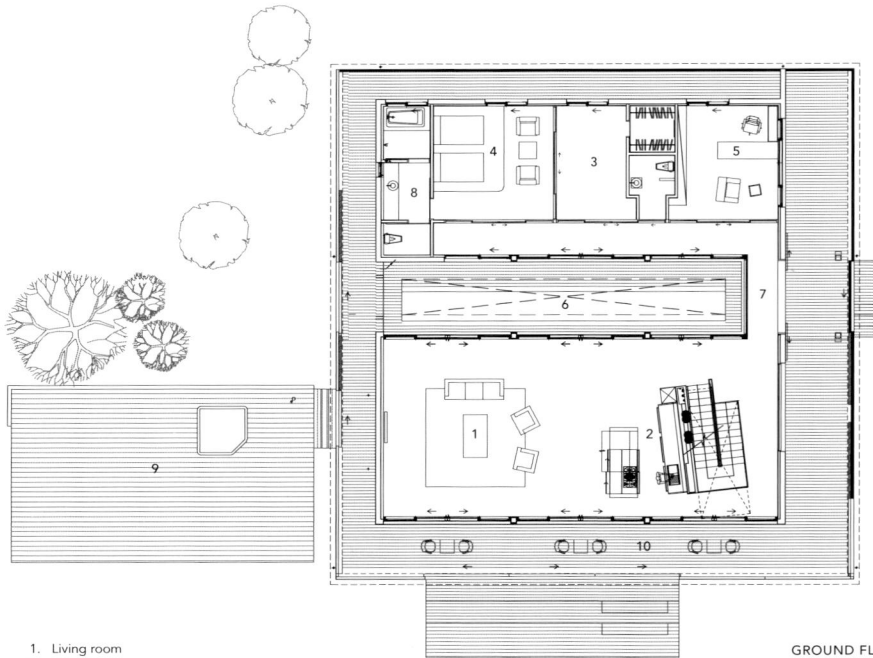

1. Living room
2. Kitchen
3. Korean-type room
4. Bedroom
5. Office
6. Courtyard
7. Entrance
8. Bathroom
9. Deck
10. Terrace

GROUND FLOOR PLAN   0 _____ 5 m

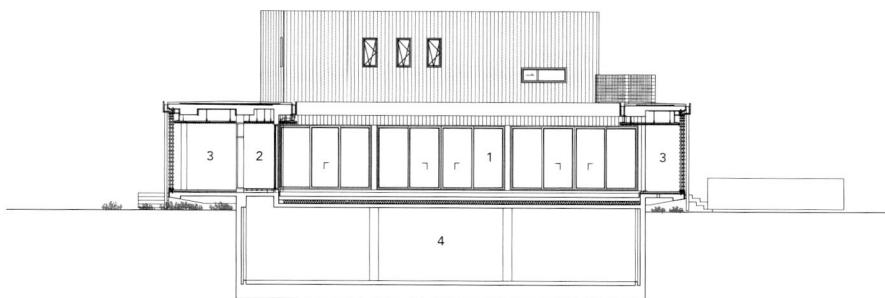

SECTION A   0   5 m

1. Courtyard   2. Entrance   3. Terrace   4. Basement

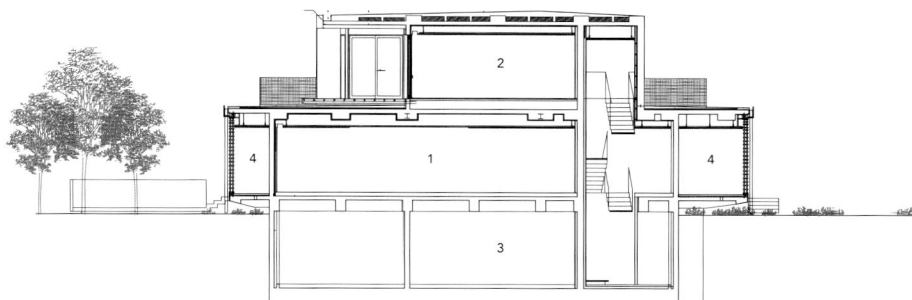

SECTION B   0   5 m

1. Living room   2. Bedroom   3. Basement   4. Terrace

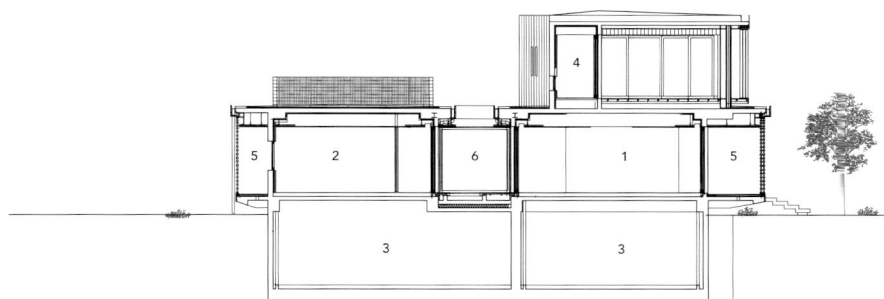

SECTION C   0   5 m

1. Living room   2. Bedroom   3. Basement   4. Bathroom   5. Terrace   6. Courtyard

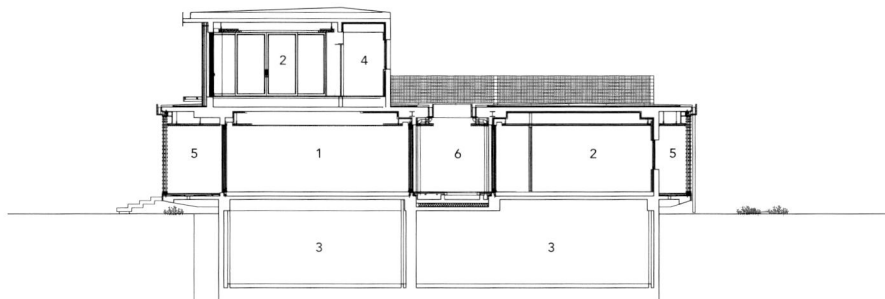

SECTION D   0   5 m

1. Living room   2. Bedroom   3. Basement   4. Bathroom   5. Terrace   6. Courtyard

20. L-SHAPED HOUSE_

HWASEONG, KOREA, 2010

The L-shaped House is situated in a small valley about one hour from Seoul. It was commissioned by a professional couple, who visit on weekends and plan to move there permanently in a few years, and is designed to be sealable while the couple work in the city.

The clients bought the land adjacent to the residence, providing large open areas to the south and east. Cho initially conceived the L-shaped House as a square orientating itself towards the mountain and trees. The architect felt the L was "a practical shape for creating private exterior spaces facing the vistas while buffeting the house from the road." Morning sunlight enters the sleeping areas of the house – the couple are both early risers. Cho included natural cross ventilation features to keep interior temperatures low and take advantage of breezes in the high humidity of summer when the house is most often occupied.

The main living space is partitioned with a moveable wall system. The master bedroom and a broad, covered deck to the south are adjacent to it. The shaded space functions as an intermediate usable area with an accordion door system. The large southern overhang permits sun into the living space only in the winter months, and air cools before entering the house in the middle of summer when the angle of the sun is much steeper. The southeastern courtyard sits in the area created by the L space of the building. It is paved with local white basalt stone, installed specifically to reflect light up into the living space, which, in turn, has one long, low continuous window. The indirect light cast off the courtyard is an ingenious way to bring light into the living room. The warm light coupled with a mix of pale woods and white surfaces from floor to ceiling, creates an inviting and casual living space. The courtyard has a minimal amount of landscaping, with one planted tree to anchor the corner, providing plenty of space for a wide variety of activities with little maintenance.

OPPOSITE, CLOCKWISE FROM TOP_ *The L-shaped form open to nature and the building at night, the roof, the entrance, the view from the west and the view from the courtyard.*

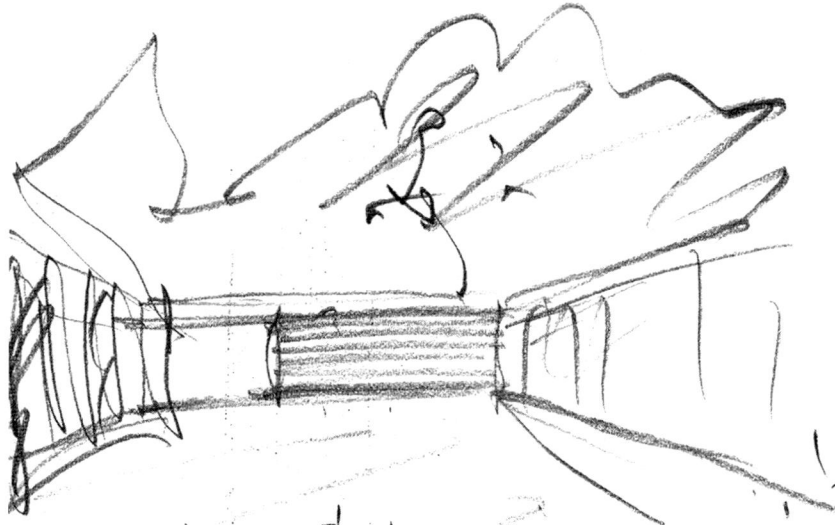

OPPOSITE, CLOCKWISE FROM TOP_ *The interior of the tea room, the wooden ceiling in the living room and the wooden ladder leading up to the attic of the tea room.*

PROJECT TEAM: Seok-gyeong Hong
LOCATION: Hwasanri, Ujeong-eup, Hwaseong-si,
Gyeonggi-do, Korea
USE: Residential
SITE AREA: 892 m² (9,600 ft²)
STRUCTURE: Reinforced concrete

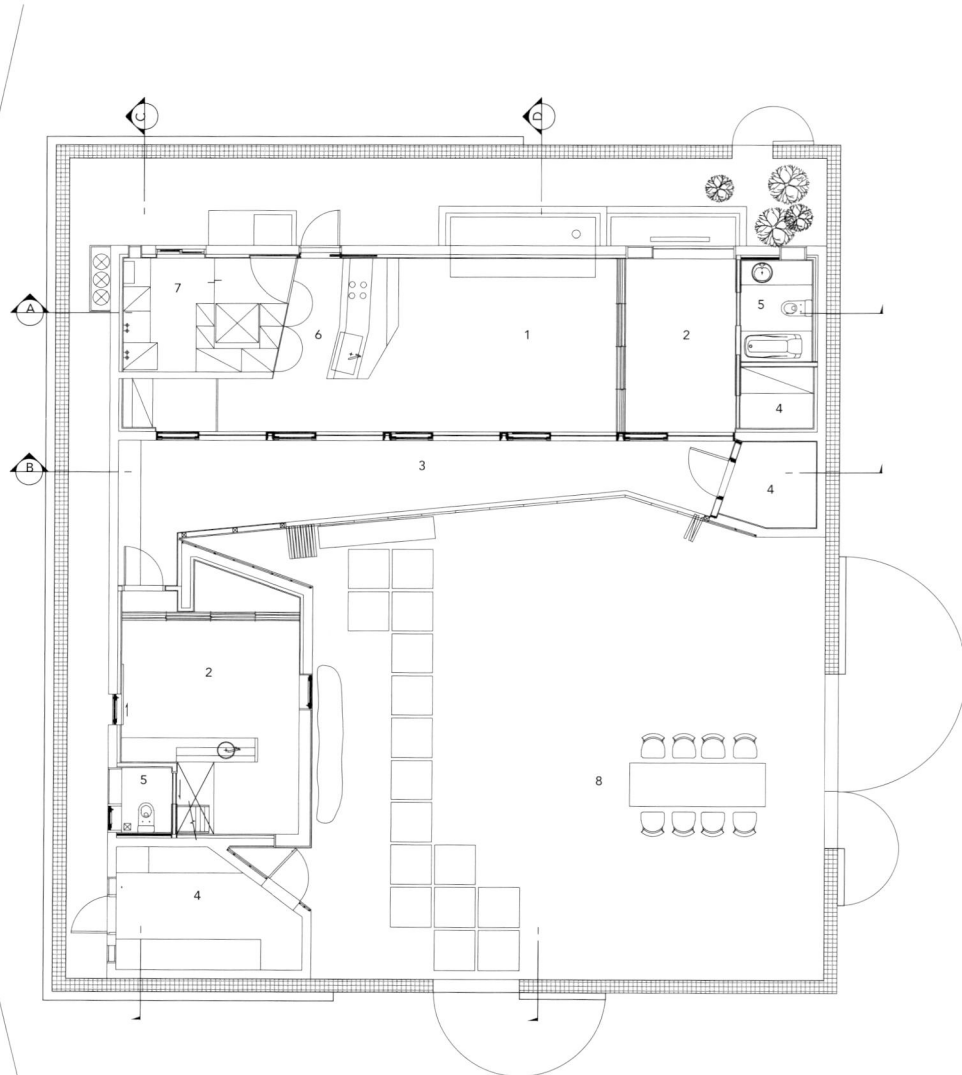

1. Living room
2. Bedroom
3. Terrace
4. Storage
5. Bathroom
6. Kitchen
7. Support kitchen
8. Courtyard

GROUND FLOOR PLAN
0   5 m

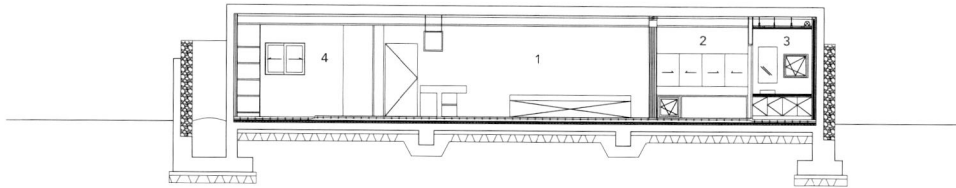

SECTION A   0   5 m

1. Living room 2. Bedroom 3. Bathroom 4. Kitchen

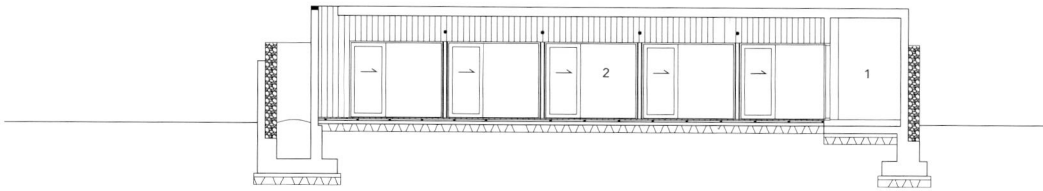

SECTION B   0   5 m

1. Storage 2. Terrace

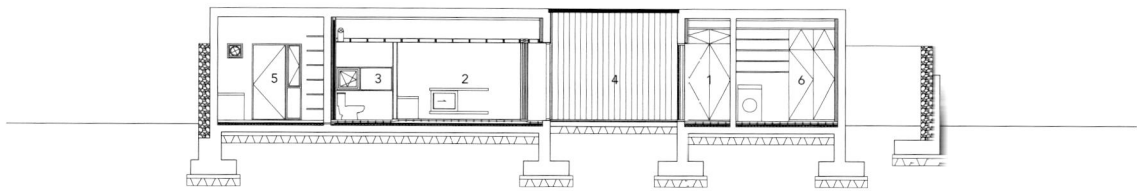

SECTION C   0   5 m

1. Entrance 2. Bedroom 3. Bathroom 4. Terrace 5. Storage
6. Support kitchen

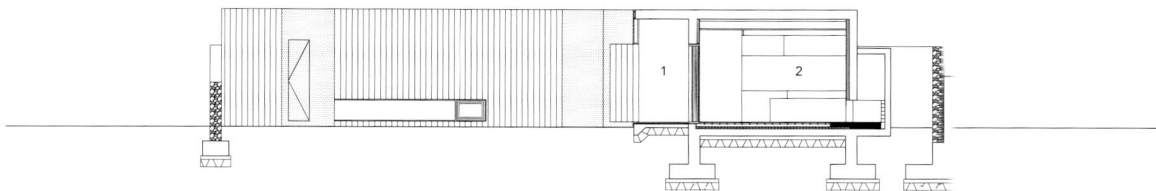

SECTION D   0   5 m

1. Terrace 2. Living room

21. TWIN TREES_

SEOUL, KOREA, 2010

Even before it was completed, the Twin Trees project became one of Korea's most talked about buildings. Cho's most celebrated structure to date, it has been widely praised as a vibrant example of Korea's progressive attitude towards contemporary architecture. Its placement alone held enormous significance. Twin Trees was erected at the former site of the Korea News Daily building, designed in 1968 by the renowned architect Swoo-Geun Kim, the grandfather of modern architecture in Korea; the building was demolished as part of an urban renewal program. Across the busy Sejongro Boulevard is Gyeongbok Palace – the former royal palace, first built in 1395, which was mostly destroyed by the Japanese in the early twentieth century, and is slowly but surely being restored to its former glory.

Cho designed a structure that took great care to incorporate the area's historical and cultural context. For the specific shape of the seventeen-storey twin towers, Cho was inspired by the large trunk, weathered and smoothed over time, of the white birch, a tree commonly found in the mountains that ring Seoul. The roundness of the forms helps to mitigate the peculiar sharp angles and odd adjacencies of the site. Cho composed the two buildings spatially so that one projects out slightly while the other subtly recedes inward, creating a pleasant sheltered public space in between them. The complex is oriented towards an ancient watch tower at the southeast corner of Gyeongbok Palace, and it also connects to Samcheong-dong, another vibrant neighbourhood.

The two towers feature a pattern of flowing horizontal lines, which seem to vary from different perspectives, allowing the eye to perceive each building mass within the flow of its surroundings. Although the exteriors appear to be simple, they are a complicated form comprised of numerous differentiated curves. The undulating curved glass curtain wall and the mullion system, composed of aluminium horizontal and steel vertical bands, define the interior and exterior of the buildings, modulating views and reflections of the city. The shadows from these regular lines fall into the office space early in the morning and late in the afternoon. The protruding mullion is clad in zinc-coloured painted aluminium, which absorbs light and lends the buildings a solid, almost primitive aspect. Cho and his team developed the steel mullions to allow maximum transparency. The mullions vary in width, but average about 1.8 m (6 ft), and were prefabricated to run precisely along the curvatures of the floor plates.

Starting from either the base or the top, the building narrows as it approaches the middle, like a waistline. The floor slabs thus all have different dimensions, and the mullion system follows this geometry while maintaining the fixed glass sizes. Where the building recedes in the form, the mullions become more dense to accommodate multiple units of curved glass. Each mullion is connected to a slip plate at the edge of the floor slab to allow the curtain wall to move independently from the building structure. The office spaces have glazed glass with adjustable screens to control light levels yet allow impressive vistas of the palace and of Bugaksan Mountain just beyond. Standing inside the Twin Trees, contemplating the palace grounds and the bustling streets, it is easy to sense the dynamism of a city and of an entire nation.

OPPOSITE_ *The undulating façade of Twin Trees.*

BYOUNG CHO_

두건물사 통협마땅들 비빙께

이룡山 반께

통협라기

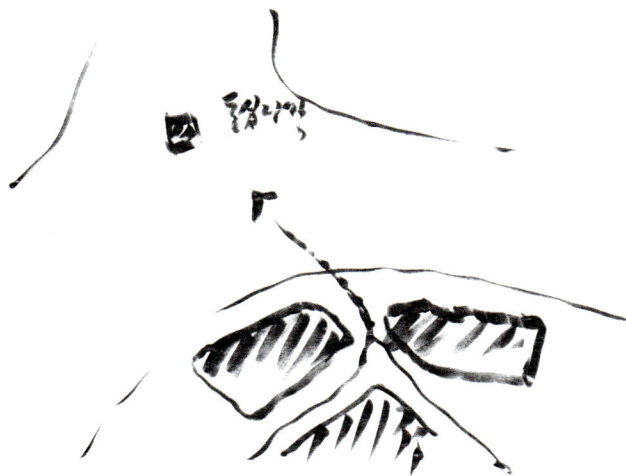

PROJECT TEAM: Woo-hyun Kang, Eric Horn, Gi-hyeon Park,
Yong-eun Pai, Nicholas Locke, Sung-hwa Kwon, Ji-young Seo,
Joo-hyun Park and Eric Druse
LOCATION: 14, Junghak-dong, Jongno-gu, Seoul, Korea
USE: Commercial and office
GROSS FLOOR AREA: 55,658.3 m² (599,101 ft²)
STRUCTURE: Post-tension system, steel reinforced concrete

OPPOSITE, CLOCKWISE FROM TOP_ *The juxtaposition of the traditional
with Twin Trees and various views of the undulating glass façade which, with
the aluminium mullion system, defines the interior and the exterior.*

OPPOSITE_ *The undulating glass façade.*

ABOVE, CLOCKWISE FROM TOP_ *The massive columns in the interior, the staircase from the lobby, the hallway and the undulating glass façade of the interior.*

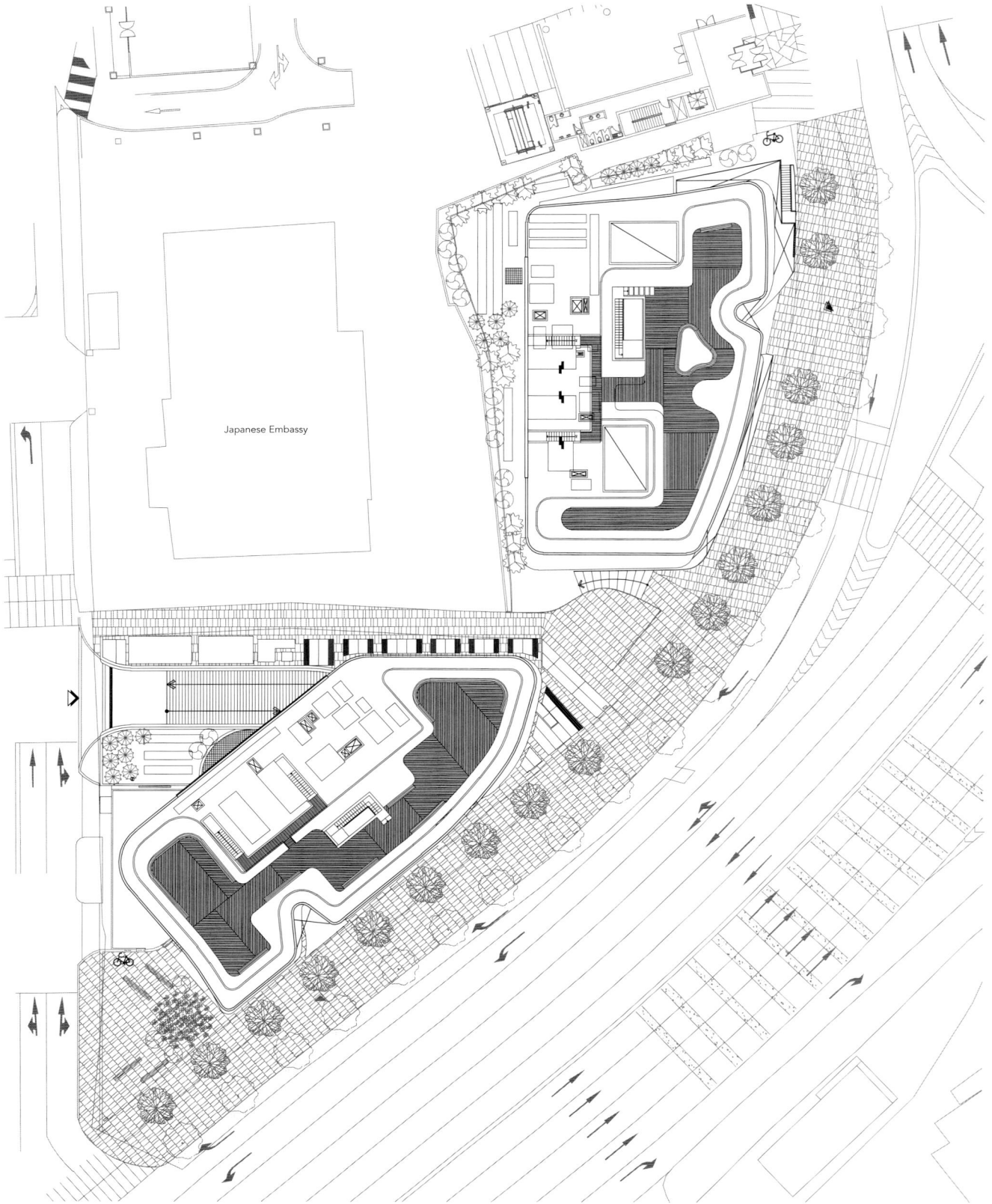

Japanese Embassy

SITE PLAN   0   10 m

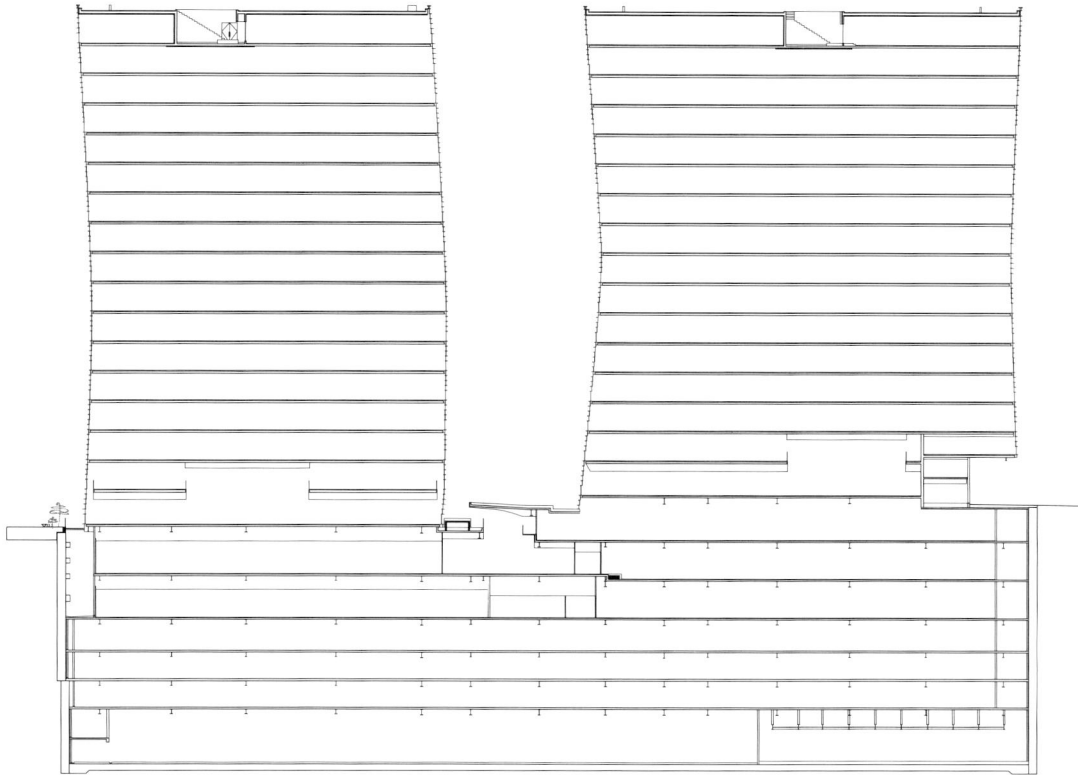

SECTION A   0   10 m

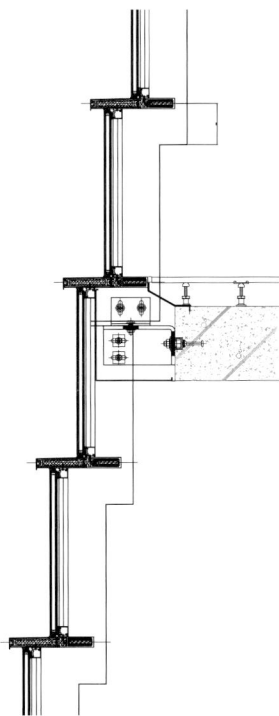

VERTICAL SECTION
VIEW OF TRANSOM

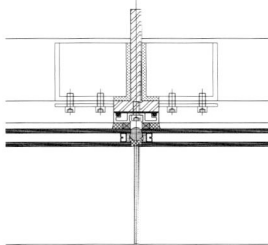

SKIN SECTIONS

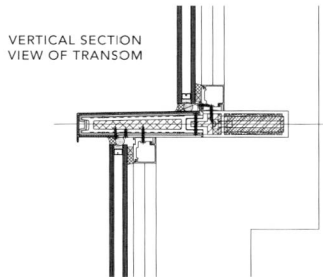

HORIZONTAL
SECTION VIEW OF
MULLION

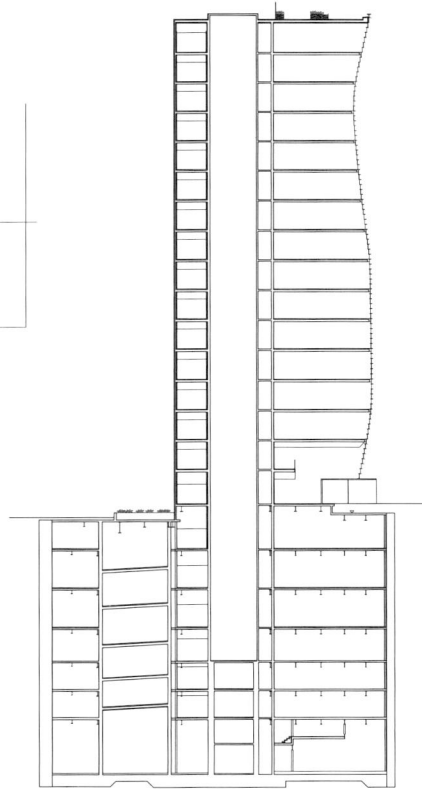

SECTION B   0   10 m

Concept sketch.

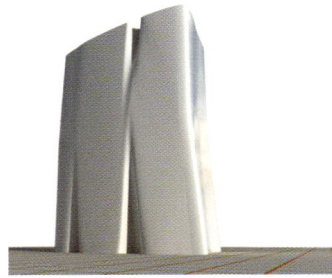

The rendering of the image of the building.

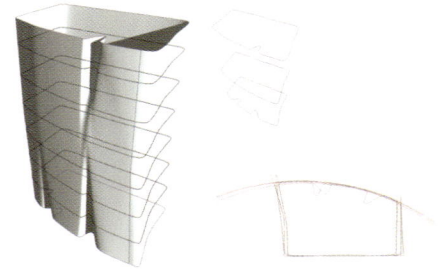

The free-form surface is defined by pure arcs and lines. To achieve this section, lines of the NURBS surface are created (inset). The basic form of the building can be defined by the top, bottom and middle sections as shown.

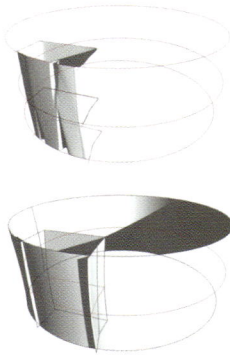

The top, bottom and middle sections are traced with circles and lines. This creates a geometry that can be constructed with standardized modules. By lofting the standardized curves a surface is created that is approximate to the original.

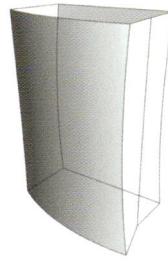

The lofted surfaces are trimmed to reveal the basic shape.

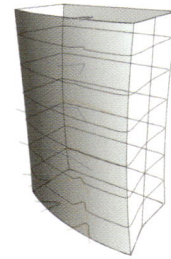

More detail has been added to the simplified surface model. Construction lines for the three 'notches' in the face of the building are created using the sample sections as guides.

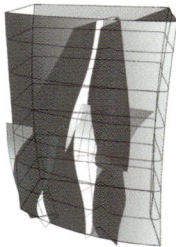

The construction lines for the 'notches' are lofted.

Here the surfaces are trimmed.

The simplified surface has sufficient detail so sections can be created from it that will inform the final construction. A horizontal section every 600 mm (24 in.) has been created, starting at the base of the surface and continuing to the top. This will be the height of each glass level that makes up the façade of the building.

To create a closer approximation of the original NURBS surface, the corners are filleted to sections of a desired radius.

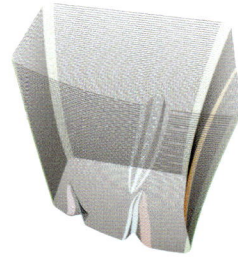

Although it would be possible to loft the simplified surface from filleted curves, the

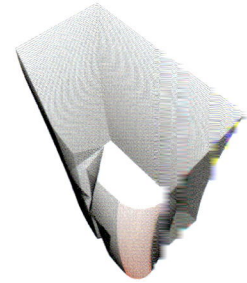

curved sections may not stay in tangent to the straight sections throughout the loft.

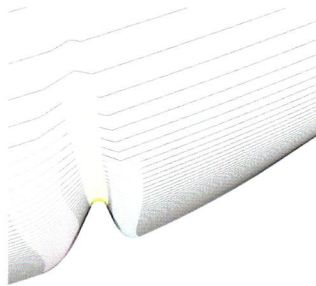

Each colour represents a fixed radius. By filleting the distinct straight sections in this manner it is possible to limit the number of different curvatures required for the façade glass from an infinite number to six or seven. This leaves a discrepancy in the surface that must be addressed by detailing or by altering the geometry of the 'simplified' surface.

The filleted sections are extruded to reveal the shape of the 600 mm (23½ in.) tall panels of glass that will make up the façade. At this point the length of glass, as well as the radius required for construction, can be calculated.

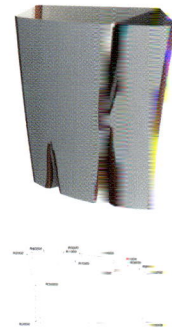

The red areas illustrate the curved glass in the façade. Below are measurements of a section generated from the simplified surface that verify that the radii have remained constant from the bottom of the building to the top.

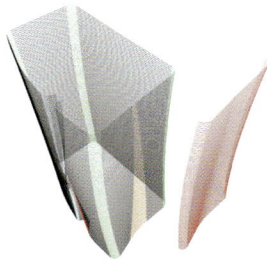

The shape of the windows in plan has been simplified so the window lengths that can cover a building of continuously altering circumference can be calculated. One side of the building is separated from the others for further study.

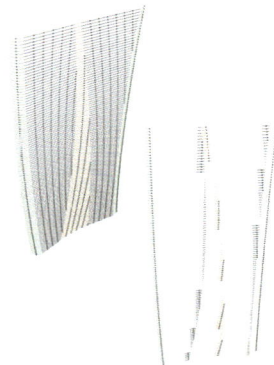

The arcs and lines defining the shape of the windows are divided by a point every 1800 mm (71 in.) starting from the left side. These points are used to divide the arc and lines to standard lengths for the glass.

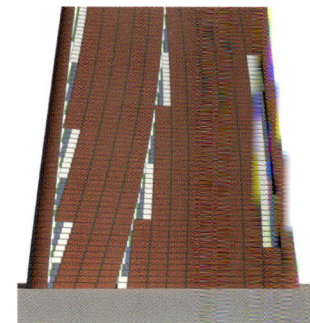

Here is a proposal for modular glass sizes for the façade. This wall shows four sizes of glass each for four radii of glass for a total of 16 glass modules.

22. SCISSORS HOUSE_

JEJU ISLAND, KOREA, 2010

Often called the Hawaii of Korea, Jeju Island is an autonomous province located in the Korea Strait, about 60 miles south of the Korean peninsula. It is a lush subtropical haven filled with exotic fruits, pristine forests, green tea farms, and honeymooning couples dressed in identical clothing. In summer, cool breezes blow north from the Pacific over the entire face of Halla Mountain, South Korea's tallest peak which stands at 1,950 m (6,400 ft) and, in winter, winds blow south from the upper latitudes.

Located on the southern coast, Scissors House pivots up a hill overlooking the Pacific Ocean. Cho designed and oriented the house to take full advantage of the natural conditions while maintaining much of the tangerine farm on which it is built. The slope of the site is terraced with retaining walls made of basalt. The house scissors between one tier and another, stepping up and pivoting around the low wall. A stone-and-moss garden faces the entrance and reaches up to the main living space and courtyard. Sliding doors along the main living and eating space open up the entire house to the sea,

which, in Jeju's temperate climate, means that the inhabitants can feel like they are living outdoors for much of the year.

The low, continuous roof provides protection against the strong winds that move over the house. The roof is a single slab of concrete, without any waterproofing or parapet, which might easily be damaged in typhoon-strength winds. During the pouring and curing process, the roof was re-trowelled every two to three hours to allow moisture to rise and form a completely watertight seal. The two main levels of the house are connected by an elegant angled staircase that wraps around an attractive inner courtyard.

OPPOSITE, ABOVE AND BELOW_ *Scissors House, seen from the east, and the courtyard with the house wrapping around it.*

PROJECT TEAM: Yoon-hee Kim, Woo-hyun Kang and Hong-joon Yang
LOCATION: Seohong-dong, Seogwipo, Jeju-do, Korea
USE: Residential
GROSS FLOOR AREA: 322.3 m² (3,469.2 ft²)
STRUCTURE: Reinforced concrete

OPPOSITE AND ABOVE_ *Views of the subtropical flora surrounding the house. The sketches show the concept of the roof as a single piece of concrete.*

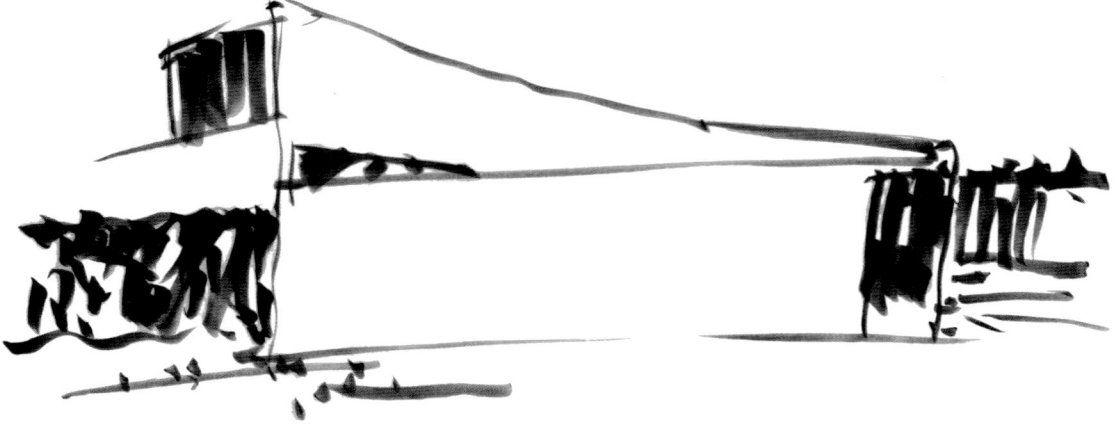

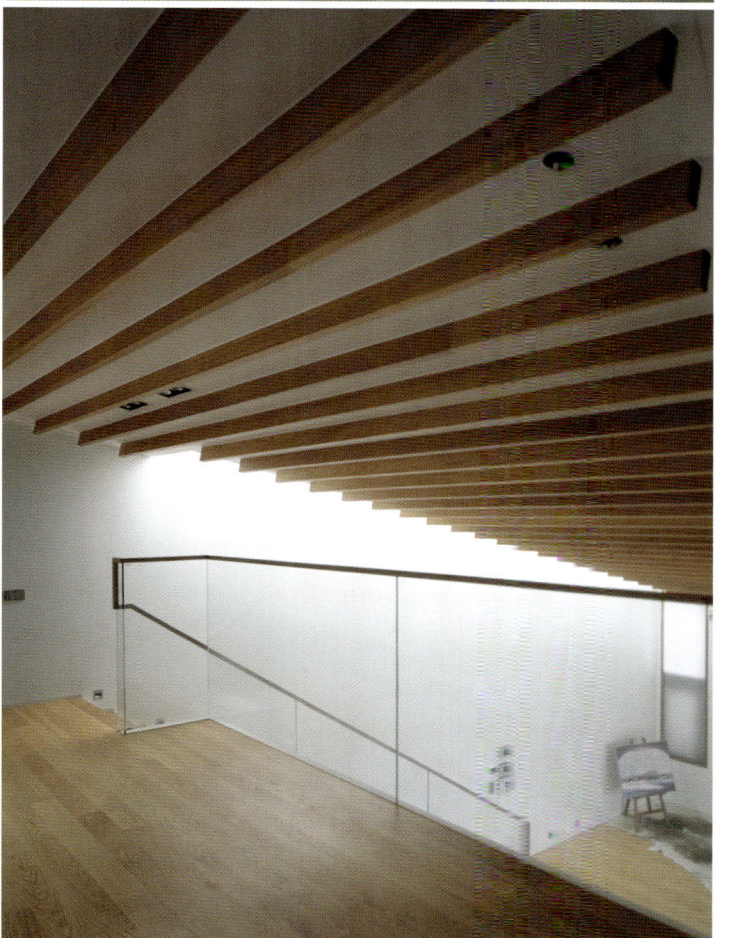

CLOCKWISE FROM TOP LEFT_ *The sloped roof and horizontal window, the undulating wood-framed window along the staircase, the wooden supported ceiling and the mezzanine.*

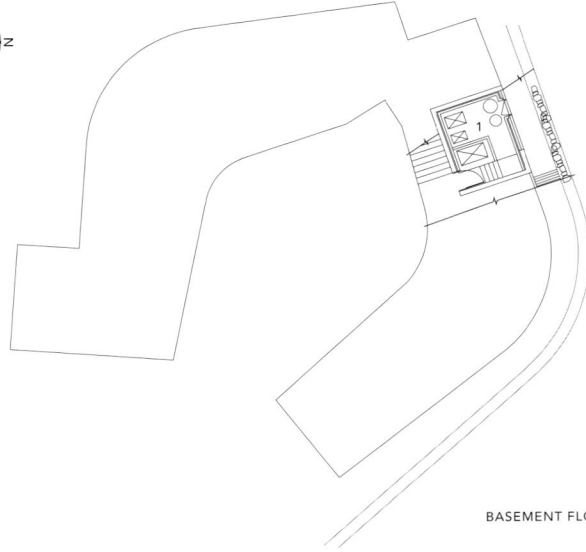

1. Utilities

BASEMENT FLOOR PLAN   0   5 m

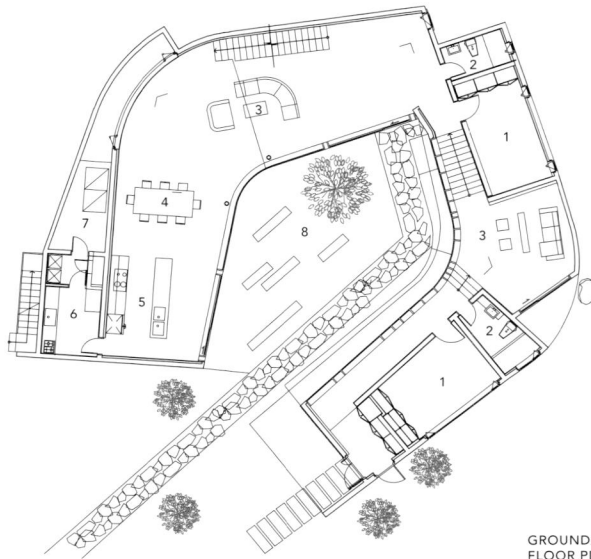

1. Bedroom
2. Bathroom
3. Living room
4. Dining room
5. Kitchen
6. Support kitchen
7. Utilities
8. Courtyard

GROUND/FIRST
FLOOR PLAN   0   5 m

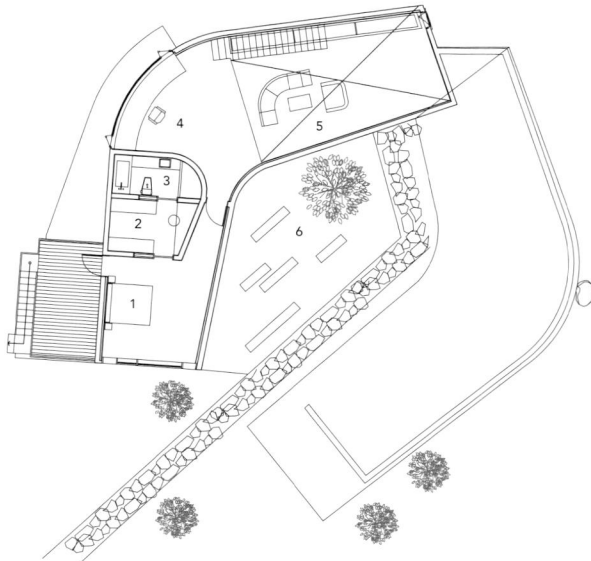

1. Bedroom
2. Dressing room
3. Bathroom
4. Loft
5. Living room
6. Courtyard

SECOND FLOOR PLAN   0   5 m

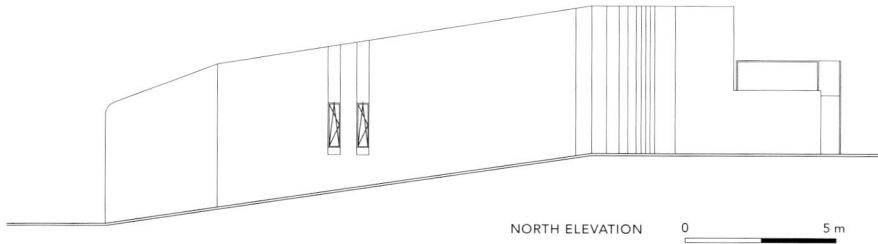

NORTH ELEVATION   0   5 m

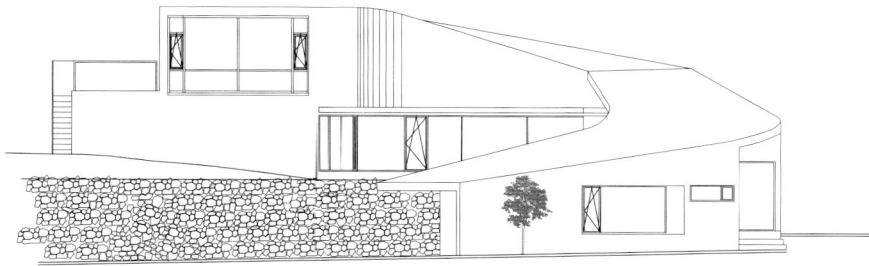

SOUTH ELEVATION   0   5 m

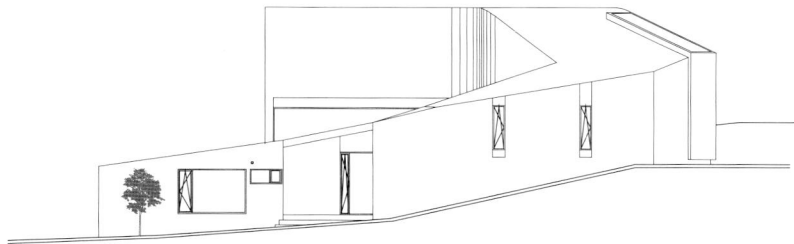

EAST ELEVATION   0   5 m

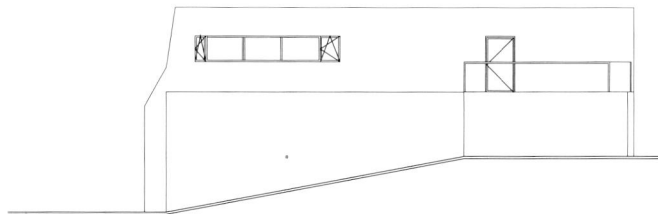

WEST ELEVATION   0   5 m

23. HEYRI THEATRE AND HOTEL_

HEYRI ART VALLEY, PAJU, KOREA, 2010

Situated in the fast-growing Heyri Art Valley in Paju, Gyeonggi Province, an hour north of Seoul, the Heyri Theatre and Hotel responds to the growing need for overnight accommodation in the area while offering a complex to host performing arts and other cultural events. The Heyri Theatre is a stunning, modern structure dominated by a large and open central space. The influence of Montana's agricultural buildings on Cho's aesthetic can truly be felt here. It feels meticulously measured and engineered, yet avoids the clichés of conventional theatres.

The theatre hosts a diverse array of programming, such as performances from young experimental acts as well as seasoned musicians and performance artists. The design of the hall anticipated the need for a flexible, open space. Measuring 11 x 20 x 7 m (36 x 65 x 23 ft), it is able to accommodate large or small performances. Seven projected VIP boxes frame the main space, stepping down to offer unobstructed views, while a suspended catwalk provides an area for the general public to watch performances. Serving the theatre, a café opens to the surrounding pine trees while an unobtrusive courtyard connects the two buildings, allowing an interaction with nature. The Heyri Theatre articulates the stipulated ethos of the master plan by engaging with the landscape in many ways.

Juxtaposed against the exposed concrete façade of the theatre, the hotel is defined by four geometric ribbons, which wrap around the building to create a multitude of transitional spaces while allowing the guests privacy and a unique experience of the surrounding natural environment. On the upper level, this overlap of the façade creates courtyards for moon viewing and relaxation in complete seclusion, an experience enhanced by built-in hot tubs. The deck allows the control of light and air entering the building. The glistening façade is composed of a series of ceramic panels, supported by a lightweight steel frame, rendering a scale to the community. Such seemingly simple gestures turn an otherwise monolithic architectural typology into one of humanistic sensibilities, finding ways to give the users a quiet, contemplative experience of nature in a rapidly urbanizing setting.

OPPOSITE, CLOCKWISE FROM TOP_ *The theatre and the hotel seen from the east side of the courtyard, the view from the north side of the courtyard, VIP booths and the façade.*

PROJECT TEAM: Jung-hui Lee, Youngjin Kang,
Hong-joon Yang, Woo-hyun Kang, Sara Kim,
Angel Tenorio, Sung-hwa Kim and Ha-hyeok Park
LOCATION: Heyri Art Valley, Beopheung-ri,
Tanhyun-myeon, Paju, Gyeonggi-do, Korea
USE: Performance hall
GROSS FLOOR AREA: 1083.1 m² (11,658 ft²)
STRUCTURE: Reinforced concrete

1. Performance hall
2. VIP booth
3. Lobby
4. Guest room
5. Control room
6. Parking
7. Utilities

SECTION A   0   5 m

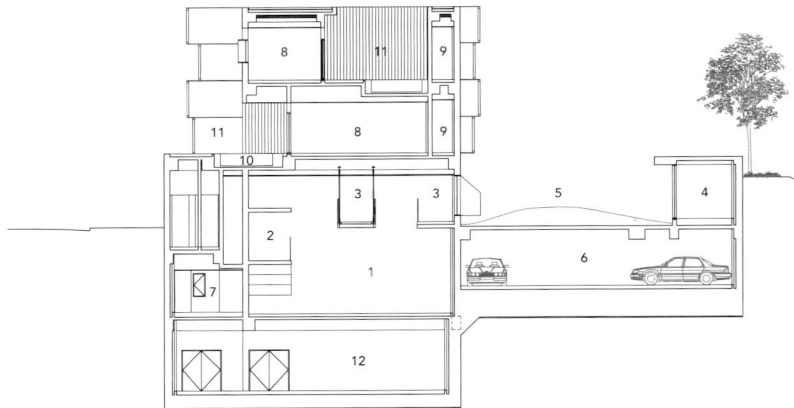

1. Performance hall
2. VIP booth
3. Balcony
4. Café
5. Courtyard
6. Parking
7. Rest room
8. Guest room
9. Hall
10. Hot tub
11. Deck
12. Utilities

SECTION B   0   5 m

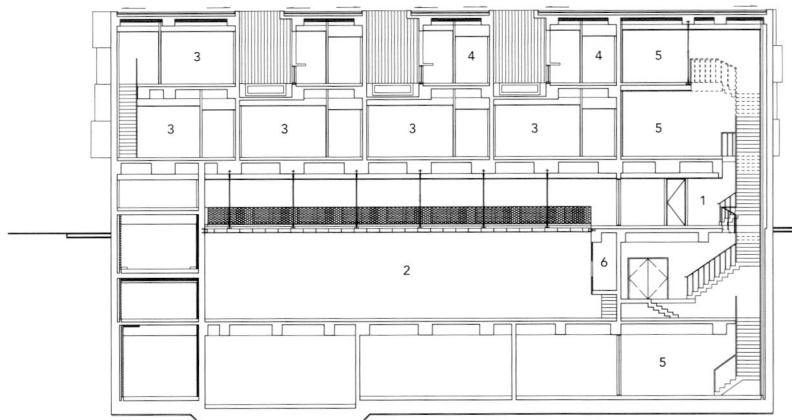

1. Lobby
2. Performance hall
3. Workshop
4. Office
5. Hall
6. Control room

SECTION C   0   5 m

OPPOSITE, ABOVE AND BELOW_ *VIP booths seen from the performance hall and the café viewed from the courtyard.*

CLOCKWISE FROM TOP_ *The research facility seen from the street, detail of the canopy construction, an aerial view of the construction site, a detail of the interior, the staircase and the rendering of the wire.*

24. KISWIRE RESEARCH AND DEVELOPMENT FACILITY_

JOHOR BAHRU, MALAYSIA, 2012

PROJECT TEAM: Yong-eun Bae, Joo-hyoung Lee, Dong-hyun Koh, Joon-won Choi, Nicholas Locke and Lane Ferris

LOCATION: Johor Bahru, Malaysia

USE: Research and development centre

GROSS FLOOR AREA: 1,800 m² (19,375 ft²)

STRUCTURE: Post-tension system, reinforced concrete

Cho designed this research and development facility in Malaysia for Kiswire Ltd, one of the world's largest manufacturers of steel wire. The complex comprises four buildings connected to each other by a system of wire. The architect wrapped the structures in the wire produced at the facility, allowing them to appear linked. Simple rectilinear volumes house offices, and an open courtyard provides shade from the intense sun, an orchid garden and an area for group activities. The inner courtyards have subtle angles, which can diminish the rigidity of the transitional spaces and allow the users to have natural ventilation across a narrow building width.

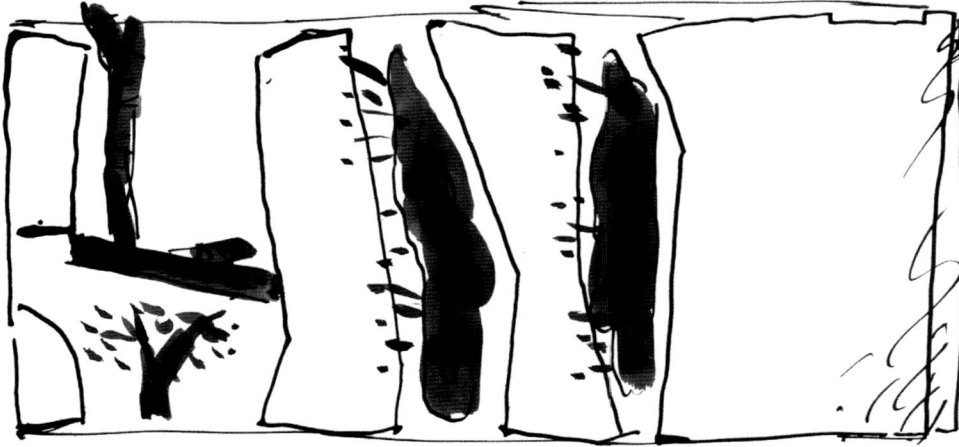

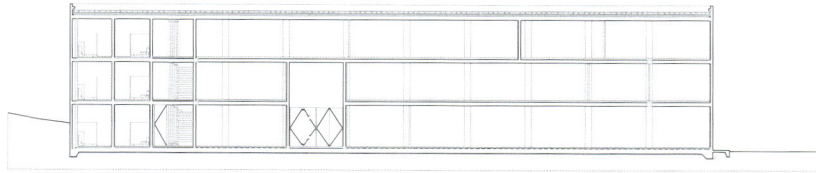

SECTION C   0   5 m

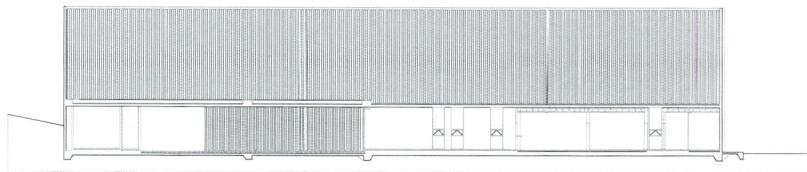

SECTION D   0   5 m

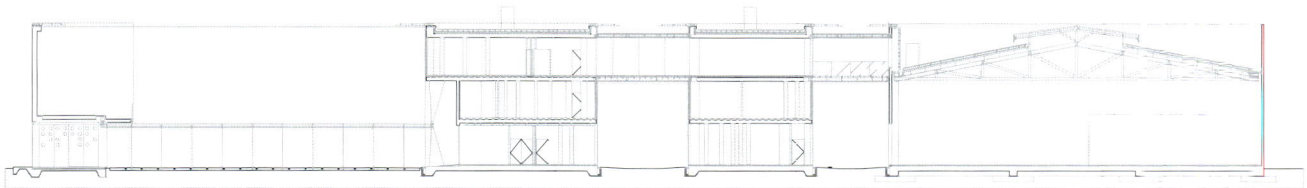

SECTION A   0   5 m

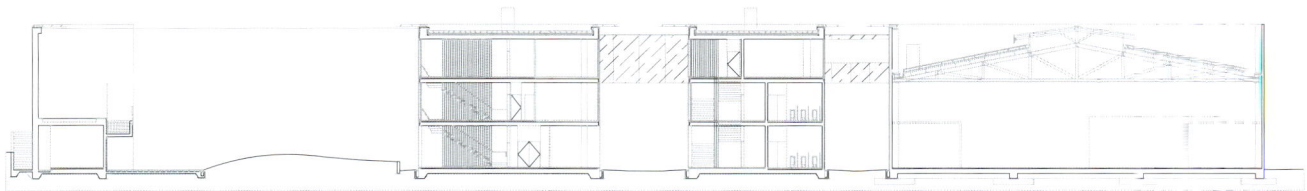

SECTION B   0   5 m

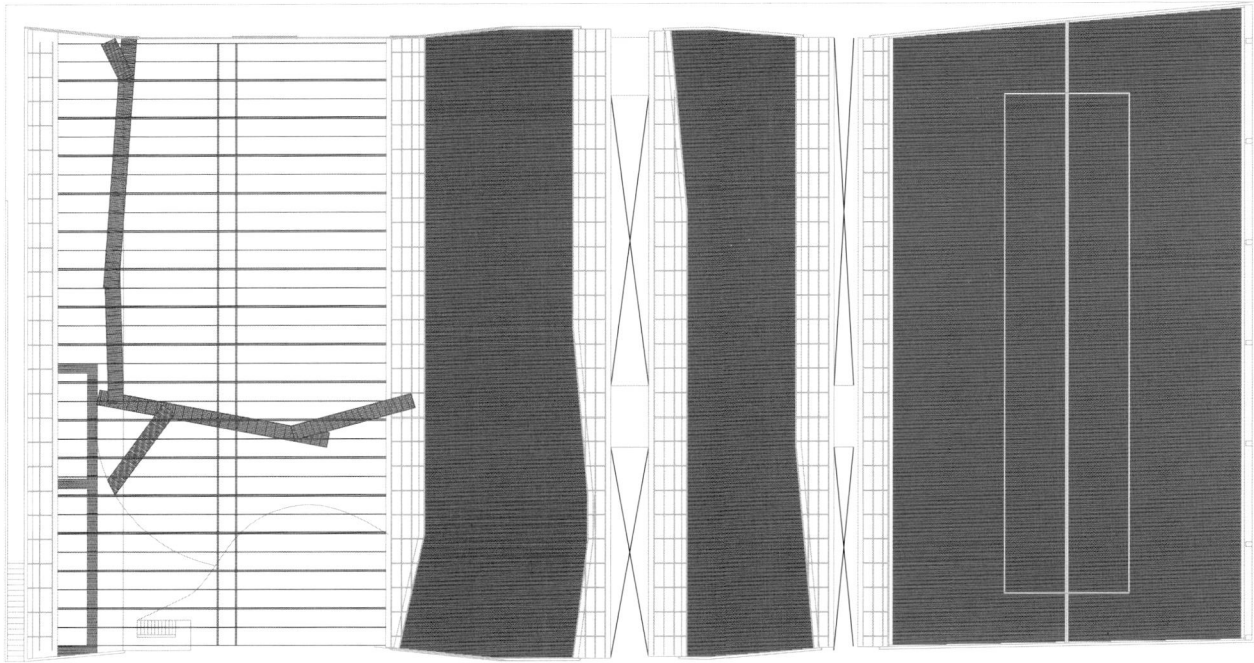

ROOF PLAN   0   5 m

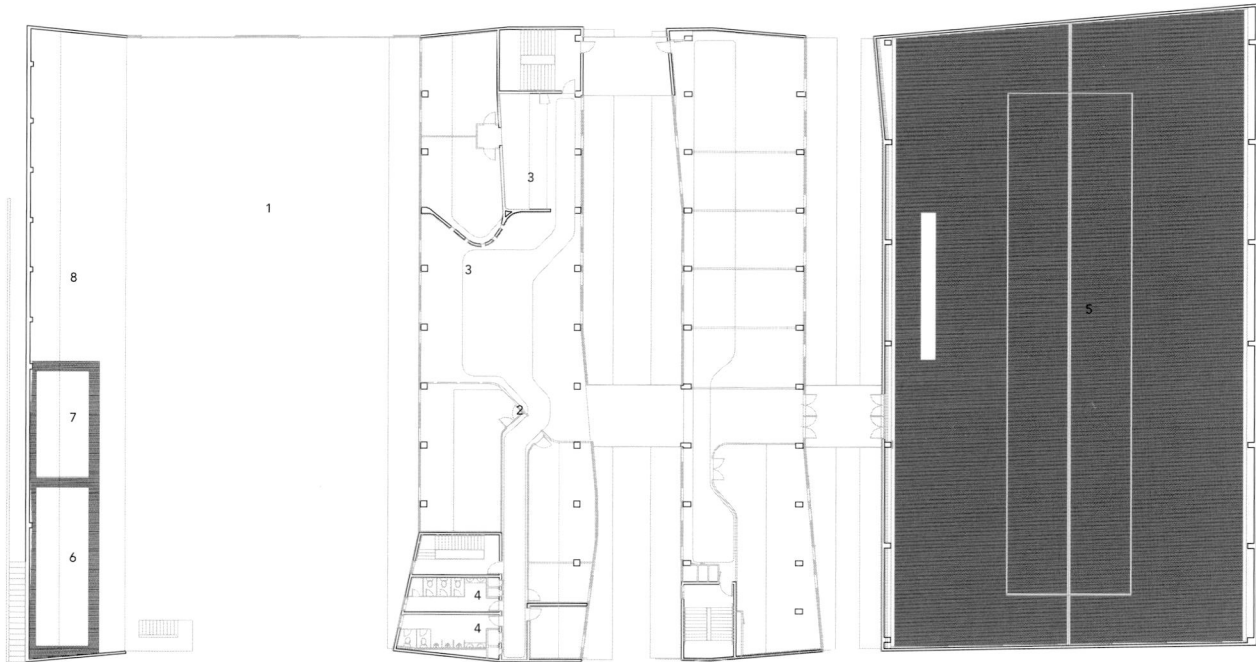

SECOND FLOOR PLAN   0   5 m

1. Courtyard 2. Lobby 3. Office 4. Bathroom
5. Water house 6. Kitchen 7. Terrace 8. Cafeteria

8

7

6

1

3

3

2

5

4

4

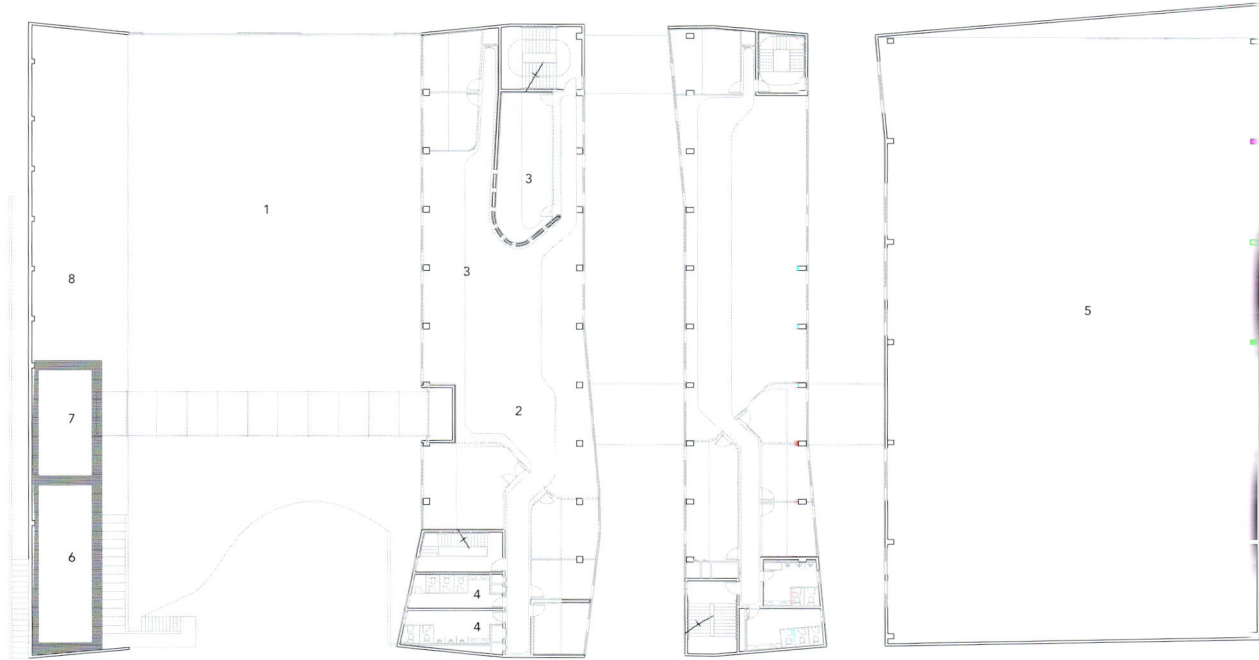

FIRST FLOOR PLAN

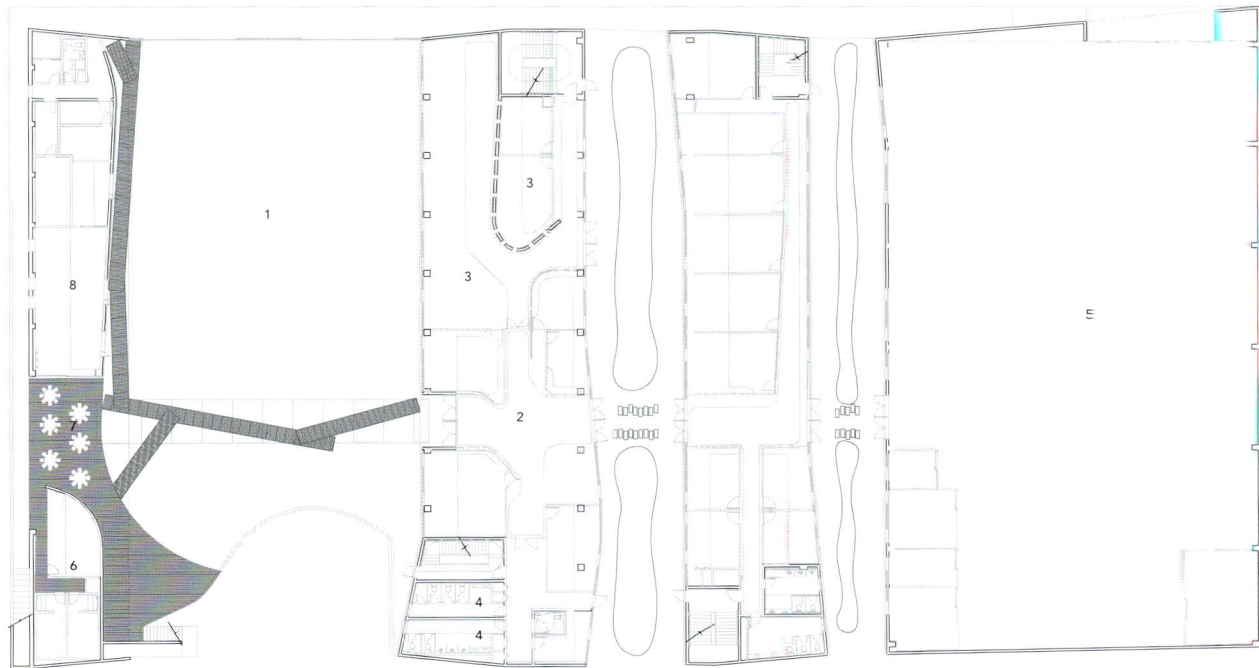

8

6

1

3

3

2

5

4

4

GROUND FLOOR PLAN   5m

25. NAMHAE SOUTHCAPE HOTEL, LINEAR SUITE AND VILLAS_

NAMHAE, KOREA, 2013

The Namhae Southcape Hotel and Villas is a resort complex on an island at the southern tip of the Korean peninsula. It comprises a hotel, villa-type residences, a golf course and other luxury amenities. Located in an area famous for its natural beauty, with mountains right up to the ocean's edge, the resort is built on rough land where the sea and sky meet. The jagged coastline and sloping hills harmonize brilliantly against the flat horizon. For Cho, the resort was an ideal opportunity to create a manmade structure that complements the natural landscape.

The master plan started out as a single horizontal line, a balance that echoed the horizon line and brought order to the haphazard terrain. "The buildings are merged into the site, harmonized with the topography, acting as part of the landscape," states Cho. He proposed simple structures and resolute forms that emphasize the island's dramatic hills. The resort occupies various slopes and ridge lines, which, according to him, "explore how nature and people can

coexist in a meaningful relationship with each other. Architecture is not an artificial object; it resonates within a place." Cho placed elements – windows, landings, rooftops, courtyards, walkways – to facilitate users' ability to observe such natural phenomena as the changing sunlight, cycles of wind, the bloom of local flora and the progression of the seasons. The "villages", or clusters of villas, are in close proximity to the golf course. The villas are divided into four types, depending on the terrain they occupy. Some are relatively narrow and placed side by side; others are arranged to follow the rolling shape of the terrain; and those closest to the sea have extensive grounds and impressive vistas. "Pocket" parks link the villages and form a meeting place of man, nature and architecture. Cho hopes that visitors to the Namhae resort will "perceive architecture as an element inherent within human life, in which nature is no longer an element to be defeated."

OPPOSITE_ The hotel building with the pre-existing community house.

ABOVE, CLOCKWISE FROM TOP LEFT_ The hotel seen from the ocean, looking down onto the complex, the hotel block within the existing topography and the approach to the entrance.

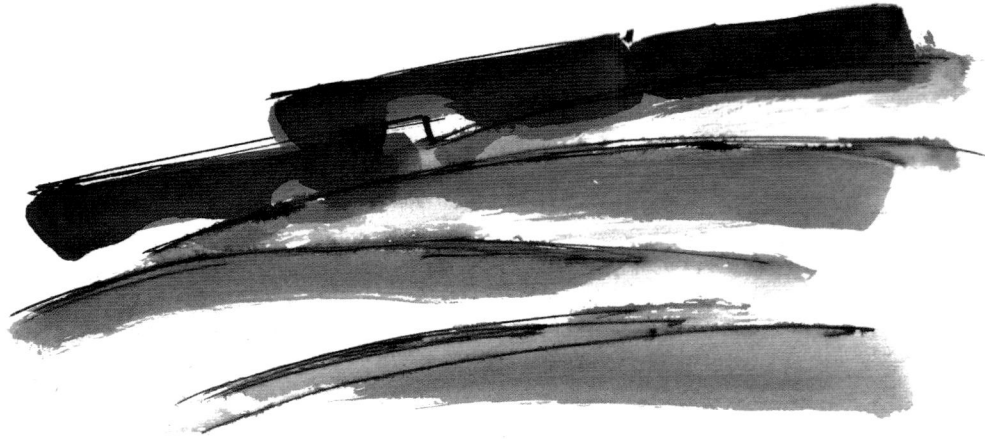

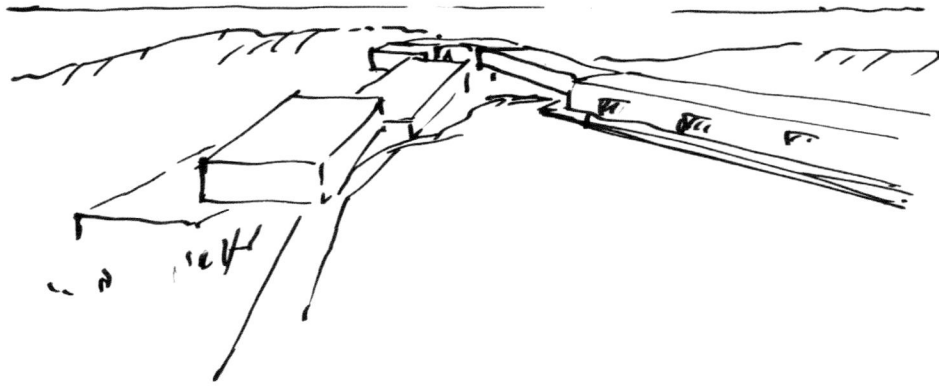

OPPOSITE, CLOCKWISE FROM TOP_ *The hotel from a distance, a rendering of the hotel blocks seen from the golf course, the hotel seen from the street, the entry way of the hotel and the hotel seen from the community house.*

PROJECT TEAM: Woo-hyun Kang, Sara Kim, Jung-yong Park, So-jin Kang, Seong-heon Oh, Yong-eun Bae, Sun-yong Choi, Nicholas Locke, Angel Tenorio, Allicia Belloescobar and Anouck Foch

LOCATION: 321, Jindong-ri, Changseon-myeon, Namhae-gun, Gyeongsangnam-do, Korea

USE: Hotel

GROSS FLOOR AREA: 6,016.9 m² (64,765 ft²)

STRUCTURE: Reinforced concrete

CLOCKWISE FROM TOP LEFT_ *A rendering of the street view of the hotel and various renderings of the guest rooms.*

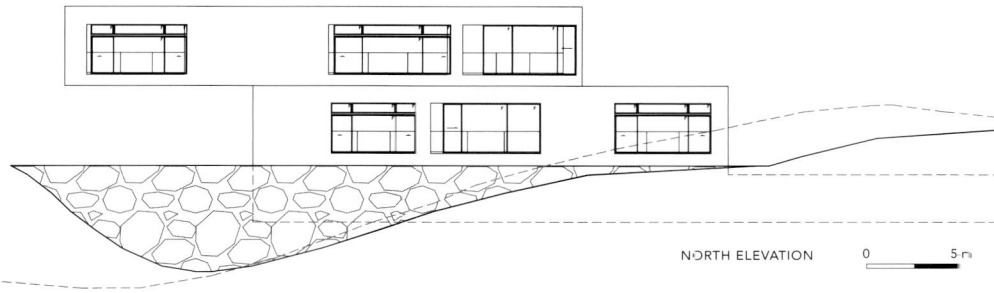

NORTH ELEVATION   0   5 m

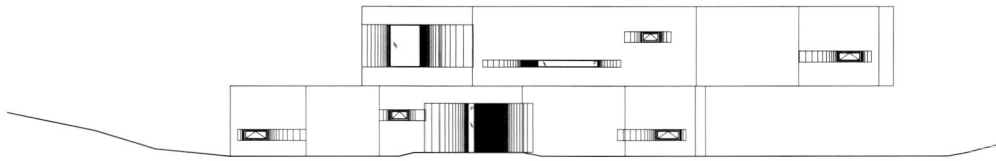

SOUTH ELEVATION   0   5 m

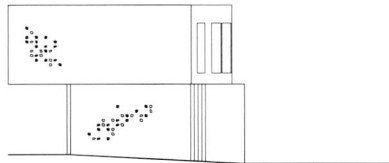

WEST ELEVATION   0   5 m

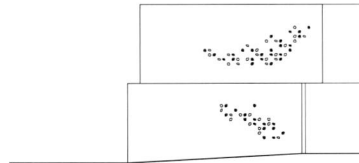

EAST ELEVATION   0   5 m

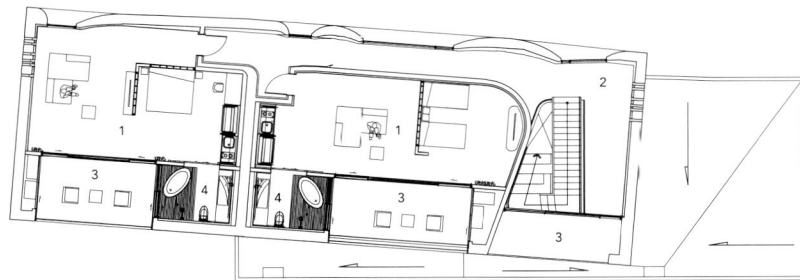

FIRST FLOOR PLAN   0   5 m

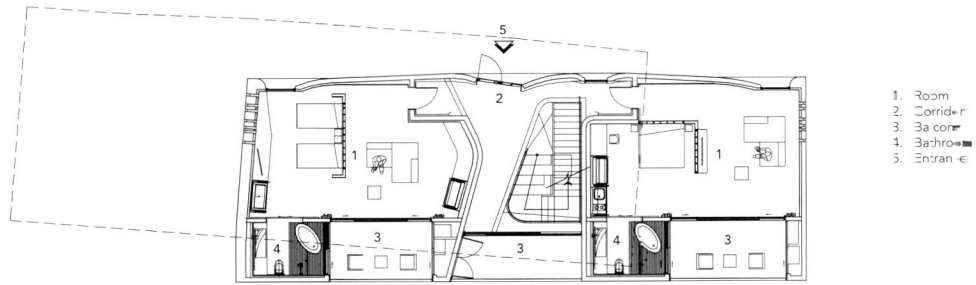

GROUND FLOOR PLAN   0   5 m

1. Room
2. Corridor
3. Balcony
4. Bathroom
5. Entrance

NORTH ELEVATION   0   5 m

SOUTH ELEVATION   0   5 m

WEST ELEVATION   0   5 m

EAST ELEVATION   0   5 m

FIRST FLOOR PLANS   0   5 m

GROUND FLOOR PLANS   0   5 m

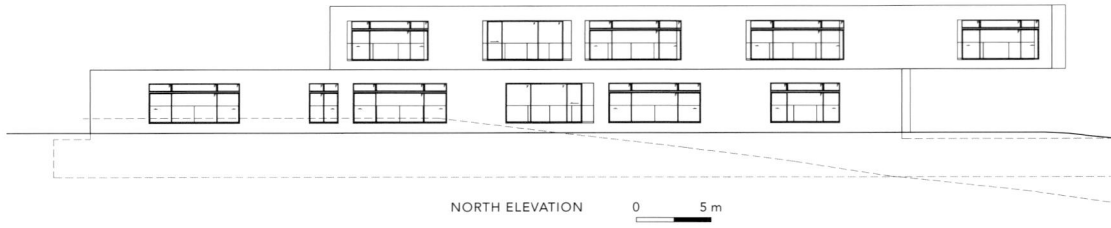

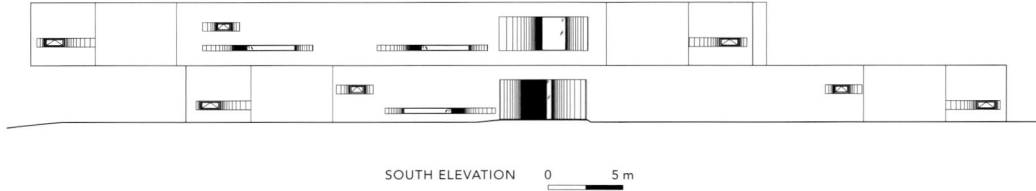

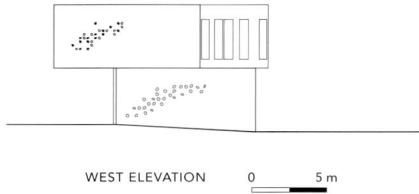

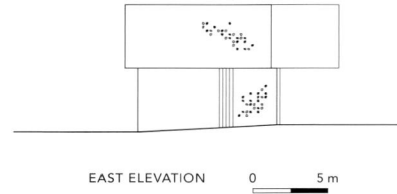

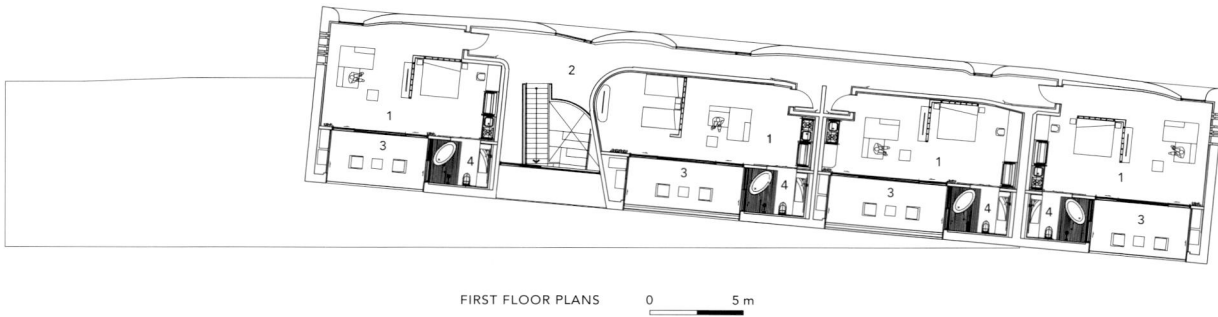

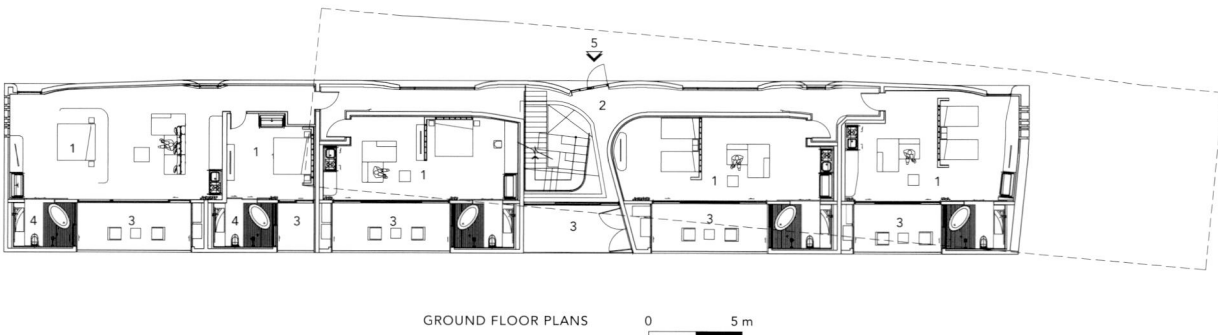

1. Room   2. Corridor   3. Balcony   4. Bathroom   5. Entrance

ABOVE_ *The guest rooms.*

PROJECT TEAM: Young-jin Kang, Hyun-jin Hwang, Kim Sung-hwa and Ho Kang
LOCATION: 243, Jindong-ri, Changseon-myeon, Namhae-gun, Gyeongsangnam-do, Korea
USE: Residential
GROSS FLOOR AREA: 512 m² (5,512 ft²)
STRUCTURE: Reinforced concrete

ABOVE AND LEFT_ *Renderings of villa type "a", hillside bay.*

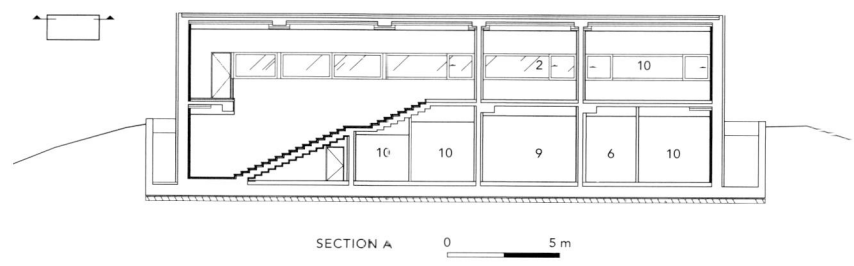

SECTION A   0   5 m

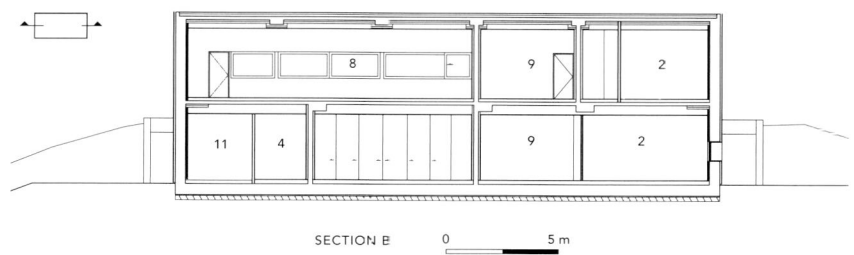

SECTION B   0   5 m

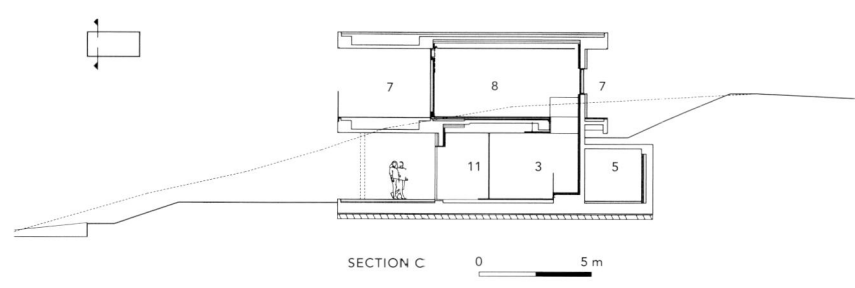

SECTION C   0   5 m

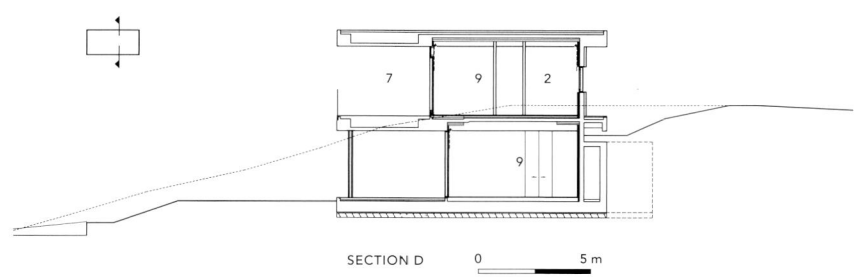

SECTION D   0   5 m

1. Master bedroom 2. Bedroom 3. Corridor 4. Room
5. Utilities 6. Dressing room 7. Balcony 8. Dining room
9. Library 10. Rest room/bathroom 11. Entrance

ABOVE_ *Renderings of villa type "b", ridge mesa.*

PROJECT TEAM: Young-jin Kang, Hyun-jin Hwang, Sung-hwa Kim and Ho Kang
LOCATION: 243, Jindong-ri, Changseon-myeon, Namhae-gun, Gyeongsangnam-do, Korea
USE: Residential
GROSS FLOOR AREA: 487.9 m² (5,252 ft²)
STRUCTURE: Reinforced concrete

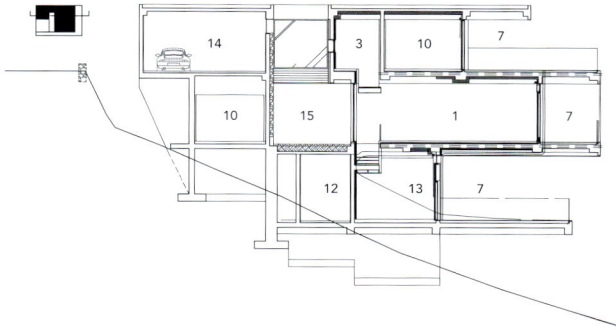

SECTION A   0   5 m

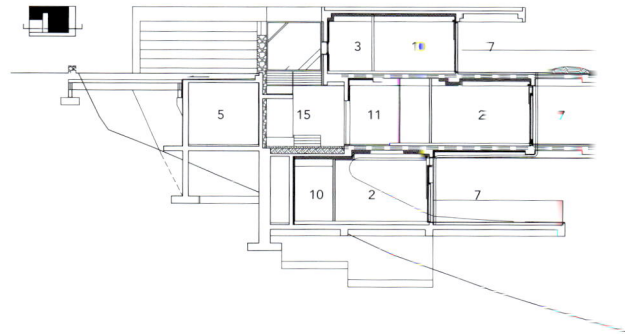

SECTION B   0   5 m

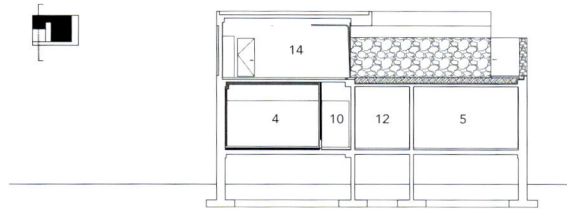

SECTION C   0   5 m

SECTION D   0   5 m

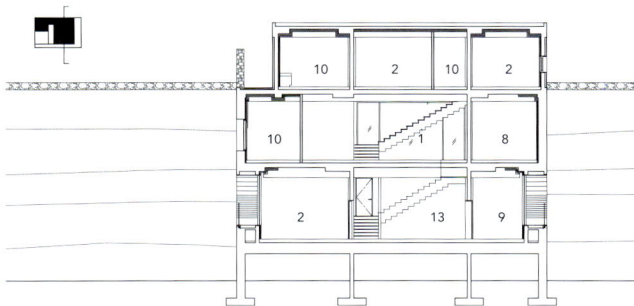

SECTION E   0   5 m

1. Living room 2. Bedroom 3. Corridor 4. Room 5. Utilities 6. Dressing room 7. Balcony 8. Kitchen 9. Library 10. Restroom 11. Entrance 12. Storage 13. Bar 14. Parking 15. Courtyard

PROJECT TEAM: Young-jin Kang, Hyun-jin Hwang, Sung-hee Kim, Ho Kang, Sook-jung Kim and Seong-heon Oh
LOCATION: 243 Jindong-ri, Changseon-myeon, Namhae-gun, Gyeongsangnam-do, Korea
USE: Residential
GROSS FLOOR AREA: 689.5 m² (7,422 ft²)
STRUCTURE: Reinforced concrete

OPPOSITE_ *Renderings of villa type "d", oceanside elevations.*

PROJECT TEAM: Young-jin Kang, Hyun-jin Hwang, Sung-hwa Kim and Ho Kang
LOCATION: 243, Jindong-ri, Changseon-myeon, Namhae-gun, Gyeongsangnam-do, Korea
USE: Residential
GROSS FLOOR AREA: 656 m² (7,061 ft²)
STRUCTURE: Reinforced concrete

ABOVE_ *Renderings of villa type "f", oceanside plateau.*

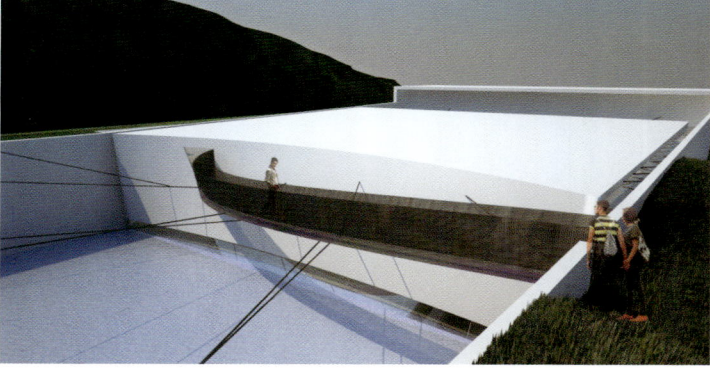

26. KISWIRE MUSEUM AND TRAINING CENTRE_

BUSAN, KOREA, 2013

The Kiswire Museum, in the Korean port of Busan, is part of a larger urban vision that Cho has been developing with city officials. The concept takes into account the dual characteristics of the neighbourhood – a haphazard industrial area set into hills with a spectacular view of the ocean – and converts unused property into spaces that encourage spontaneous interactions and civic participation. The old Kiswire factory is being transformed into a commercial and recreational centre.

The museum, which Cho is designing to be the focal point of the new neighbourhood, features a wide-open, columnless space with a spiralling ramp, object displays, a library and service rooms. A massive suspended roof, constructed of pre-cast post-tension concrete, serves as an anchor for the activities happening underneath. The roof's edges are left open to natural light, creating a feeling of suspension as well as ventilation. A curving wall facing the training centre defines the interior museum space, and side halls lead to a café and the training centre, regulating visitor circulation and establishing small, loosely defined areas for eating and resting.

PROJECT TEAM: Yong-eun Bae, Hui-jeong Yoon, Dong-un Co, Gyu-yeong Kim, Hye-eun Choi, Sara Kim, Joon-won Cho Sun-yong Choi, Ha-young Choi, Ha-heol Park and Jae-gi Kim
LOCATION: 26-3, Mangmi-dong, Suyeong-gu, Busan, Korea
USE: Museum
GROSS FLOOR AREA: 1,922.4 m² (20,69 .5 ft²)
STRUCTURE: Reinforced concrete, exposed post-tension wire system

OPPOSITE, CLOCKWISE FROM TOP LEFT_ *The training centre seen from the street, the outside of the training centre, the deck, the interior, an aerial view, the museum's water garden and ramp, the wire ramp in the museum and the training centre seen from the water garden.*

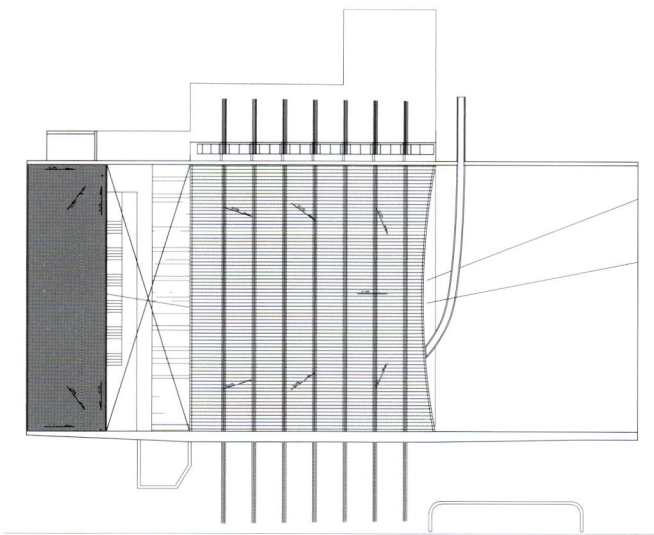

ROOF PLAN 0 5 m

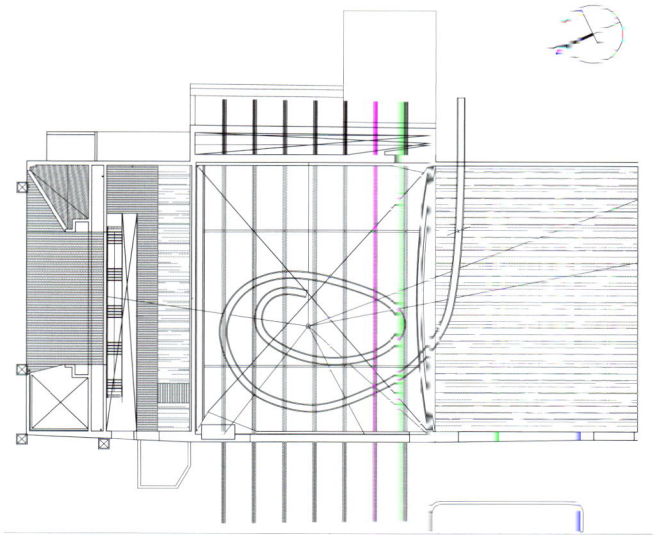

GROUND FLOOR PLAN 0 5 m

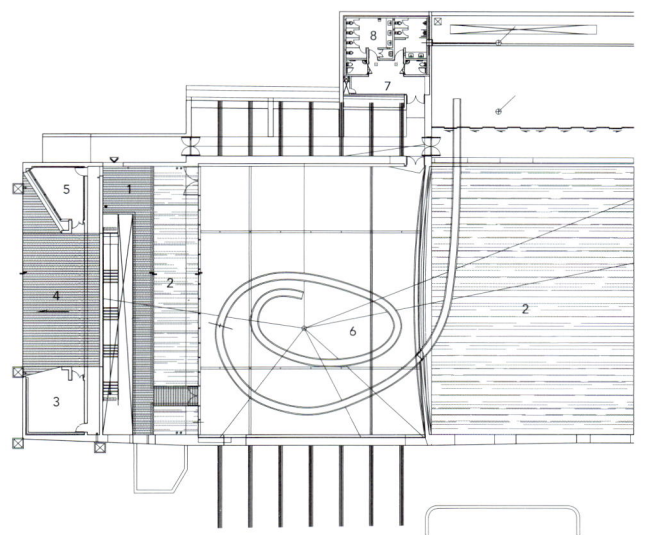

BASEMENT PLAN 0 5 m

SECOND BASEMENT PLAN 0 5 m

1. Deck 2. Water garden 3. Storage 4. Stage
5. Waiting room 6. Exhibition space 7. Hall 8. Restroom

SECTION A

0   5 m

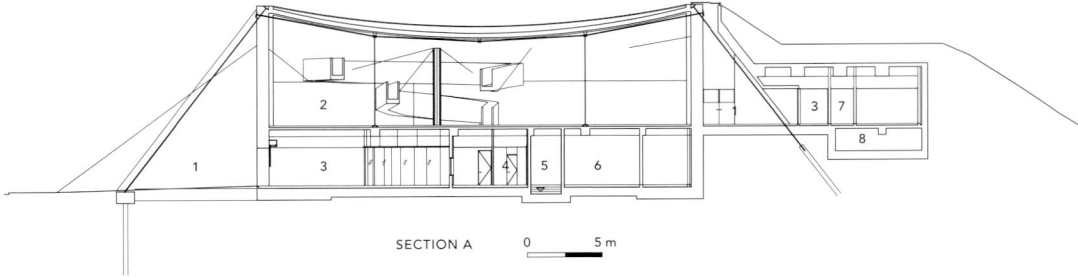

1. Entrance 2. Exhibition space 3. Hall 4. Janitor's room 5. Corridor 6. Utilities
7. Rest room 8. PIT

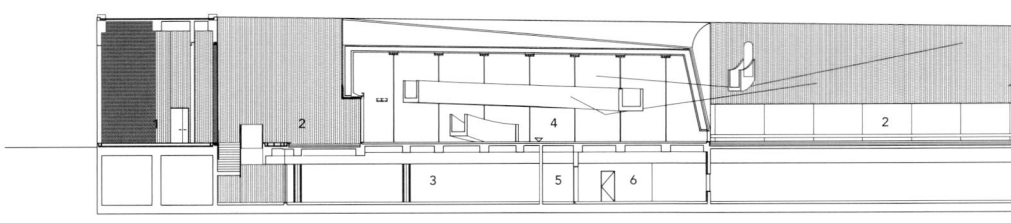

SECTION B

0   5 m

1. Stage 2. Water garden 3. Storage 4. Exhibition space 5. Hall
6. Janitor's room

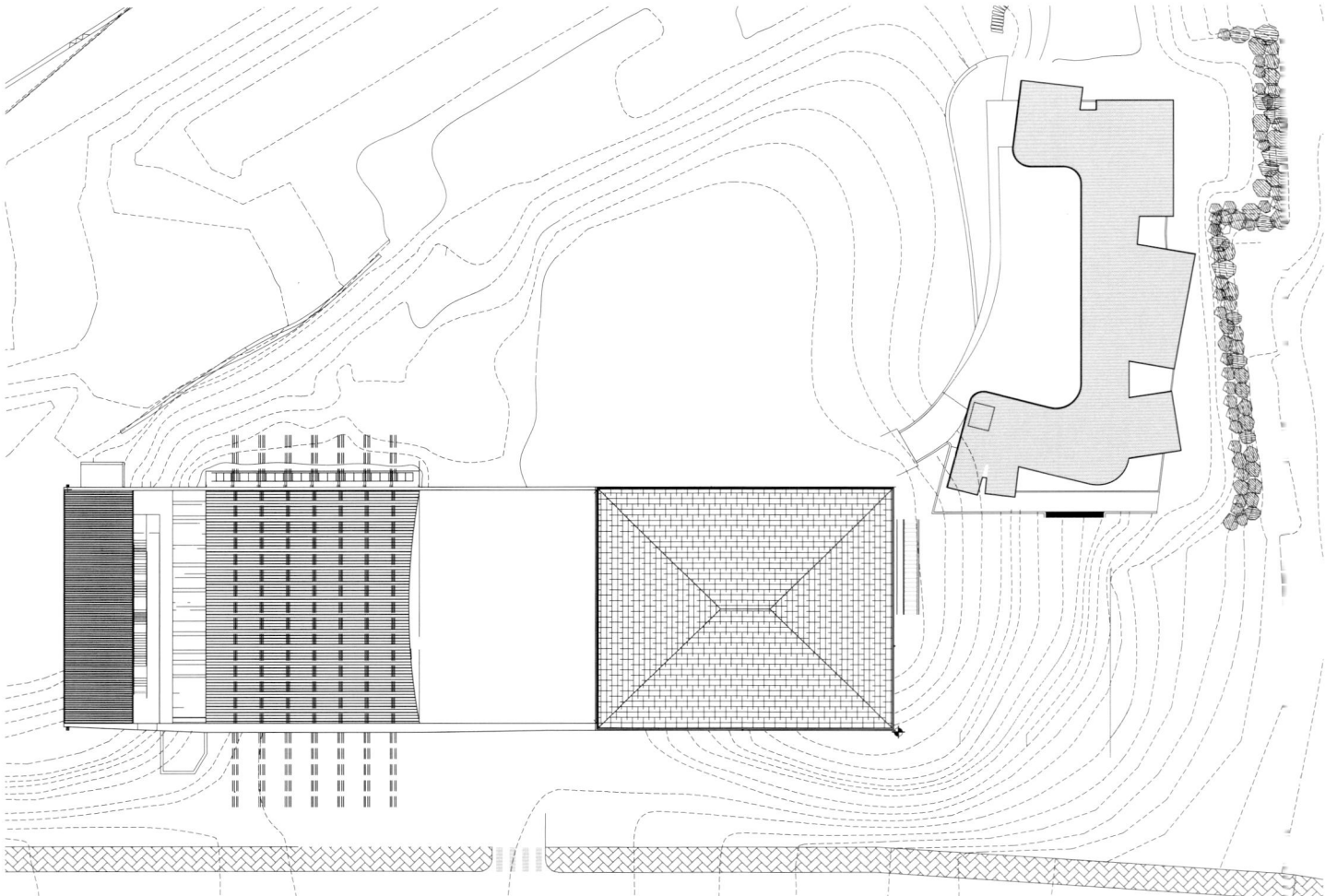

SITE PLAN

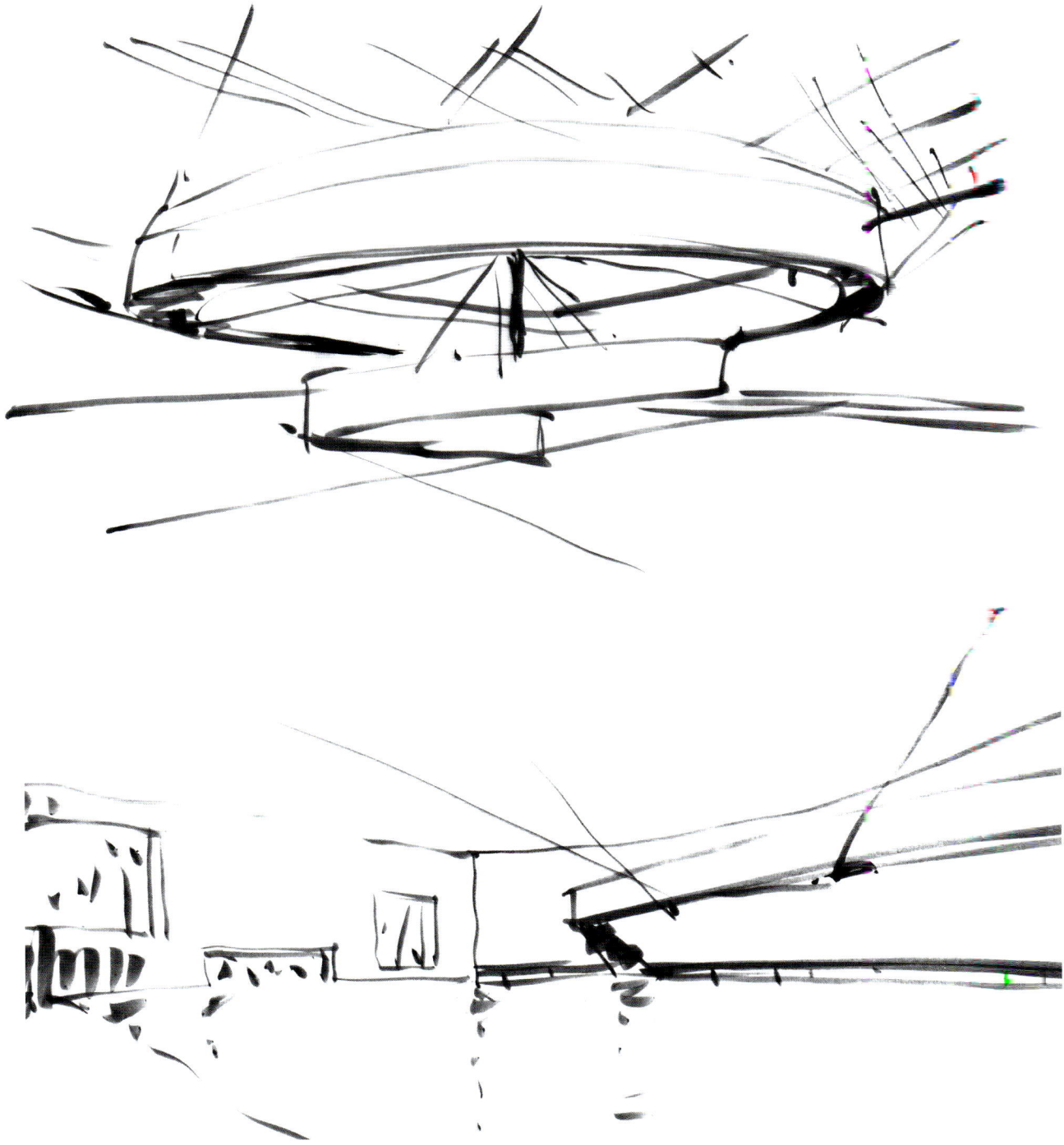

NORTH ELEVATION 0 ___ 5 m

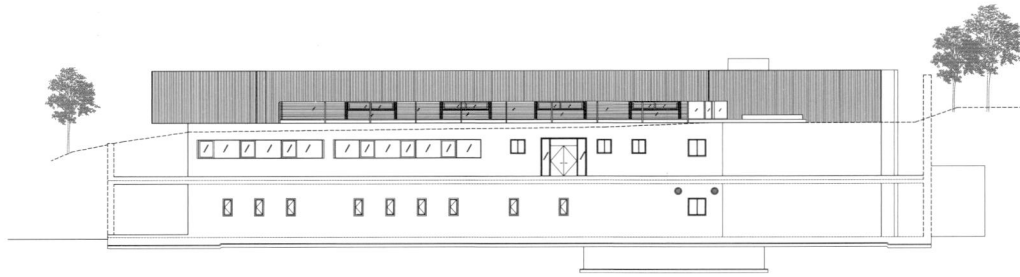

SOUTH ELEVATION 0 ___ 5 m

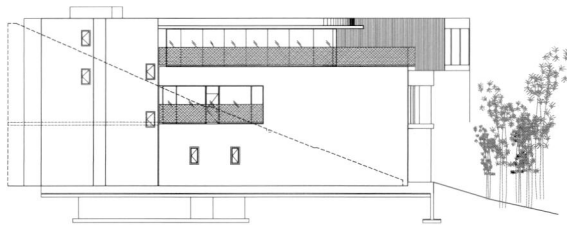

WEST ELEVATION 0 ___ 5 m

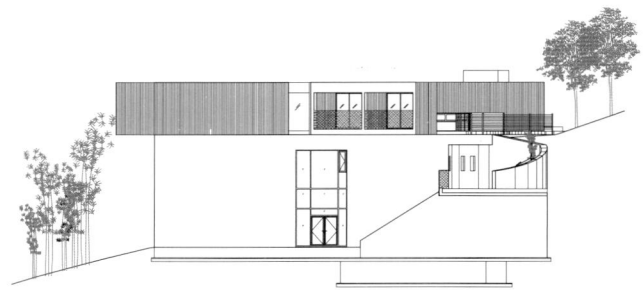

EAST ELEVATION 0 ___ 5 m

CLOCKWISE FROM TOP_ *Rendering of an aerial view and the dormitories.*

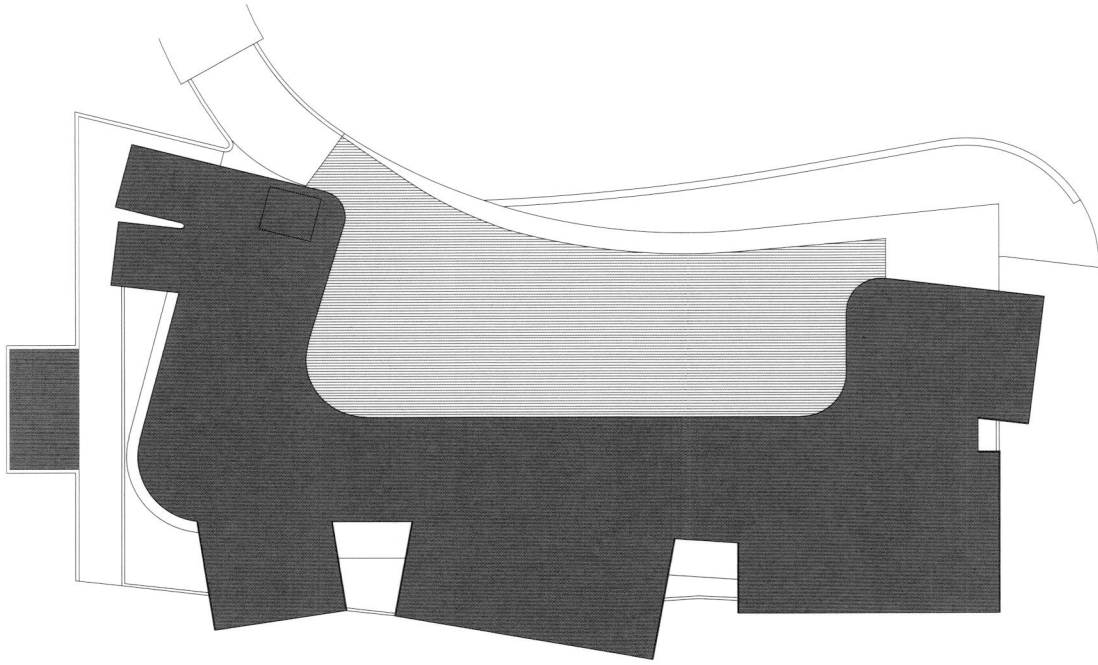

ROOF PLAN   0   5 m

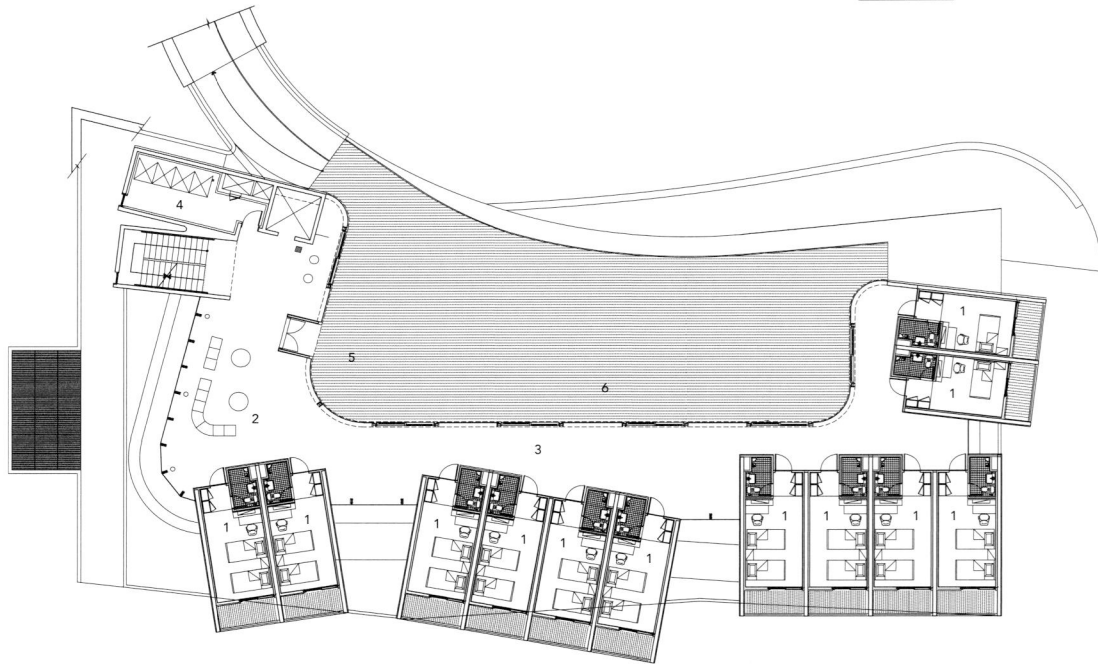

GROUND FLOOR PLAN   0   5 m

1. Unit
2. Lounge
3. Corridor
4. Laundry room
5. Entrance
6. Deck

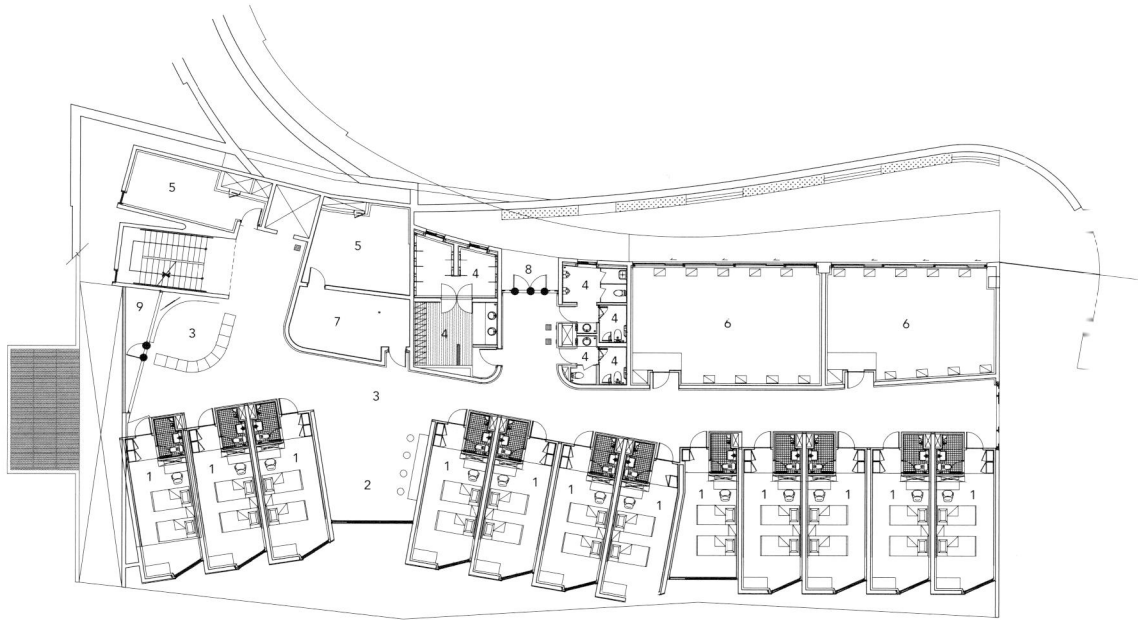

BASEMENT PLAN   0   5 m

1. Unit
2. Lounge
3. Corridor
4. Rest room/bathroom
5. Storage
6. Multi-use hall
7. Laundry room
8. Entrance
9. Deck

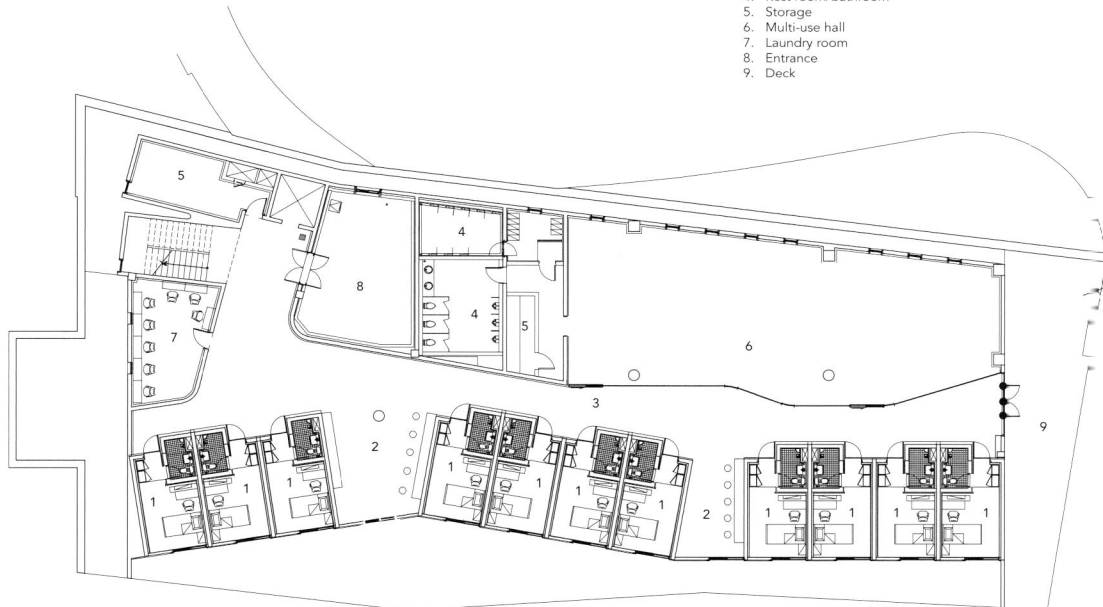

SECOND BASEMENT PLAN   0   5 m

N

PIT PLAN

1. Unit
2. Lounge
3. Corridor
4. Rest room/bathroom
5. Storage
6. Multi-use hall
7. Media room
8. Utilities
9. Courtyard

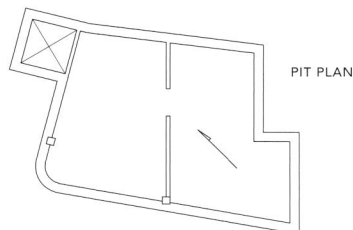

27. KISWIRE HEADQUARTERS_

TOKYO, JAPAN, 2009–

The headquarters of Kiswire Ltd, one of the world's largest manufacturers of metal wire, is located in Jungang-gu, the heart of Seoul's central business district. Cho, who also designed Kiswire's new research and development facility in Malaysia, decided to use the company's product, steel wire, as a main element of his design. The narrow structure is clad with steel wire with an external steel bracing structure that is completely independent from the clean glass workspace.

The use of steel wire is abundant in infrastructures, but highly uncommon in building envelopes. Cho used the wire not only to represent the company, but also to emphasize the thin vertical face of the building and to give passersby something interesting to look at in a neighbourhood dominated by nondescript mid-rise buildings. The building's nine storeys are divided by the structural bracing and steel wire façade, which make the structure appear to

be one single mass. Cho explains, "Our idea to use wire came from observing the looms and other instruments that weave the wires fibres together and organize them in a dynamic, functional form. In the Kiswire building, the wires are a new element woven into the urban fabric of the Jungang-gu district." The wire varies in thickness and concentration, providing diffused natural light and a sound screen for the inner glass box. The wire mitigates reflections from the glass and casts a subtle shadow on the interior.

OPPOSITE_ *The Kiswire Headquarters seen from the street.*

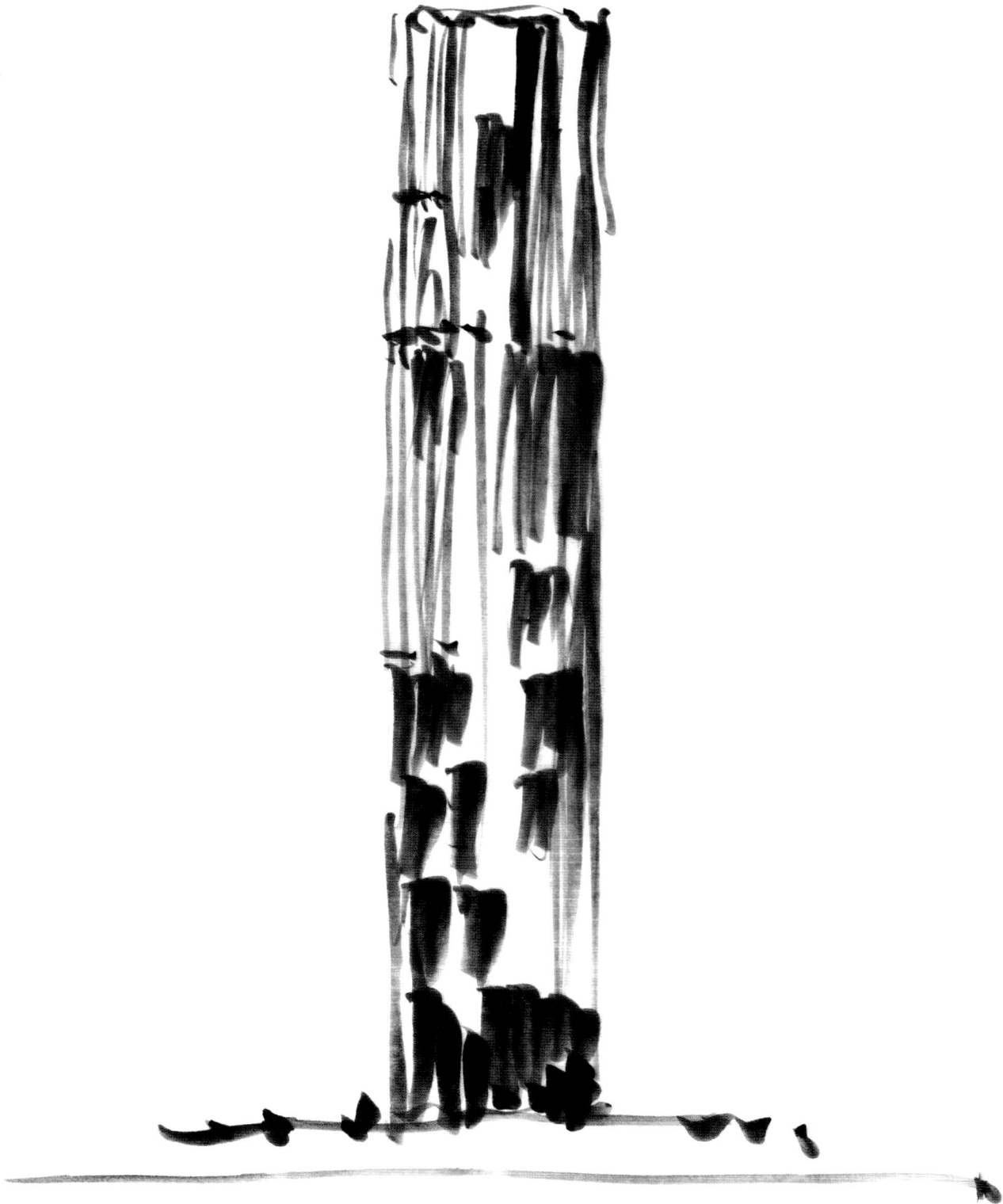

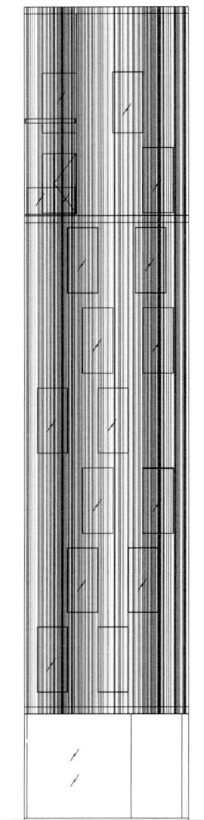

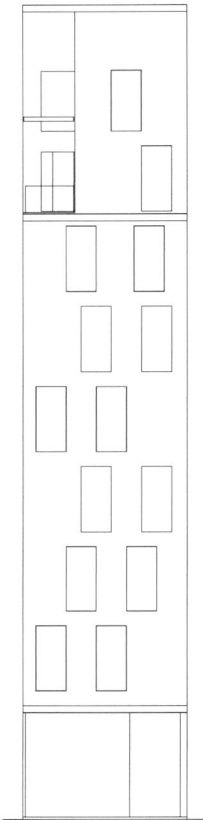

FRONT ELEVATION   0   5 m   FRONT ELEVATION   0   5 m   ALLEY ELEVATION   0   5 m

PROJECT TEAM: Nicholas Locke, Greg Hale, Dong-hyun
Go and Eric Druse
LOCATION: 4-5, Jinmajeong, Ilbongyodae, Jungang-gu,
Tokyo, Japan
USE: Office headquarters
GROSS FLOOR AREA: 910 m² (9,795 ft²)
STRUCTURE: Reinforced concrete, external steel frame

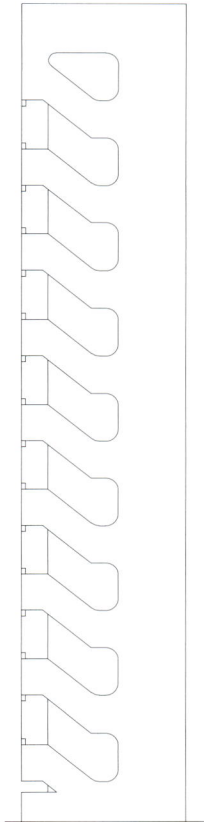

BACK ELEVATION   0 _____ 5 m

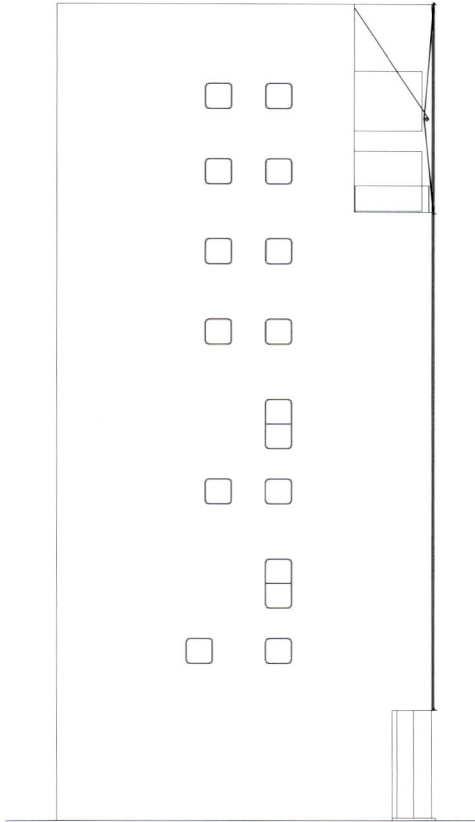

SOUTH ELEVATION   0 _____ 5 m

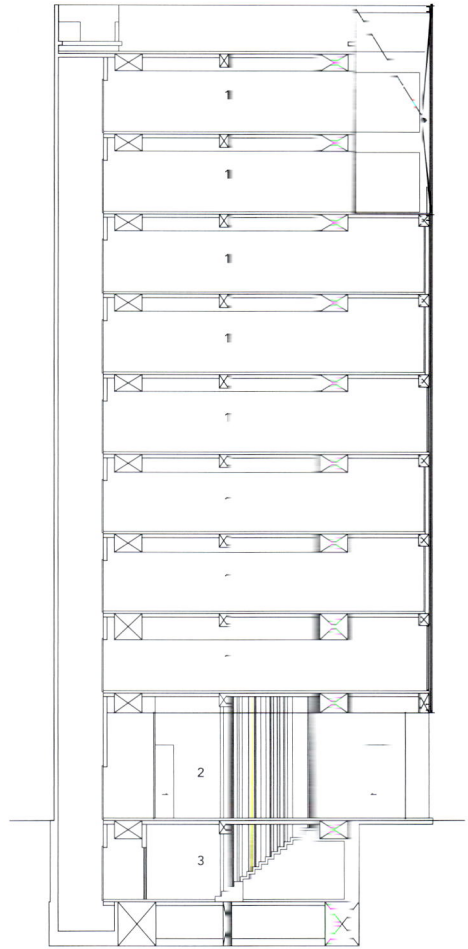

SECTION A   0 _____ 5 m

1. Office
2. Wire Gallery
3. Shop

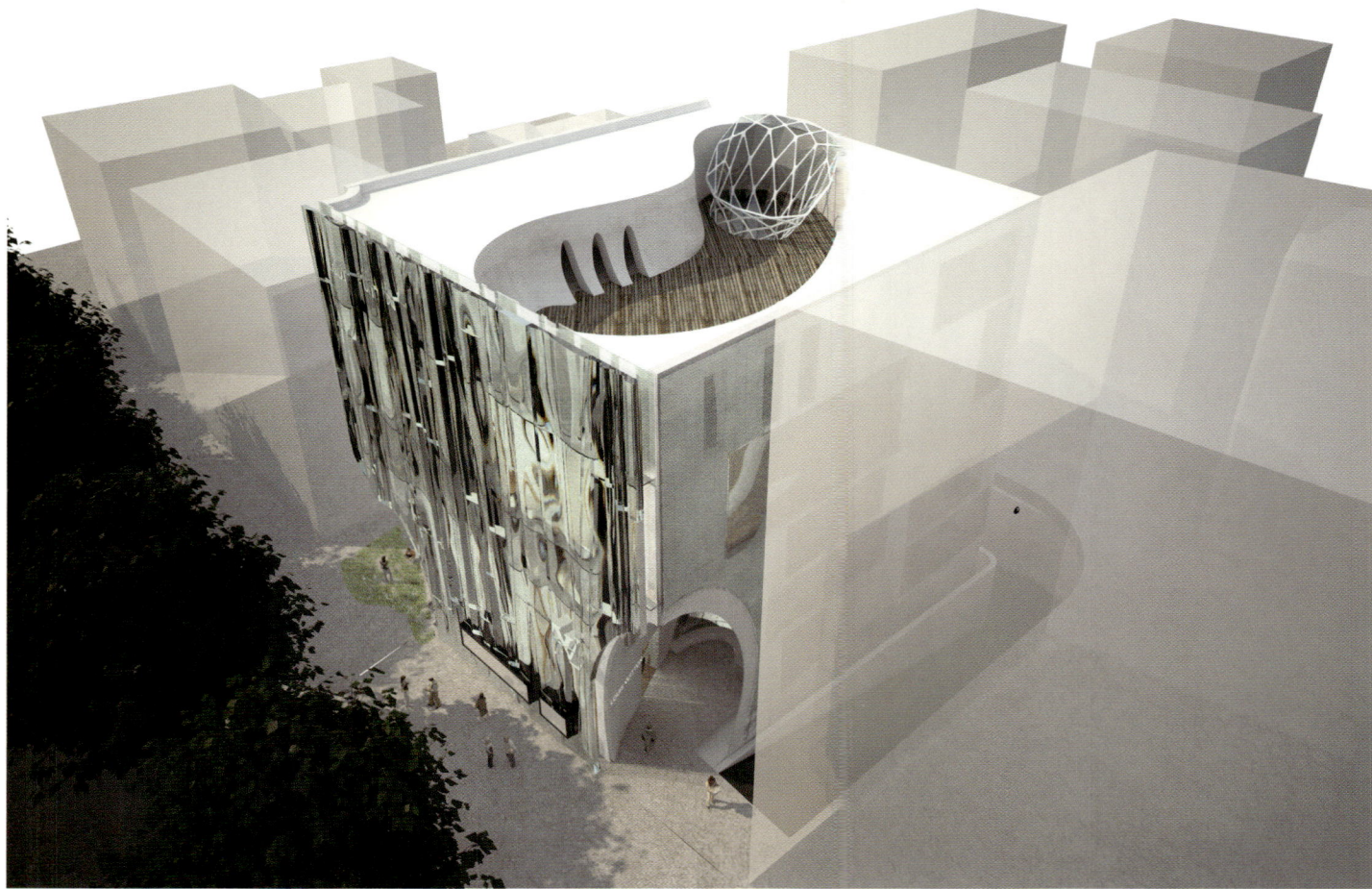

28. MAISON LOUIS VUITTON_

SEOUL, KOREA, 2011–

Cho was invited to participate in a competition held by the luxury group LVMH for a flagship Louis Vuitton boutique in Seoul's fashionable Gangnam district. Cho's design maximizes the use of space inside a square form, and features a shimmering glass façade. The neighbourhood is, in Cho's opinion, "largely rigid and opaque", and many buildings prevent passersby from looking in. In contrast, the store, with its play of light, glass and stainless steel mesh, will invite people to stop, look and come inside.

The form of the façade is a series of continuous concave and convex curves, with angles that constantly diffract and distort light and generate faceted reflections. Cho envisions them as providing perspectives with a cinematographic quality to highlight the Louis Vuitton collections and displays. Inside, natural light is diffused through the stainless steel mesh and triple-glazed glass. The display floors are in a stepped arrangement, and two concrete masses provide enclaves for entry and rest. The building is punctured at an

angle by what Cho calls a "green tunnel", interdecio aring natural light and air through the centre of the building. t is a swel structure with operable windows for the interior retail and VIP paces. The green tunnel stretches from the café terrace to the entry way and can be sealed with translucent fabric in inclement weather. It also serves as a seasonal display area at roof level. The structure contains two trusses on the third and fifth floor, which, in conjunction with the cores, three perimeter walls, and two concrete bearing walls, allow all levels to be column-free, and give the interior designers maximum flexibility to arrange displays and environments.

OPPOSITE_ *Renderings of the street view and an aerial view.*

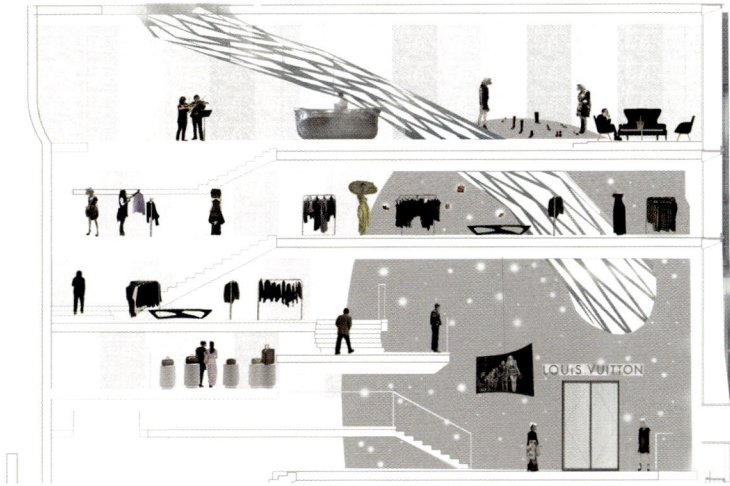

ABOVE AND OPPOSITE_ *Studies of sections of the building.*

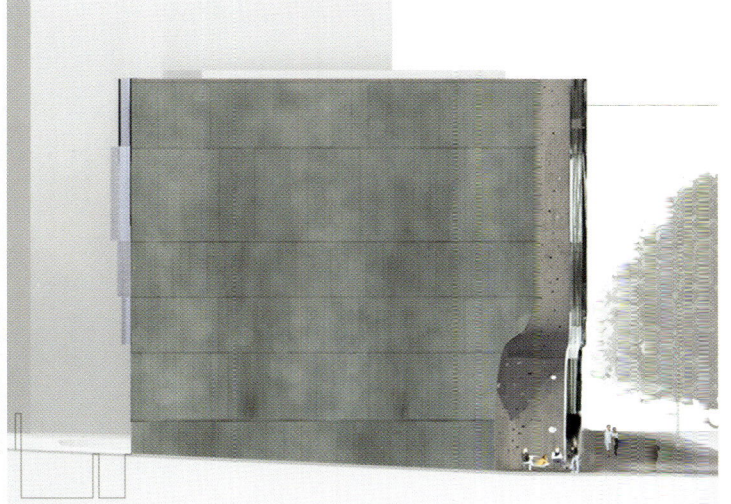
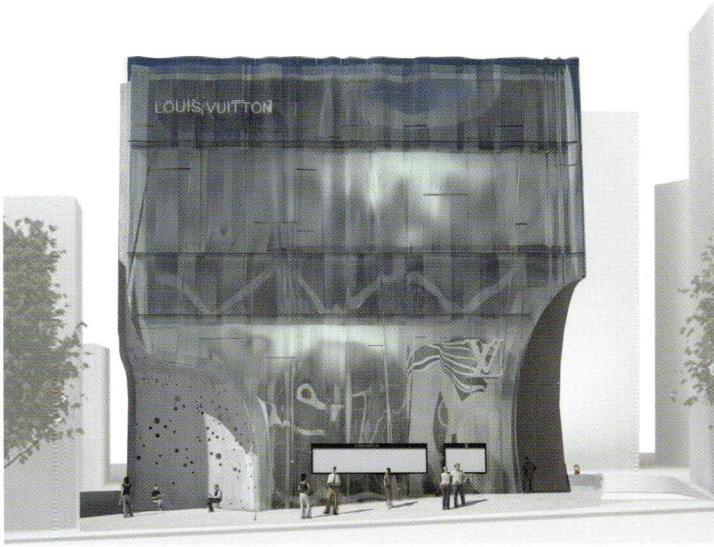

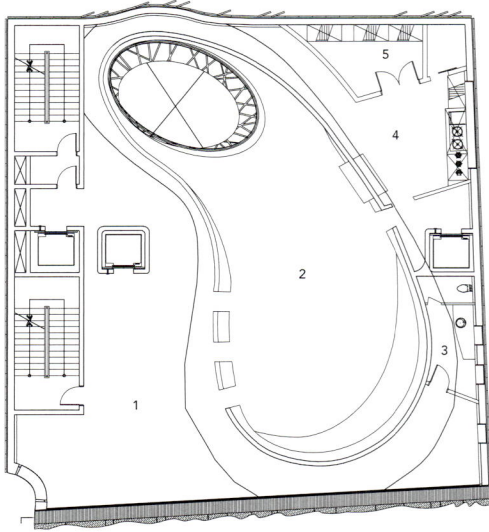

FOURTH FLOOR PLAN   0   5 m

1. Indoor café 2. Terrace café 3. Rest room
4. Kitchen 5. Storage

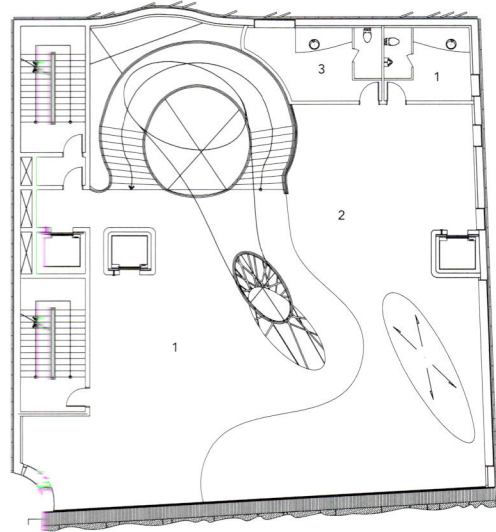

THIRD FLOOR PLAN   0   5 m

1. Women's space 2. VIP space 3. VIP rest room

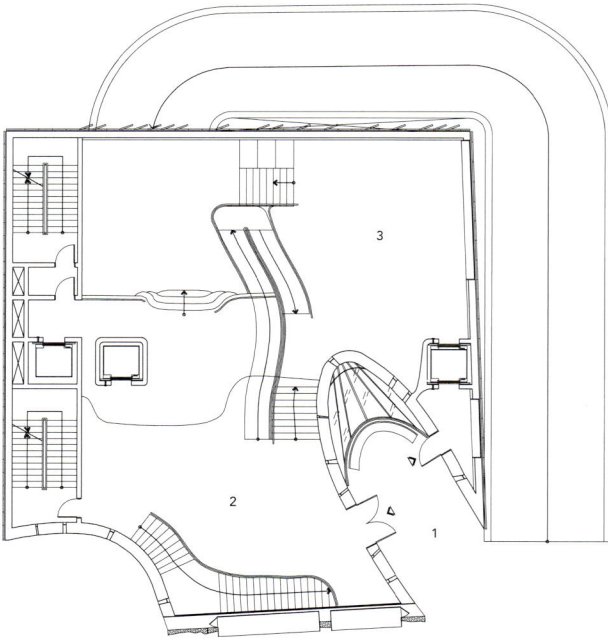

GROUND FLOOR PLAN   0   5 m

1. Entrance 2. Exhibition space 3. Travel room

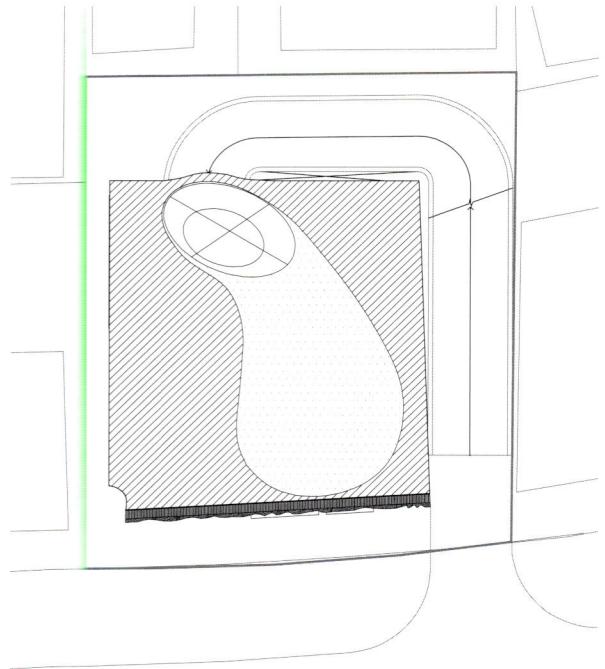

SITE PLAN   0   5 m

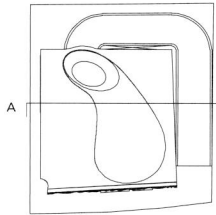

1. Café terrace
2. VIP area
3. Women's area
4. Travel world
5. Exhibition space
6. Men's area
7. Parking

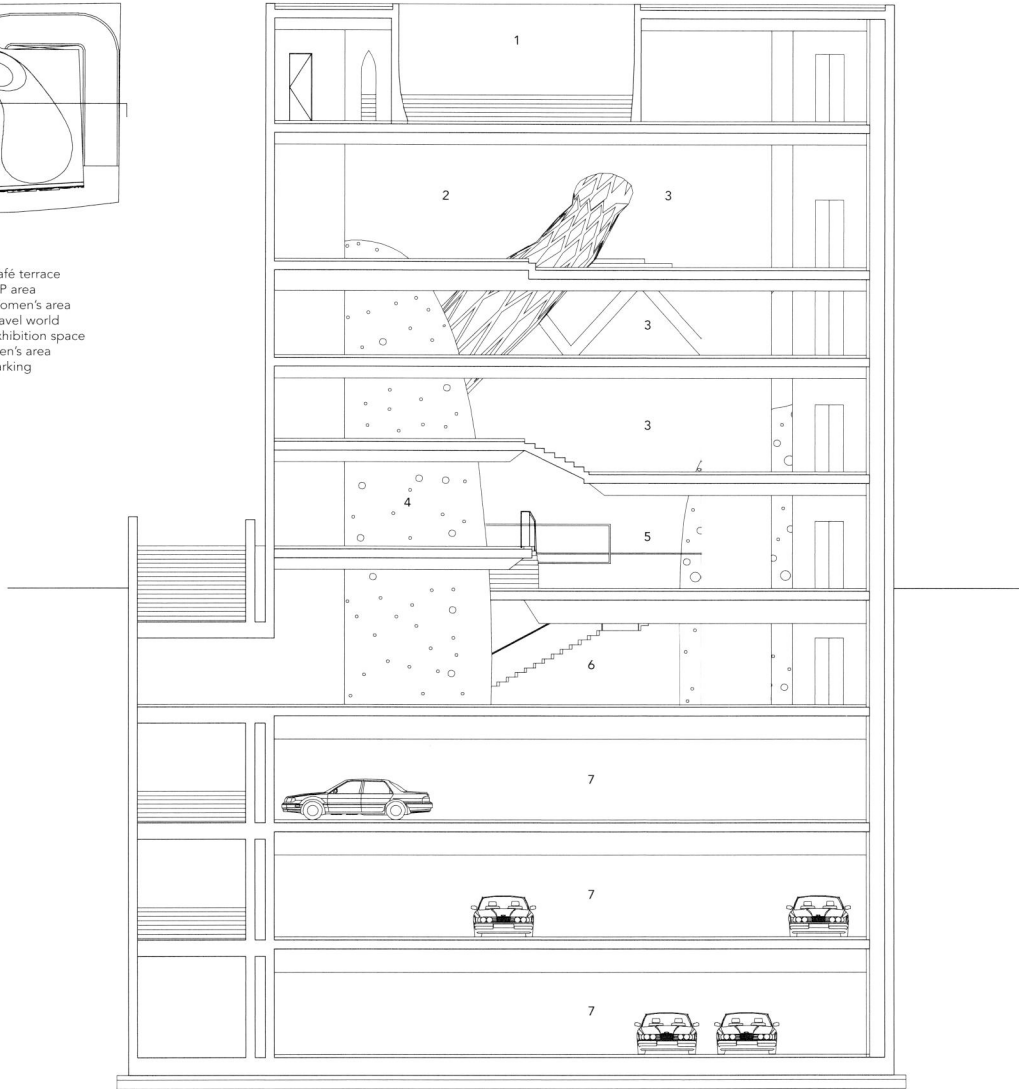

SECTION A   0   5 m

PROJECT TEAM: Sara Kim, Nicholas Locke, So-jin Kang,
Hong-joon Yang and Jae-gi Kim
LOCATION: 99-18, Cheongdam-dong, Gangnam-gu, Seoul, Korea
USE: Retail "Maison", sales facility, cultural facility
GROSS FLOOR AREA: 3,850 m² (41,441 ft²)
STRUCTURE: Reinforced concrete, steel truss, post-tension
concrete

29. LODGE STUDIO_

MONTANA, USA, 2005–

The Lodge Studio sits at the base of the Rimrock Bluff, a 120 m (400 ft) sandstone wall defining the northern edge of Billings, Montana. The concrete rhombus-shape structure opens to the expansive views overlooking the entire Yellowstone Valley. Two wooden boxes merge inside, making two connected rooms. There are two exterior covered patios in the front and rear in which to enjoy making and listening to music and artworks, or watching a passing thunderstorm.

The material and construction details are designed to be rather raw and simple. Inside the space visually opens towards the lower side of the hill. From each side, the view of the landscape divides interestingly into two different directions.

PROJECT TEAM: Eric Horn and Nick Panchau
LOCATION: Billings, Montana, USA
USE: Studio
GROSS FLOOR AREA: 137 m² (1,474.6 ft²)
STRUCTURE: Reinforced concrete, light wood frame

ABOVE_ *The shell for the two plywood boxes is made of cast-in-place concrete with a board form that leaves the exterior rough. The roof is flat to express the shell-like monolithic block that aesthetically matches the surrounding rocky landscape.*

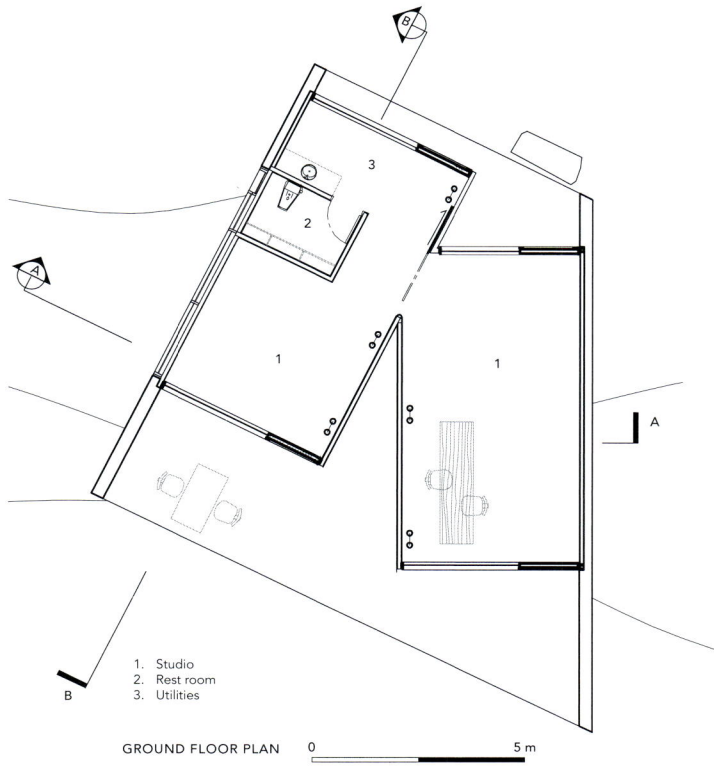

1. Studio
2. Rest room
3. Utilities

GROUND FLOOR PLAN   0   5 m

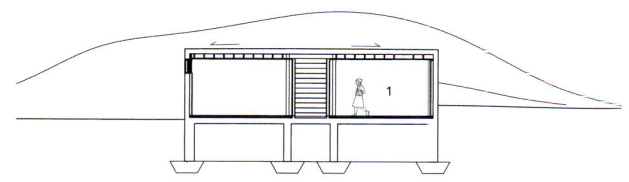

SECTION A   0   5 m

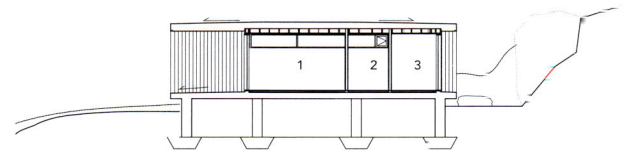

SECTION B   0   5 m

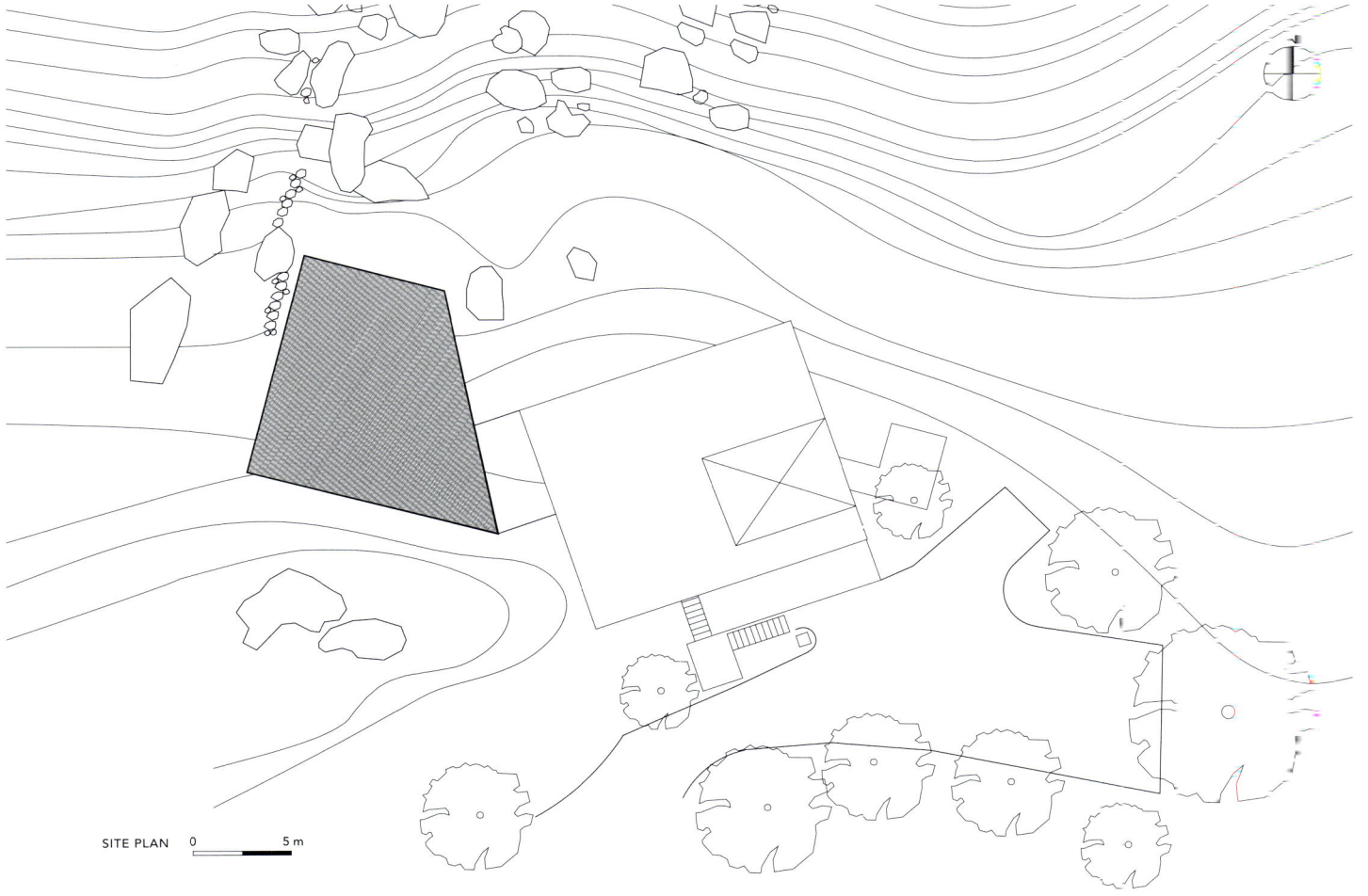

SITE PLAN   0   5 m

2009 광주디자인비엔날레 Gwangju Design Biennale

THE CLUE

30. ONE EARTH, ONE SUN_

GWANGJU DESIGN BIENNALE, 2009

The exhibition began with themes shared by people around the world and with their participation. The words "international" and "global" are usually used interchangeably to mean "transcending national boundaries". However, the word "international" may be defined as "specific relations between different countries", whereas the word "global" encompasses the whole world and all places on the planet.

On Earth, which rotates on its own axis and revolves around the sun, there are many cities. Cities are located in 24 time zones due to the movement of the Earth, and in these cities different cultures are formed with diverse lifestyle patterns and within different environments. Nonetheless, we all share the same light under a single sun.

This exhibition aimed to show how all cities might accept and respect their differences, just as all humankind coexists under the same Sun. Our planet Earth is like a gigantic clock. It revolves 360 degrees counter-clockwise, one rotation per 24 hours. This means that the Earth rotates at 15 degrees per hour. Therefore, the Sun also rotates 15 degrees at the celestial equator. Accordingly, on the sundial the hour hand interval is 15 degrees. Earth is divided into 24 time zones, each with a 15-degree difference in longitude. Thus 24 cities in 24 time zones were selected to be featured in the exhibition.

OPPOSITE_ *The Gwangju Design Biennale, 2009.*

Clue One *"One Earth, One Sun"*

31. METAMORPHOSIS OF SAM-RA-MAN-SANG_

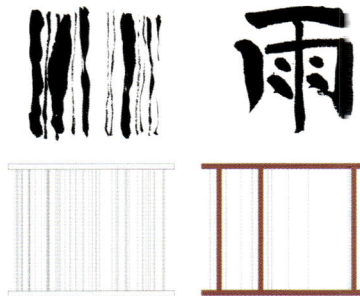

INTERPRETED IN A CONTEMPORARY INDUSTRIAL PROJECT: STEEL WIRE BY BYOUNG CHO

These six words, which represent Sam-Ra-Man-Sang or the natural world, have been chosen and expressed in architectural poems created with a contemporary industrial product, steel wire.

These words are selected from physical phenomena found in nature rather than just concepts or abstract ideas. The words can be interpreted in contemporary architectural language, particularly utilizing the contemporary industrial product, steel wire.

RAIN_
Thin concrete columns stretch towards the sky
Empty space between
Penetrated by silver lines

A crisp rain shower in a deep forest
The sound of light reflects delicately
Thus as in the forest of rain

TREE_
Curtains of calmness drawn closed
Around four-sided space
Filled with serenity
Silent anticipation of the outer world's future

Thus calm silence is shaken by excitement

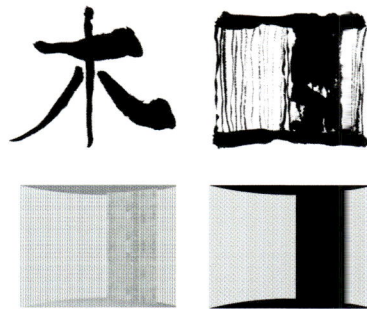

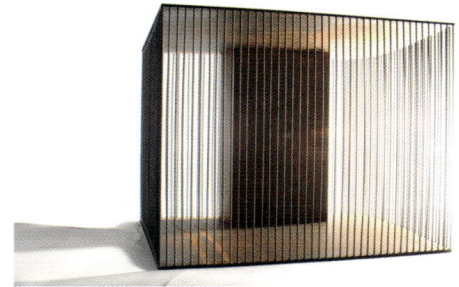

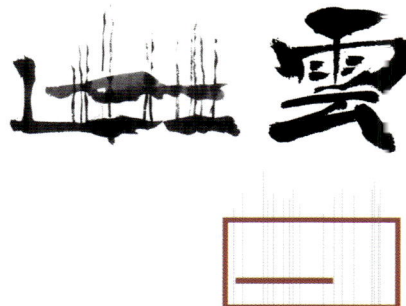

CLOUD_
Space rising through a field of wires
Accepting great mass
A densely laminated wooden platform

Vertical force and horizontal gravity coexist
Upon recognition of each other

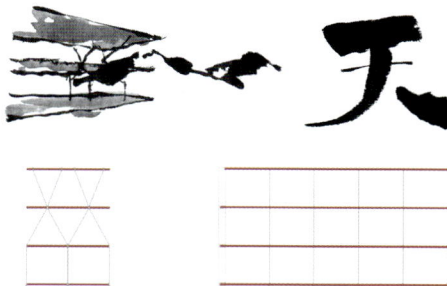

SKY_

Layers of space dissolve in transparent and
reflection
Glass dematerializes
Reflecting the void and the sky

Thin wires disappear
Suspending the ultimately flat materiality of the glass
And space in between

"Dematerialized Definition"
Thus revealed
Apparent through transparency
And the reflection of thin silver wires

EARTH_

Earth is always present

Dig deep and go down within
Hear the vibrating sound of earth

Vibrating sound of earth
Deep and delicate
Like the ringing of a cello in a small dark room
Running through silver wires
Towards the outer world as sunlight
Falling down to your eyes
Bouncing delightfully between the lines
Through the vibrating sound of earth

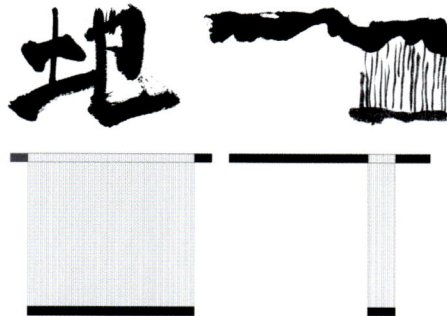

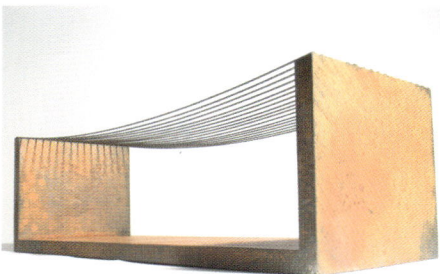

WIND_

Reflective silver lines
Stretching for miles under tension
Neither gravity nor axis of space exist in the empty
room

There is only tension

32. DRAWINGS AND PAINTINGS_

ABOVE_ Landscape, *watercolour on newspaper, 1995.*

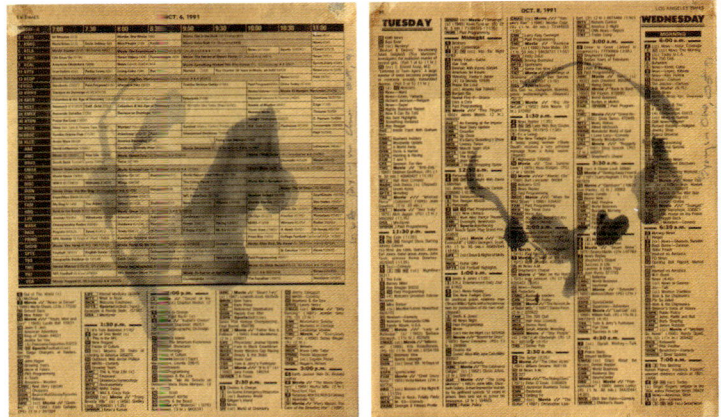

ABOVE_ Skull, *black ink on a poetry book by Kathleen Millay, Horace Liveright, New York (published in 1928), 1991.*

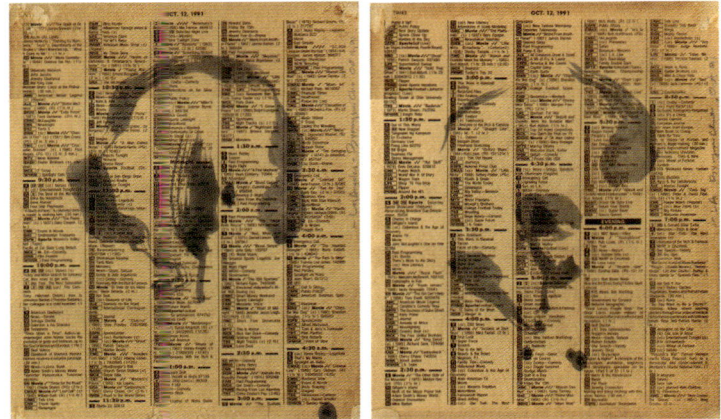

ABOVE_ Skull, *black ink on newspaper, 1991.*

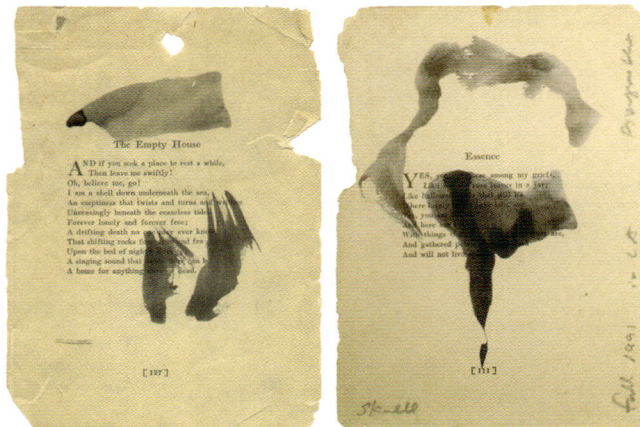

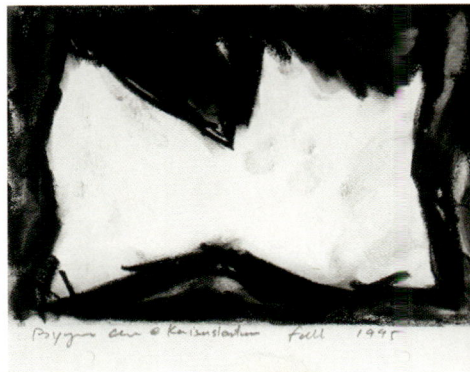

ABOVE_ Landscape, *oil paint stick on paper, 1995.*

CLOCKWISE FROM TOP LEFT_ Landscape, *pencil on brown paper, 1995;*
Reflection, *black ink on Korean paper, Nam Hae, Korea, 2011;* Reflection, *black
ink on Korean paper, Nam Hae, Korea, 2011;* Landscape of Namhae, *ink on
Korean paper, Nam Hae, Korea, 2011.*

33. SCHOOL WORKS_

EXPERIENCE AND PERCEPTION BY BYOUNG CHO_

What interests me most in my architecture is how the user can live within it – in other words, how it will be experienced, and how it will change and be perceived with the passage of time, rather than how to decorate it or to make it look nice. Moreover, I regard such experiences of using architecture as a phenomenon that has an organic relationship with memories and emotions from the past, as possessed by people, and expectations for what will take place in the future in a specific era and time. It thus continuously evolves in a novel manner, rather than being something subjective that changes according to different situations and people. The process that creates

and presents this phenomenon is the architecture I seek to realize. Thus, I place more value on its relationship with history, culture and social reality, in broad terms, and on programs of the project, users, and realistic problems of surrounding conditions, in narrow terms, as I stated earlier, rather than on completeness of the building itself. Consequently, I do not hesitate to introduce with boldness what is normally considered non-beautiful, in order to induce stronger relationships.

A series of urban renewal projects, including projects in the cities of Lugano, Boston and Montreal, are relatively large-scale projects

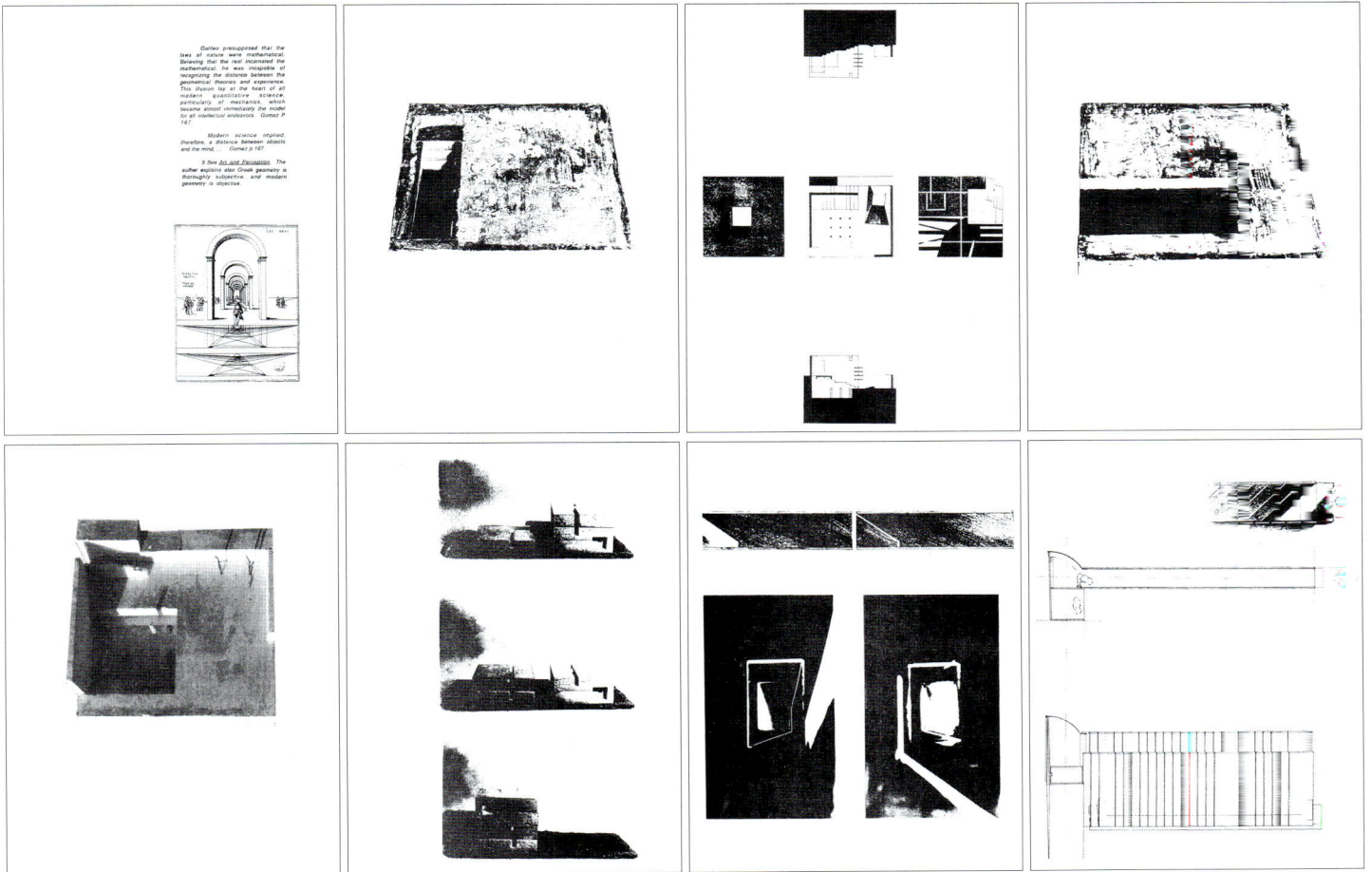

that attempted to present memories of the cities, memories of places and a direction for the future. However, the origin of the concept for each project was extracted from very small, delicate and common things, as seen in individual building projects in the later phases. Also, elements that are like seeds of the extracted concepts are projects that consider old buildings, whether big or small, or physical prototypes of the site as a starting point for architectural projects. The employed architectural methodology intends for the importance of the place, the era and the aesthetics of the prototype to be perceived more strongly through minimum modifications. More specifically, while a physical prototype of the site is maintained, it is intended to offer a taste of the old prototypes as they were, and to make available to one the experience of a time quality offered by something new within the framework of the prototype.

Such relationships between the new and the prototypes should be something in which the objects and humans as well as the qualities of time and place are organically entwined like a single creature, breathing and alive. Moreover, they should not be understood as independent entities, but should be understood within their relationships, namely how the user can participate in it and live within it.

CURRICULUM VITAE_
BYOUNG CHO

REGISTRATION_

Licensed and Registered in the state of Montana, USA and Illincis, USA
Member of the American Institute of Architects, AIA
Member of the National Council of Architectural Registration Boards, NCARB
Registered in Seoul, Korea (KIA)

EDUCATION_

Harvard University, Cambridge, Massachusetts, USA

1991   Master in Architecture
1991   Master of Architecture in Urban Design Award
1990   Attended Harvard ETH Student Exchange Program, Zurich, Switzerland
1990   Travelling scholarship to Turkey, Federal Government of Switzerland

Montana State University, Bozeman, Montana, USA

1986   Bachelor of Architecture
1986   Winner of New Sweden Student Urban Design International Competition

AWARDS_

2013   **AIA Honor Award, Montana Design Award** for the design of Heyri Theatre and Hotel
2013   **AIA Honor Award, Montana Design Award** for the design of L-shaped House
2013   **AIA Honor Award, Montana Design Award** for the design of Oisoo Gallery
2013   **AIA Design Award, Northwest and Pacific Regional** for the design of L-shaped House, Hanil Visitors' Centre and Guest House
2013   **AR House Award** for the design of L-shaped House
2010   **AIA Citation Award, Northwest and Pacific Regional** for the design of Earth House
2010   **Soo Kun Kim Prize** for Earth House
2009   **AIA Honor Award, Montana Design Award** for the design of Earth House
2009   **AIA Honor Award, Montana Design Award** for the design of Hanil Cement Information Centre and Guest House

2009	**AIA Honor Award, Northwest and Pacific Regional** for the design of D-shaped Concrete Box House
2009	**KIA National Award** for the design of Hanil Cement Information Centre and Guest House
2008	**KIA National Award** for Areomsol Kindergarten
2007	**AIA Honor Award, Montana Design Award** for the design of Concrete Box House
2006	**AIA Citation Award, Northwest and Pacific Regional** for the design of C-shaped Metal Roof House
2006	**AIA Citation Award, Northwest and Pacific Regional** for the design of Camerata Music Studio and W-Residence
2005	**National Architectural Culture Award of Korea** for the College of Arts and Architecture, Paeje University
2005	**KIA National Award** for 'H' Camerata Music Studio and Gallery
2004	**AIA Honor Award, Montana Design Award** for the design of Camerata Music Studio
2004	**AIA Honor Award, Montana Design Award** for the design of U-shaped House
2004	**AIA Honor Award, Northwest and Pacific Regional** for the design of Uri Village
2004	**AIA Honor Award, Northwest and Pacific Regional** for the design of the Village of Dancing Fish
2004	**Vanguard Design Firms**, Architecture Record, USA
2002	**AIA Honor Award, Montana Design Award** for the design of Uri Village
2002	**AIA Honor Award, Montana Design Award** for the design of the Village of Dancing Fish
2001	**AR+D Award**, highly recommended
2001	**Phi Beta Kappa Teaching Award**
1999	**KIA National Award** for a multi-family apartment, Young-in, Korea
1998	**A-Chun Prize, KIA** for 'L'-shaped House
1998	**CRI-ARC Award** for Cho's Studio/Residence

PUBLICATIONS_

2007_

*Contemporary Korean
Architecture: Megacity Network*,
Jovis Verlag GmbH, Germany:
Concrete Box House, Village of Dancing Fish

2010_

Carles Broto, *Houses Now*,
Links Books, Spain:
Earth House

Industrial Architecture, Liaoning Science
and Technology Publishing House:
Hanil Visitors' Centre and Guest House

Materials Bible,
Loft Publications, Spain:
Earth House

Phyllis Richardson, *Nano House*,
Thames & Hudson, UK:
Earth House

FEBRUARY_
W magazine (USA):
Hanil Visitors' Centre and Guest House

MARCH_
Dwell online (USA):
Earth House

APRIL_
Dwell magazine (USA):
Four-box House

MAY_
Archello (the Netherlands):
Twin Trees and Coastalscapes Libya

JUNE_
CasaBella magazine (Italy):
Earth House, Hanil Visitors' Centre
and Guest House, Heyri Theatre and Hotel

Dezeen online (Germany):
Earth House

Dwell magazine (USA):
Four-box House

JULY_
Architonic online (Switzerland):
Earth House

Código 06140 magazine (Mexico):
Earth House

Dezeen online (Germany):
Hanil Visitors' Centre and Guest House

Wallpaper magazine:
Hanil Visitors' Centre and Guest House,
Twin Trees, Heyri Theatre and Hotel

AUGUST_
ArchDaily online:
Scissors House, Earth House, Hanil Visitors'
Centre and Guest House

Architectural Record magazine:
Scissors House

Architecture Asia magazine (Malaysia):
Earth House

Architizer online:
Heyri Theatre and Hotel, Camerata Music
Studio, Earth House, Scissors House

Designboom online (USA):
Heyri Theatre and Hotel, Scissors House

E-architect online (UK):
Scissors House

Interni magazine:
Scissors House

Interiors (Russia)

Wallpaper magazine (UK):
Scissors House

SEPTEMBER_
L'Architecture d'Aujourd'hui (France):
Earth House

Arhitext: Thresholds (Romania):
Scissors House

Detail magazine (Germany):
Hanil Visitors' Centre and Guest House

Floornature online:
Earth House, Scissors House

Indian Architect & Builder magazine (India):
Earth House

Mark magazine, no. 27 (the Netherlands):
Hanil Visitors' Centre and Guest House

SDU Publishers' Book (the Netherlands):
Hanil Visitors' Centre and Guest House

OCTOBER_
Architecture Now!, vol. 7:
Hanil Visitors' Centre and Guest House,
Three-box House

*Architectural Record: Serious Concrete
online*:
Hanil Visitors' Centre and Guest House

Structural Concrete journal:
Hanil Visitors' Centre and Guest House

NOVEMBER_
A+A (China):
Hanil Visitors' Centre and Guest House

Designboom magazine online:
L-shaped House

mur+betong magazine (Norway):
Hanil Visitors' Centre and Guest House

Taiwan Architect magazine, no. 436 (Taiwan):
Earth House

DECEMBER_
Detail online (Recycling):
Hanil Visitors' Centre and Guest House

EcoLogik online:
Hanil Visitors' Centre and Guest House

New Trajectories, New York:
Hanil Visitors' Centre and Guest House

2011_

Building Materials, Liaoning Science
and Technology Publishing:
Twin Trees

JANUARY_
Fabric Formwork magazine (Chile):
Hanil Visitors' Centre and Guest House

Stuttgart University magazine:
Hanil Visitors' Centre and Guest House

FEBRUARY_
Urbanism & Architecture (China):
Hanil Visitors' Centre and Guest House

MARCH_
CasaBella magazine (Italy):
Earth House, Hanil Visitors' Centre
and Guest House, Heyri Theatre and Hotel

Chosun Daily Newspaper:
Twin Trees

RBA revistas Arquitectura y diseño:
L-shaped House, Earth House

Tectónica blog (Spain):
L-shaped House, Earth House

APRIL_
ArchDaily (USA):
L-shaped House

Archiportale & edilportale (Italy):
Hanil Visitors' Centre and Guest House

Architecture Lab online:
Scissors House

Designboom magazine online:
L-shaped House, Twin Trees

MAY_
The Archive Team:
L-shaped House, Earth House

Minimalistas blog (Spain):
L-shaped House

JUNE_
Concept Asia:
Twin Trees

Cubes Concepts Asia:
L-shaped House

Hi-Design International
(Shenzhen, China):
Twin Trees

AUGUST_
Dwell Asia:
Twin Trees, Concrete Box House,
Earth House

Madison (China):
Twin Trees

SEPTEMBER_
Dwell Asia:
Earth House

Earthworks magazine
(South Africa):
Twin Trees

Future magazine (Spain):
Twin Trees

OCTOBER_
Design Bureau magazine
(Amy, Chicago, USA)

DECEMBER_
AEC café website:
Twin Trees

2012_

100 New Buildings, China:
Kiswire Museum, Libya Greenscapes

Convergent Flux, Birkhauser, Switzerland

High-rise Office Buildings, Hi-Design
International, Shenzen, China:
Twin Trees

New Houses, Guangzhou JiaTu Culture
Communication Co.

Oceanreading, China, Shenzhen Ocean
Readings Culture Communication Co. Ltd:
Twin Trees

Wood Features Building, China, Artpower
International Publish Co., Ltd.
L-shaped house

MAY_
Designboom magazine online:
Maison Louis Vuitton

2013_

Victoria Ballard Bell and Patrick Rand,
Materials for Design 2, Princeton
Architectural Press

Office, Braun, Switzerland

Phillip James Tabb, *The Greening of
Architecture*, Ashgate Limited, London UK:
Hanil Visitors' Centre and Guest House

The World Architectural firm selection,
BySpace, China:
Twin Trees

JANUARY_
Bright magazine, the Netherlands:
Earth House

FEBRUARY_
Disajn magazine, Sweden:
Camerata Music Studio

JUNE_
Archidaily:
Heyri Theatre and Hotel

Architizer:
Camerata Music Studio, Hanil Visitors
Centre and Guest House, L-shaped
house, Twin Trees

DesignBoom magazine online:
Heyri Theatre and Hotel, Hanil Visitors
Centre and Guset House

Dezeen magazine:
Hanil Visitors' Centre and Guest House

JULY_
The Architectural Review, vol. 139:
Hanil Visitors' Centre and Guest House

LIST OF ARCHITECTS/INTERNS_
1993–2013

Gwangwon Ann

Jun-ho Ann

Yong-eun Bae

Allicia Belloescobar

Byeong-gwon Cheon

Hyeon-jin Cho

Ung-hui Cho

Yeong-muk Cho

Ha-seung Choi

Ha-young Choi

Hye-eun Choi

Hyeyeon Choi

Joon-won Choi

Sun-yong Choi

Steven Clarke

David Cook

Eric Druse

Lane Ferris

Anouck Foch

Dong-hyun Go

Greg Hale

Mark Hanna

Hyemi Hong

Kyung-jin Hong

Seok-gyeong Hong

Seok-hyeon Hong

Eric Horn

Hyun-jin Hwang

Sang-min Hyeon

Su-yeong Jeong

Moon-hyeon Jo

Yong-joon Jo

Greg Jonason

Eungi Kang

Ho Kang

In-ae Kang

So-jin Kang

Woo-hyun Kang

Young-jin Kang

Kody Kato

Dong-woo Kim

Eun-jeong Kim

Eun-mi Kim

Gyeong-sun Kim

Ho-joong Kim

Hui-jun Kim

Hyeon-seong Kim

Jae-gi Kim

Jeon-am Kim

Jun-ho Kim

Junyeon Kim

Kyu-young Kim

Minhui Kim

Minseok Kim

Minyoung Kim

Samcheol Kim

Sara Kim
Seung-hyun Kim
Sook-jung Kim
Sung-hwa Kim
Yoon-heui Kim
Yukon Kim
Yun-seong Kim
Huig-yeong Kwon
Sung-hoa Kwon
Dae-ho Lee
Jea-ha Lee
Jin-wook Lee
Joo-hyoung Lee
Jung-hui Lee
Seung-jae Lee
Dong-won Lim
Seonyeong Lim
Nicholas Locke
Tae-hyun Nam
Yeowool Noh
Seong-heon Oh
Gi-hyeon Park
Hae-seong Park
Ha-hyeok Park
Joo-hyeon Park
Jung-yong Park
Sung-jun Park
Branden Shigeta

Joon-seok Seo
Minhui Seo
Dong-hee Shin
Seungh-yeon Shin
Wonil Son
Matthew Stewart
Jiyoung Suh
Angel Tenorio
Adam Whalen
Hyeong-seok Woo
Sumin Woo
Hong-joon Yang
Wonmo Yang
Huijeong Yoon
Dimitris Zoupas

Structural Engineers:
Dong Yang Structural Engineers Co., Ltd
K Structural Engineers Co., Ltd

Mechanical / Electrical Engineers:
Sun Hwa Mechanical Engineers Co., Ltd

Construction Company:
C&O Construction Co., Ltd
Hanil Construction Co., Ltd
Hyo Sang Construction Co., Ltd
Jae Hyo Construction Co., Ltd
Youngmook Cho

PICTURE CREDITS_

Every effort has been made to trace the copyright owners of the images contained in this book and we apologize for any unintentional omissions. We would be pleased to insert an appropriate acknowledgment in any reprint of this publication.

All photographs by Wooseop Hwang, except for the following:
Jongoh Kim: 29 (above), 30, 37–38, 45–46, 54–55, 58–59, 74–75, 80, 83, 86 (left), 90 (above left and above right), 119 (above left and above right), 123 (above)
Yongkwan Kim: 19, 48–50, 61, 62 (below left), 68–69, 70 (below left and below right), 86 (right), 87, 90 (below), 99, 102, 131 (below), 132 (above left), 137–38, 141, 171, 172 (above right centre), 174, 248–49
Wanson Park: 16–17
Kyungsub Shin: 175

ACKNOWLEDGMENTS_

Material co-ordinators: Sook-jung Kim and Sojin Kang of bcho architects

First published in the United Kingdom in 2014 by
Thames & Hudson Ltd, 181A High Holborn,
London WC1V 7QX

Byoung Cho © 2014 Thames & Hudson Ltd, London
Text © 2014 Lieux Design and Byoung Cho Architects

Designed by Steve Russell

British Library Cataloguing-in-Publication Data
A catalogue record for this book is available from the British Library

ISBN 978-0-500-34291-6

Printed and bound in China by Toppan Leefung Printing Limited

To find out about all our publications, please visit **www.thamesandhudson.com**. There you can subscribe to our e-newsletter, browse or download our current catalogue, and buy any titles that are in print.